PRAISE FOR *UNSTUFF YOUR LIFE!*

"Living in chaos? Mellen has written the book to help . . . those willing to take even a small sip of Mellen's Kool-Aid may enjoy a more organized, efficient, and well-managed life."
　—*Publishers Weekly*

"Mellen is an accomplished organizer and coach for people who wish to streamline their lifestyle and possessions."
　—*Library Journal*

"With a good sense of humor and a considerable amount of compassion . . . *Unstuff Your Life!* is an extremely helpful and practical book, always pointing us to the bigger picture."
　—Sharon Salzberg, author of *Real Happiness*

"Whether it's your home or your head, Andrew Mellen shows how to achieve organizational success!"
　—Peter Walsh, author of *It's All Too Much* and *Enough Already!*

"I read *Unstuff Your Life!* cover to cover and LOVED IT! I have been doing everything Mellen suggests and although I thought I was organized, I am even more so now."
　—Bonnie McEneaney, author of *Messages*

"As someone who is severely organizationally challenged and resistant, I was entirely skeptical that *Unstuff Your Life!* would make a difference. I am happy to say that Andrew Mellen's organizational strategies and concepts really work!"
　—Rosalind Wiseman, author of *Queen Bees & Wannabes*

UNSTUFF
YOUR LIFE!

SECOND EDITION

UPDATED & REVISED 2ND EDITION

UNSTUFF YOUR LIFE!

Kick the Clutter Habit and Completely Organize Your Life for Good

ANDREW MELLEN

FIRST
LINE PRESS

1⃤ FIRST LINE PRESS

First Line Press

unstuffbook.com

St. Petersburg, FL, USA

Library of Congress Control Number: 2024908789

Paperback ISBN: 979-8-9874774-2-7

E-Book ISBN: 979-8-9874774-3-4

Cover and text design by Alex Hennig

Art direction by Jazmin Welch at fleck creative studio

For my mother, Frances Mellen; my father, Jordon Mellen; and my maternal grandmother, Bess Osborne—who, each in his or her own way, taught me about Like with Like and putting my things away.

I wasn't the neatest kid, so I guess it finally took.

CONTENTS

INTRODUCTION

We are what we repeatedly do.
Excellence, then, is not an act, but a habit.
–ARISTOTLE

GENTLE READER; less-than-gentle reader; kind, overwhelmed, unfo-
cused, slightly desperate reader—I'm back with an updated version of
this how-to book just for you!

So welcome (or welcome back) to my world. I hope you find
everything you need to get and stay organized for good.

And what does my world look like?

Well, on a personal level, I have a comfortable home where I can
find anything in 30 seconds or less. I have art on the walls and cleaning supplies under the kitchen sink. I'm not a minimalist, not that
there's anything wrong with it if *you* want to be a minimalist.

Minimalism doesn't work for me on two levels. First, the focus
with minimalism is still on stuff. It's like a stuff diet where I have to
constantly count belongings just like I would calories. Second, minimalism feels like dogma—more rules I have to follow without question, and if or when I don't, I'm supposed to feel bad about myself.
Yuck. Who needs any system where imperfection equals shame, guilt,
or feeling like a failure?

So I have stuff—enough stuff to make my life comfortable, convenient, and beautiful. But just enough stuff that staying organized doesn't require a ton of maintenance. I want to use my precious time for activities and relationships, not for managing inanimate things.

On a professional level, as a speaker, author, coach, and organizer (andrewmellen.com), I travel around the world literally and virtually, working with individual clients and companies, helping them become more efficient, effective, and clutter free.

My clients vary widely in life experience and economic background, and they come from all walks of life. They run the gamut from struggling, hustling artists and award-winning yet just-as-frazzled filmmakers to overwhelmed entrepreneurs and harried CEOs, from globetrotting digital nomads to deeply rooted stay-at-home parents. They also include small businesses, multinational corporations, world-class museums, tiny not-for-profit organizations, and more than a few houses of worship. What they all have in common is too much to do, not enough time to get it all done, and *way too much stuff*!

I've been lucky enough to speak on stages from SXSW to TEDx and lead seminars and workshops in settings ranging from house parties to stadiums, all the while spreading the gospel of unstuffing one's life through a delightfully nonsectarian evangelism. I've appeared in print everywhere from *O, The Oprah Magazine, The New York Times,* and *Fast Company* to *TIME, Real Simple,* and *The Wall Street Journal*; on radio and TV (*CBS News Sunday Morning,* NPR, Oprah & Friends, *Martha Stewart Living Today,* HGTV, DIY, and others); as well as on many podcasts, streaming channels, and blogs.

Like the Johnny Appleseed of stuff, I travel far and wide planting the seeds of organization and liberation every chance I get. Strangers are still fascinated by my line of work, and it seems every conversation eventually comes around to their stuff and what I think they should do about it. I am grateful every single day that I get to share this work with people hungry to change how they think about, feel about, and interact with stuff.

SOME NOTES ON THE SECOND EDITION

Within this updated and revised edition of my *Wall Street Journal* bestselling book, you and I get to work together using the same step-by-step process that I've shared with clients and workshop attendees everywhere since 1996. Using this method, you, too, can create a functional home you love and/or an efficient office or workspace that supports your creativity and productivity. These simple steps—none of which are complicated, all of which have been tested over multiple decades of practical application—will guarantee your success in getting organized *even if you've tried and failed multiple times in the past.*

From entering and exiting your home with your keys, bag, wallet, and mobile phone always in tow to facing the challenges of large-scale spaces such as attics, basements, garages, and even off-site storage facilities—we cover it all in these pages. So whether you want to get a handle on your kitchen, your car, your office, your computer, or your closet, you'll find complete instructions right here.

I've avoided discussing common areas like living rooms and family rooms, not because they don't matter but because the principles and techniques laid out for all the other clutter hot spots are easily applicable to these spaces, too. Once you've mastered them and applied them to your most challenging problem areas, you'll be able to apply them consistently throughout your entire home.

From your nightstand or entertainment center to your medicine cabinet or coat closet, you'll easily eliminate expired medicine, obsolete technology (videotapes, DVDs, CDs), board games with missing parts, broken emery boards, and tweezers that no longer tweeze—until each room, each drawer, each space is neat, clean, and clutter free. Likewise, you'll tackle digital clutter like emails, photos, PDFs, and other files—as well as the machines, cords, and cables no longer needed to access these materials.

Simply stated, after you finish reading and working through this book, you will always know where anything and everything is located in your home, office, devices, and car. Vehicle registration? Got it. Spare keys? You bet. Social Security card? No question. Aunt Betty's famous piecrust recipe? That great photo from your bucket-list trip last summer? Your current tax bill? Without a doubt, you will have it in front of you before you break a sweat.

And you will never again find yourself drowning in stuff—whether it's papers, photos, sporting goods, magazines, collectibles, digital files, or clothing. Through a series of activities and exercises, you will replace your currently ineffective habits with powerfully successful habits, freeing up hundreds if not thousands of previously wasted hours.

The ideas and instructions laid out in this book form a road map to freedom from clutter. My clients know that I avoid absolutes when speaking with them, but I promise you that, in this instance, the always and never mentioned here are about to come true for you.

It may be hard to read that and not get a little excited while also feeling some skepticism creep in. That's fine. These steps have been repeatedly tested and are exacting and precise without being rigid. Almost everything here is open to exploration, if not debate. I'll seldom ask you to do something without explaining why. I never liked it when my mom told me, "Because I'm the mom—that's why!," so I'll avoid doing that with you. You'll see in the chapters ahead that there is plenty of room to customize your approach and the appearance of your spaces.

I've worked hard to provide complete instructions and information so that you can release any resistance to change that crops up when I suggest a new way of doing things. After all, if your previous attempts at getting organized had been successful, you wouldn't be reading this book, would you? So trust me to give you good orderly direction, and I'll trust you to make it fit your lifestyle and budget.

HOW TO USE THIS BOOK

As you read this book, you may get the urge to ask why you can't just do *some* things the way you've always done them, whether that's sorting the mail or folding the laundry. Here's why: a piecemeal approach gives you a piecemeal result. By consistently applying these techniques across the board, you are guaranteed to experience powerful and significant relief in every place you've ever been stuck on stuff.

So before playing devil's advocate and touting minor miracles of successfully finding the insurance policy buried in a pile of catalogs, I'll ask again: If your way of finding and organizing things was working so well, would you really have picked up this book? And wouldn't you already know where your car keys are—every time you reach for them?

While I'll frequently use the word *work* to describe our efforts together, think of this more as training. Imagine yourself an Olympic athlete (maybe you are) training for the race of your life—with one major difference: winning isn't based on beating anyone to the finish line; it's about setting yourself free from behavior that no longer serves you. The good news is you don't have to change overnight and you don't have to be perfect. That's a promise.

You could also think of this work as a gift you're giving yourself. Each chapter offers a concise and manageable focus and a set of skills broken down into easy-to-accomplish, project-sized pieces. By the time you finish each chapter, you will have mastered another problem area. So whether you read only one or two chapters or tear through the entire book, each step along the way will bring you closer to regaining control over your things, your time, and your life. That's the prize to keep your eyes on.

I've been asked, "What if I stop and start this process? What happens then?"

Nothing tragic, of course. You'll delay that big rush of completely kicking your clutter habit as quickly as possible, but again, there's no race to the finish line, so you may certainly take a break (or breaks).

And because each chapter is its own unit of study, you can't lose the skills you've learned previously.

There is a natural rhythm that you'll develop as you move from chapter to chapter, but a pause here and there won't delay your results too much. So if you want or need a break, take one—just don't stay away too long!

Likewise, I've been asked, "What if I don't want to start with Chapter 1 because I want to start somewhere else? It's the basement that's making me crazy!"

I understand. You're feeling particularly jammed up or stymied, and you've selected this book because you want some powerful and immediate help with a significant problem in your life. You feel like there's no time to waste. But you should still start with Chapters 1 and 2. (You've waited this long to clean out your basement; a few more days won't make that much difference.)

The first two chapters lead you through an exploration of your particular relationship with stuff and teach you the most fundamental skills for unstuffing. Together, Chapter 1 and Chapter 2 lay the proper foundation for the work you'll face in subsequent chapters.

After those two chapters, you'll have a basic working knowledge of the techniques we build on in the remaining chapters. So if you'd like to read and work through Chapter 1 and Chapter 2, and *then* skip around, go for it. Give me the first two chapters to teach you the fundamentals, and I'll give you the confidence of knowing that the building blocks of organization are well within your grasp.

I also suggest you read each chapter through first without worrying about having to do anything. Read as if you were reading an article or short story, not studying for a test or grasping for a life vest. Then return to the beginning and work your way through the chapters again, completing whatever exercises and tasks are assigned. That way, if you do skip around, you'll do so from an informed point of view.

To help guide you through the activities and exercises included here, I have created a companion workbook you can purchase through many of the same vendors that sell this book. It contains all of the book's exercises, questionnaires, worksheets, and checklists in one convenient spot so you can reference your work at any time. The workbook also includes exclusive bonus content you won't find anywhere else.

If you prefer to use your own notebook, that's fine, too. The basic forms and lists included in the workbook are available for download at unstuffbook.com.

With these resources, my goal is to guide and coach you toward making clear and informed decisions about whatever you're trying to accomplish. The distance between being prepared and being hasty is not that far in time allotted but vast in results achieved.

As you get in touch with the reasons for the choices you've made historically around any number of issues, whether that's bills or tools or toys or clothes or food or dishes or [insert confounding item here], you'll begin to recognize that you often got into trouble the minute you stopped paying attention to what you were doing in the moment and began thinking about something else.

So remember: no multitasking. Leave that to us professionals. Just kidding. Even we can't successfully multitask, which I demonstrate in my book, *Calling BS on Busy*. For best results, focus on what you're doing while you're doing it so you don't trip yourself up.

If you're panicking now, thinking I just took away your superpower, in most cases doing one thing at a time is actually the quickest way to get more done with fewer mistakes. It turns out getting organized is not about doing more; it's about doing less.

So even though it may feel foreign to start with, practice staying present by doing one thing at a time. This is one of the easiest ways to avoid forgetting who you were supposed to call back or where the lid to the face cream is. Because you can't forget what you never knew. If you were walking around the house looking for the ringing phone with the top to the face cream in your hand, were you actually paying enough attention to remember later where you set that lid down as you reached for the phone?

Probably not.

A key to this work's effectiveness is to move deliberately—and slowly—and to take on only one area at a time, allowing enough space for new habits to develop. Then you can build from there.

Perhaps you're thinking, *But I'm in desperate shape! I need help now, and I can't wait for things to change gradually.*

To you, I say, great, you're in the perfect place. Remember this feeling of desperation. It's the last time you need to feel this unsteady and out of control—and a desire to avoid this feeling again can be powerful motivation if you actually remember it. So take a moment and commit it to memory.

Are your palms a bit clammy? Is your breathing shallow and labored? Are you itchy? Hungry? Angry? Distracted? Ready to toss this book across the room? Note it all and refer back to it when you're tempted to quit doing this work.

I won't leave you without some immediate relief, though. That feeling of swirling, unformed impending doom is usually a great fiction, a product of our unique and remarkable imaginations. Through stories we tell ourselves over and over again—perhaps even unconsciously at this point—we create and recreate these states of panic. Unless you're being held at gunpoint with a demand that you produce a specific mislaid document, there's little about being late and disorganized that merits this degree of unease.

Now, you may be an adrenaline junkie who *wants* to be organized but also really craves the rush of panic, and if so, you have two choices:

1. Use this book to break that habit of deliberately creating a level of chaos that makes you feel alive while also undermining any sustainable level of happiness and serenity.
2. Set this book aside.

If you're not ready to choose option one, it's probably not the right time for you to read this book. It will ruin your buzz. Once you've read this book, you'll never again be able to rush around the house frantically searching for your keys or your purse or your cell phone or your living will without hearing my voice or, even better, your own voice reminding you, *This isn't brain surgery; no one is lying open on the table. There is enough time to find or accomplish this.*

There is a pervasive, tremendous lie most of us tell ourselves and reinforce each day—that there is not enough time to accomplish what is really important to us. But there *is* enough time for what's truly important. Anyone who's cared for a sick or dying friend or loved one knows that time shifts when the illusory veil of immortality is removed. The bills get paid, food gets prepared and eaten, but superfluous phone calls or texts are not replied to. Low-priority events go unattended. The things that are really important find a way of receiving adequate attention, if not complete attention. And the baloney (or bullsh*t, if you prefer) falls away.

Tim McGraw's great song "Live Like You Were Dying" and Jack Kornfield's succinct summation "The trouble is, you think you have time" both remind us that, of course, we *are* dying. Each day we age. And we can never know when our last day will come. So if we can hold that in our being without feeling maudlin about it, we will gain clarity that our time really *is* limited and that what's important *is* what we really want to spend our time doing.

That's what this book is all about. I don't think paying bills and filing papers and cleaning out the junk drawer is or should be that important. It's just *stuff*. The messes that surround you are keeping you from what is important. So I'm suggesting that you commit enough time to break some old bad habits, replace them with some new useful habits, and then get on with the rest of your life.

Once you've trained yourself to unstuff consistently, you'll never have to waste a precious moment of your day looking for your house keys or wondering where the phone bill is as they're turning off your service. You won't find yourself riffling through the same clothes over and over in search of the one clean shirt you actually enjoy wearing.

It seems antithetical, I know, to spend this time once never to have to spend it again. But there is no free lunch. As with so many other things, either you're going to pay up front for being disorganized or you're going to pay on the back end, and unfortunately, when you pay on the way out it's always more expensive than if you had simply paid at the beginning.

Here's an illustration: The free trial that then became a recurring subscription 30 days later may have felt like a bargain when you signed up because you promised yourself you'd cancel before the first charge landed. But six months later when you finally spot the charge on your credit card statement and realize you've never actually used the thing, is it still the bargain you imagined? Probably not.

Now multiply that by every deferred decision and broken promise, and you can see how quickly it all adds up. Heartbreaking what a little math can do, right?

The time you spend *now* learning simple and easy ways of organizing your life will lay a foundation for uncomplicated and productive time in the future. Now, not "someday"—that mythical land where time stands still and you're scrapbooking all your vacations, baking 10 dozen cookies for the church bazaar, sewing your children's clothes, and finally learning to fly-fish on the Colorado River.

That place doesn't exist. Not even for Oprah or Martha Stewart. It's useful to remember that they have staff. And since you probably don't, it's time to surrender "someday." "Someday" doesn't exist. But today does. So welcome to it. Grab it, seize it, cherish it, and make it your own.

Let's begin!

1

YOU ARE NOT YOUR STUFF

You can't think your way into right action,
but you can act your way into right thinking.
–BILL WILSON

Nothing can be done without hope.
–HELEN KELLER

Sometimes letting things go is an act of far greater power
than defending or hanging on.
–ECKHART TOLLE

WHAT WE'RE GOING TO COVER IN THIS CHAPTER

- Half-Measures, Staying on the Hook, and Perfectionism
- What Stuff Is and Isn't
- You Are Not Your Stuff
- If I'm Not My Stuff, What Am I?
- Your Core Values
- Aligning with Your Core Values
- The Stuff Behind the Stuff
- The Promise

IN THE BEGINNING, God created man. And then, apparently right after that, She must have created stuff. Because it's everywhere. You can hardly move without tripping over stuff. And since stuff is probably not going away, we need to get right with it. Because otherwise stuff will never be right with us.

Please get something to write with and either your companion workbook or your own notebook. We're going to do a little writing. I suggest that if you're not using the companion workbook, whatever you use is reserved only for this work. Please don't use an existing journal or a series of Post-it notes. You'll want to refer back to this work often, and it should be cohesive, bound together, and easy to find.

Next, visit unstuffbook.com/stuff to download the Stuff Questionnaire, or you can find it in the companion workbook. For reference, the questions are also listed below.

As you're reading and answering the questions, keep in mind that there are no right or wrong answers to them. They are not intended to humiliate you or to expose your faults and foibles. That's true for all of this work—there's no hidden "gotcha" agenda here. The intention is always to examine the role stuff plays in your life. You won't be graded on your answers, because this isn't a test—it's an exploration.

Take your time, write out your answers (or dictate them into a note or other transcription app), and tell yourself the truth. You're the only person who's going to be reading this. We're not looking for pretty; we're looking for honest. So resist answering them according to how you wish you felt if this were an ideal world. Also avoid answering them as if you have already finished this book and your stuff is well under control.

Stuff Questionnaire

1. Do you often feel stuck?

2. Can you identify what you feel stuck in or by?

3. How often do you feel overwhelmed?

4. Do you feel that there's something else you should be doing but can't ever seem to get to it?

5. Are there things you tell yourself you'll do as soon as some other things are finished?

6. Do you ever finish those other things and actually get to the things you've put off?

7. How often, if ever, do you feel caught up (i.e., everything on your to-do list has been checked off)?

8. Do you ever complain of being bored or of having too much time on your hands?

9. If so, how do you address that? What do you do to fill that time?

10. Do you stop what you're doing when anyone calls or texts and shift all your attention to them?

11. Do you do this regardless of whether it's an emergency or just an everyday call?

12. Do you always agree to do a favor for someone whether it's convenient for you or not?

13. If so, do you ever feel put-upon or get resentful as a result?

14. Do you think that saying no makes you a bad or selfish person?

15. Do you ever get resentful when people say no to you?

16. Is there ever an appropriate time for you to say no? When?

17. Do you take no personally? Do you sometimes think they might have said yes to someone else under similar circumstances?

18. What's the difference between an excuse and an explanation?

19. How often do you say *because* or *but* when explaining things?

20. Do you think you're often offering valid explanations for things and not making excuses?

21. Have you ever had a disagreement with someone over this interpretation?

22. Does your stuff seem to have a life of its own?

23. Do you often set something down and swear it moves sometime during the night?

24. How often during a week do you misplace something you need—keys, wallet, cell phone, bag?

25. Are you mostly upbeat except when you think about your stuff?

26. Do you remember a time when you used to feel optimistic, and now you just feel beaten down?

27. Do you have piles of papers around but swear you can find anything in them?

28. Have you ever freaked out—becoming panicky or unreasonably upset—when someone moved your stuff?

29. Have you ever lost something that was important to you because someone confused it for trash?

30. If that has happened, do you feel you had any responsibility for this, or was it only the other person's fault?

31. Do you get nervous when the phone rings or a text arrives?

32. Do you screen your calls?

33. Has stuff made living in your home challenging?

34. Have you ever fought with someone you love over stuff?

35. Does your stuff seem to force you into smaller and smaller living spaces?

36. Do you sleep to one side of your bed because you have a pile of stuff next to you?

37. Do you sometimes have difficulty breathing?

38. Do you spend more time tidying up, looking for things, or decluttering than doing the things you love?

39. Is looking for things threatening to overtake your passions?

40. Are you often just a few minutes late to get somewhere?

41. Do you tell yourself that being late is not a big deal?

42. Do you think that the people you love are more important than stuff?

43. If someone looked only at your behavior, would they objectively see that?

44. When you're feeling blue, do you think that shopping will get you out of your funk?

45. Does the act of buying something give you a warm and fuzzy feeling?

46. Have you ever said, "I'd die without_____"?

47. If you answered yes to the previous question, were you talking about a person or a thing?

48. Do you often speak in absolutes (such as "I always..." or "I never...")?

49. Do you have stories about most of the things you own?

50. Do you like to tell them to your friends and family? How about strangers? Anyone who'll listen?

51. Do they find the stories as fascinating as you do?

52. Do you think you spend more time talking about stuff or about things you've done or plan to do?

Wow, congratulations! That's a lot of questions. Thanks for taking the time to answer them all. Did you answer them all? If you didn't, please go back and do so. And, yes, I am serious.

As you review your answers, make note of any patterns that are revealed about your relationship with things, about your relationship with time, and about your relationships with people. Again, these questions are not designed to shame you or to hurt you in any way. They're here to help you identify where you're stuck on stuff and where stuff is stuck on you.

I've often seen that light bulb go on behind clients' eyes when they first recognized that what they thought they were spending their days doing was not what they were actually doing. Or it was getting done but with a heap of resentment or resistance or avoidable delays.

So use the information gathered from your answers to clarify whether you are in fact spending your time doing the things you think you're doing *and* that these are the things you want to be doing. If, instead, you discover that you are caught in a cycle of activities and tasks that may be necessary but are also consistently pushing their way ahead of things that matter more, in the following pages you'll learn how to reverse that process and put the necessary tasks back in their proper place.

If you find that you spend more time with things than with people and that doesn't please you, here, too, you will learn how to manage your possessions so that you are not spending valuable time interacting with them when you could be enjoying the company of friends and family.

HALF-MEASURES, STAYING ON THE HOOK, AND PERFECTIONISM

I don't have rules about much, but I am sure that half-measures are useless. Actually, they're worse than useless; they undermine our ability to accomplish anything of significance in our lives. So if you're someone who has a history of enthusiastic beginnings followed by rapid losses of interest or a history of picking and choosing how you'll participate in something, constantly reevaluating your commitment and efforts, I'm strongly suggesting you let that go for the rest of our time together. Remember, this is voluntary—hopefully, no one showed up at your door and said, "Read this book and get your act together or else." If they didn't, then this is something you think is worth doing. So I'm going to support you in doing it fully.

What's laid out before you is a feast of tools and tips and questions and suggestions to help you unstuff your life in whatever ways are valuable to you. And whatever those are, I want you to do them completely. Not three-fourths of the way, not seven-eighths of the way—all the way. You won't know what could have been possible if you let yourself off the hook.

And, believe me, I've heard all the excuses masquerading as explanations by now: Your bestie has tried and failed at this before or so-and-so's bestie told them that it didn't work; you recently read a study that said this could never work for someone with your particular challenges or circumstances; you're too busy; you're not smart enough; you're too smart—you'll figure out all the angles (there are no angles); you're too fat, too thin, too tall, too short, too old, not old enough; someone's on their way over; someone's just about to leave; you're just about to leave; you've got somewhere else to be or to get to; you'll do it "later"; you don't see the point . . . The list goes on.

As a reformed perfectionist and control enthusiast myself, I also understand the corollary notion that if you can't do something perfectly, there's no point in attempting it at all. I now know this is baloney. Of course there's a point in doing something imperfectly. If there wasn't, most things in life would never get started, and even fewer would ever get finished.

More importantly, there's a big difference between imperfectly and incompletely. You can get a perfect score on a math test, but if you're looking to get a perfect score on life, you may need to redefine what perfect looks like. First of all, life doesn't always add up, and second, unlike a math test, no one's grading you on life (except maybe

God, depending on how you define God—but I'd like to think She grades on a curve anyway).

So let's shift our thinking about how we evaluate our efforts and use a model in which effort expended equals results achieved. That way, we can get off the thankless merry-go-round of telling ourselves, *Everything has to be perfect the first time or it's a waste of time.* Instead, we recognize that if we are diligent, if we don't let ourselves off the hook, if we apply ourselves 100 percent, then we are guaranteed to receive a 100 percent return on the experience.

And when that experience is unstuffing our lives, of turning chaos into order and moving from confusion to organization, no whole-hearted effort is wasted. The outcome may not be perfect, but if that's the case, we're free to try again. Hmm, so maybe with enough earnest attempts, we actually can get a perfect score on life?

If you still haven't answered all 52 questions, please go back and do that now. Believe me, I can sit here longer than you can. So just do it and get it over with. Besides, what's coming next is so great that you'll be bummed to miss it, and it won't make a lick of sense if you haven't answered every single one of those questions!

WHAT STUFF IS AND ISN'T

All this talk about stuff, but what exactly *is* stuff?

Stuff (noun): Miscellaneous unspecified objects, as in "The trunk is full of stuff."

I love that definition. Stuff is the vaguest of vague objects. Not only is it miscellaneous, it's also unspecified. How perfect is that?

So now that we know what stuff is, let's talk about what stuff isn't. Stuff isn't people. Stuff isn't animals—companion, barnyard, or wild. And it isn't plants. Stuff is nothing that's alive, so let's add that to our definition.

Miscellaneous *inanimate* unspecified objects.

That's what we've got piling up around us and possibly dragging along behind us, and that's the subject of this book—the accumulation of so many individual specified things that they have now morphed and blurred into a mass of miscellaneous inanimate unspecified objects.

Understanding what stuff is and isn't makes the next part easier.

YOU ARE NOT YOUR STUFF

As we now know, stuff doesn't breathe. So, at least in this instance, you're off the hook. You are not your stuff.

Radical, isn't it? You are not your stuff.

But Madison Avenue and social media might have you believing otherwise. They'd argue that you are completely your stuff. That you're nothing if you're *not* your stuff. That the world is watching and constantly evaluating and judging you based specifically on your stuff. That's a rather bleak outlook, and it's surprisingly pervasive. But we know better.

Say it out loud with me: "I am not my stuff."

Cool. How'd that sound? Convincing? Say it again.

"I am not my stuff."

Louder.

"I am not my stuff."

Louder still.

"I am not my stuff!"

Now go to the window, open it, lean out, and shout, "I'm mad as hell, and I'm not going to take it anymore!"

Just kidding! Please don't do that. But I appreciate your willingness to consider it. You're a good sport.

On one level, I'd like to think we could all identify where our sweaters or our computers or our music collections end and we begin. But many people cannot distinguish between themselves and the objects that surround them—the shoes, the clothes, the cars, the phone, the jewelry, the trips, the addresses, the job. They may know that they are not literally any of those things, but somewhere, in some subtle or not-so-subtle way, especially when they feel that others are watching, the lines get blurred.

They start to feel like the car or the phone *is* an extension of themselves, that it's an expression of their thoughtfulness, their talent, their success, their discernment, and their taste. Maybe these items even start to feel like the best parts of themselves. And just like that, they find they are defining themselves in part by what they own.

The solution for this is not the total rejection of possessions. It's not the stuff's fault. Nor am I suggesting that you get rid of everything you've worked very hard to accumulate. Instead, I'm suggesting that in our hurry to gather more and more things around us, we become confused as to what serves us and what is just a distraction.

Think for a few moments about how you or someone you know talks about the things that surround them. Have you ever said or heard someone say, "Man, I love my [new] _____."? How about "Oh my God! I don't know how I've lived without this _____ for all these years! This is going to change my life!"?

We usually leave it at that, but how often is acquiring something new actually exponentially transforming our lives? Maybe the invention of the modern washing machine. Or the wheel. Or the phone. But a particular phone? A new app? Really?

My computer has certainly made writing this book easier, but I do know how I lived before I had one. I used a typewriter. And before that, sheets of paper and lots of pens and pencils. I think I also played more tennis and rode my bike more often.

So let's try to distinguish between comfortable or convenient and life altering. Hyperbole can be fun and certainly dramatic, but when it comes to unstuffing your life, you're going to want to accurately describe the scale of an event and its impact on your behavior and your choices.

Let me share an illustration from my own life. As a teenager, I collected record albums. I loved music. (I still do.) I lugged those albums all over the Midwest for years. Milk crate after milk crate full of records. Collecting them gave me an identity and allowed me a place to get lost. I owned albums I never listened to because I liked the cover art or because I thought a particular artist or record was a good addition to my collection. This was especially true of some obscure artists that I thought would impress others with the breadth of my musical tastes.

And books—same story. Books I had read and would never read again. Books I would never take the time to read but looked good on my shelf or seemed like something I might read someday. And if I'm being honest, books that I secretly wished demonstrated how well-read I was so if you happened to visit me, you'd judge me favorably.

Since I was a little less organized back then, my books weren't sorted or stored in any kind of order, just randomly shoved onto any free shelf. Because of this, it'd be easy to miss the fact that I had multiple copies of *Catcher in the Rye*. When I actually needed to find a book, I'd search through hundreds of them, trying to remember something distinct about the spine or cover to narrow it down. *Catcher*, in particular, benefited from that burgundy cover with yellow print. Not every book was that easy to find.

Most of those books are now gone. Today, I buy books that interest me and that I'm committed to reading and owning. I sometimes swap books with friends. And I borrow a lot of books from public libraries, both physically and digitally. Once I let go of the concept of ownership as the highest value of a book, it became much easier for me to just enjoy a book without having to keep it forever.

There are plenty of books that you should purchase. Books you use for work. Books you study and need to write in. I'd like to think this book is one of those books. Cookbooks, books for pleasure, favorite books that you'll read again and again—all worth purchasing. But if what you want is simply the knowledge contained inside the book or the thrill of a great mystery, consider all the different ways you can have that experience that also don't require you to add another possession to your life.

All of those albums are now gone, too. Some have been replaced with their digital counterparts, but only the ones I still listen to. I let them go long before I started helping others unstuff their lives—because technology gave me a way to listen to the music without the burden of dragging around the physical items. That was the right choice for me.

For an audiophile who loves vinyl, that probably would not be a great choice. She would just need to make sure she had room for those albums and the willingness to lug them with her if she ever moved to a different house. We each get to decide what serves us today that we want to hold onto and what used to serve us in the past that we can now release.

To be clear, the experience of getting rid of my records was bitter-sweet. I loved those albums, and I had a great deal invested in them, the money being the least of it in some ways. I had part of my identity tied up in them. I thought of them as a visible, easily readable piece of me out in the world.

I know now that what other people think of me is both beyond my control and far less important to me than my own comfort, happiness, and ultimately, what I think of myself. Because I am not my stuff.

You are not your stuff. We are not our stuff.

Now, it's easy to say that what we think of ourselves is the most important thing, which I believe is true, and that what anyone else thinks about the kind of cars we drive, or whose name is on our clothing, or what we're reading or listening to is unimportant, which is also true—but it's not as easy to live that second truth. That's the inside work that we all need to do to unstuff our lives. Because even if other people care more than is appropriate or even healthy, we can't control them. We can control only ourselves.

So instead of projecting into our friend's or neighbor's mind, which is never very comfortable, let's just say that, going forward, what other people think of us is none of our business—unless they make it our business by sharing it with us. And given that few of us, if any, can actually read minds, let's take all that energy and funnel it into much more fun and productive pursuits.

IF I'M NOT MY STUFF, WHAT AM I?

Have you ever fought with someone you cared about over a thing? Something misplaced, or borrowed and not returned, or returned soiled or damaged? Did they seem genuinely sorry? Was that enough?

While it's not acceptable for someone to lose or destroy your belongings, accidents happen. As a result, you may decide that you'll never lend out anything ever again. You might take it a step further and decide to never have anyone in your house again, either. Because even under your watchful eye, accidents may happen there, too.

Rather than holding on to things tighter in an attempt to preserve them indefinitely, could you decide instead to loosen your grip even more? To entertain the idea that all things are impermanent, even you? To shift your relationship with things toward one of appreciation while they're intact and acceptance when they break or fail? This may influence you to lend out the Honda and keep the Rolls-Royce in the garage—that's a fine compromise. But how important do you want to make any one thing really?

What is worth ending a relationship over? You can usually get another thing, even something as special as a cashmere sweater that was on sale for so little money it's both thrilling and embarrassing to mention. It's a little harder to replace the friend you've known since kindergarten.

So if we think of ourselves as guardians of these things but not as their God, as stewards responsible for the care and maintenance of these objects but not as their parent, then we can be appropriately vigilant *and also* reasonably detached when something about their condition or even existence shifts. We can feel sad or disappointed or relieved and still not feel called to do anything other than feel. That sounds liberating to me.

YOUR CORE VALUES

What is important to you? This is not a rhetorical question.

Your core values lie at the very center of who you are. If you've ever heard anyone mention their moral compass, core values provide direction for that compass. When what you do and what you value are in sync, your life is in balance, and the direction and purpose of your life are easy to articulate and pursue.

Once you know your core values, you can eliminate activities that don't align with them, such as

- accumulating things that don't serve you or support you in achieving your goals,
- spending time on activities that distract you from accomplishing the things you're passionate about or paid to do, and/or
- doing things you are passionate about but not adequately compensated for and then feeling like a martyr or growing resentful.

We may at any time experience acting in opposition to our core values for any number of reasons—feeling that we "should" do something we know isn't right, doing something we're "expected" to do when we feel we have no choice, or doing something without thinking because it's what we've always done.

So let's do a few core-value exercises and get the clarity we need to live in harmony with those values. Start by going to unstuffbook.com/values and downloading the Core Values Worksheet, or you can find it in the companion workbook. You'll notice it contains some questions and a list of values. The values list is not exhaustive, but it is comprehensive. If one of your values is missing from it, feel free to write it in. As a favor to other readers, if you do identify any values missing from the list, please send an email to hello@andrewmellen.com with your additions or suggestions so I can update these tools. That way, we all benefit from our collective wisdom.

There are no universally right or preferred answers to these exercises. The right answers are the truthful ones. If you value something that you judge as unappealing or wrong or stupid, either shift your feeling or shift your values. When you're finished with the exercises, return to this book.

Excellent. Now, what are the five qualities that you cannot imagine living without, that are essential to who you are and how you want to live? Write them in your companion workbook—maybe put them on a Post-it on your bathroom mirror. Keep them close since these values are at the very center of who you are. And that's most definitely not stuff.

ALIGNING WITH YOUR CORE VALUES

Now that you know what's important to you and have a clearer understanding of what you value, it's time to put those analytical skills to use on something practical. Return to your answers on the Stuff Questionnaire you filled out earlier in this chapter. Evaluate your responses, looking for where your core values are reflected in those answers. Write next to your answers each core value that you see reflected there.

If you see none of your core values in an answer, put a zero there, and write what you do see reflected instead, whether that's fear, resentment, reticence, resistance, envy, or something else. Just note it. Remember that you have nothing to fear from the truth—you're doing private work, and your frank assessment of your behavior will only help to clear the way for the kind of change you desire.

If you value love and kindness and find that you're mostly scared and resentful, how do you get from here to there? What are the choices you need to make to shift your conscious or unconscious stance from one of resistance to one of receptivity? How do you let go of things that you don't value or don't serve you to make room for and embrace the things that you do value and will serve you?

Remember, there are no universal answers to these kinds of questions. But I do believe there are universal tools for discovering your answers, and those are open-mindedness, willingness, honesty, and quiet reflection. You don't need to become a monk to learn how to hear something beneath the constant chatter of your mind. Five minutes of doing seemingly nothing besides sitting still, focusing on your breath, and reflecting on the earlier questions (as well as others that may start to come to you once you begin this process) can quiet your thoughts down enough to reveal some answers. Let's try it now.

You'll start by setting a timer for five minutes. Focus on your answers to the first questions, your core values, and the questions of how to bring your behavior into alignment with your core values. Ask, almost in a prayer, for the ability to find what you have been responsible for in the past or present and what you can change for the better now and in the future. If it helps you, you may dim the lights, but do not sit in the dark.

If you find that you're starting to judge yourself or calling yourself names for any of the places where your behavior is not yet in alignment, or even for doing this exercise, recognize that. And then, rather than tightening up or resisting it, just look at it. Look at it as if you were observing someone else who was judging themselves. Approach the tension or judgment with a degree of curiosity rather than disappointment or anger, and you should be able to refocus on the questions before you.

It may be that the entire five minutes are filled with just judging and looking, with just spinning around mentally and only brief glimpses of the questions. That's fine. The goal is simply to begin or resume a process of sitting still and reflecting.

When the timer goes off, write down anything that seems noteworthy from your quiet time.

Do this five-minute practice for 30 days consecutively, and you will be amazed at the clarity you obtain around your behavior and effective ways to shift it in your favor. With patience, you will learn both what you have been doing that runs counter to your core values and ways to do things differently to yield superior results.

THE STUFF BEHIND THE STUFF

Some of the mental noise and distractions mentioned in the last section may occur in the form of stories. We tell ourselves stories all day. Some out loud and some as chatter running just in the background, barely audible to our subconscious. We make up new reasons or reinforce established reasons why something should or shouldn't be done, or why if it is done, it should be done a particular way. We spend a lot of time trying to figure out what something means—whether that's guessing at the motivations behind someone's behavior or evaluating and assigning value to stuff.

Let's set the analysis of others' behavior aside for now. What I want to focus on are the stories we tell ourselves about our stuff. I call these stories "the stuff behind the stuff."

I'm not suggesting that these stories are deliberate lies, although some may be untrue. What I am suggesting is that we often take an object and weave a narrative around it until that object becomes bound up in that story. Any interaction with that object means also interacting with the story, so much so that the story almost stands guard over the object, acting as the first line of defense. You have to get through the story to get to the object.

This complicated relationship between story and object is why so many people struggle with any part of getting organized, particularly that first step. It often doesn't matter what the goal is—whether it's finding a proper home for the object or sifting through piles of stuff to possibly purge some surplus items. Usually the story has so much power over folks that they stand immobile in the face of it—it's become an effective barrier to any change, even a change as simple as putting something away.

NOTABLE NOTE

One of my favorite statistics is that the average adult tells 200 lies a day.[1] This doesn't mean we're all liars, but it does mean that we may have a more fluid and subjective relationship with the truth than we like to acknowledge. Hopefully, you find this amusing and the source of some humility and relief rather than an affront to your integrity. By embracing this concept, it may be easier to laugh at some of the stories you tell yourself (and others) and, by extension, easier to let both some stories and some items go and go more quickly.

1 Jerald M. Jellison, *I'm Sorry, I Didn't Mean to, and Other Lies We Love to Tell*, Chatham Square Press, 1977.

So getting to and through the stuff behind the stuff is key to this process. Your grandfather's top hat is still going to be your grandfather's top hat. And if the story is that your grandfather wore that top hat at his wedding to your grandmother, that's not going to change, either. What is going to change, I hope, is the imperative that story places on your grandfather's top hat:

"You must keep me. I'm 85 years old, and that wedding was the reason you're here today. You'd be a terrible grandchild if you got rid of me."

We think nothing of discarding a gum wrapper once we've taken out the piece of gum and put it in our mouth. At a core level, that top hat is no different from the gum wrapper. They both exist, they both served a purpose, and they both might have no more purpose to serve in our lives at this time.

You must know, of course, that the top hat is not your grandfather. That bears repeating. That top hat is not your grandfather. It's just an article of his clothing. So I'm not suggesting that you get rid of your grandfather. You might be hearing that. In fact, the story, the stuff behind the stuff, might be actively telling you that.

Hey! He's suggesting you toss your grandfather in the trash or send him off to Goodwill. Your grandfather would never do that to you, you ungrateful brat. Put me down!

But if you're done with the hat, if that hat, practically speaking, is a burden, if it's taking up room that you need for something you do use, such as one of your own hats or bags, or if it makes you sad to look at it, or if it's literally falling apart on your closet shelf and could never be worn again by anyone, let alone your grandfather, then you can reverently and respectfully let go of the hat. Even when the hat is gone, you can still celebrate your grandparents' wedding. You can still appreciate the history woven into that hat.

Don't turn everything you own into a ball and chain. Actual balls and chains will be enough. Let the hat be just a hat. And if you're done with the hat, then you are empowered to release the hat back to the universe for its next chapter, a chapter that may not include you.

THE PROMISE

I can't promise you that if you're single, by the time you finish working through this book you'll be happily married (if marriage even interests you). I can't promise you that your boss will start treating you better, that you'll finally get along with the person in the next cubicle, or that you'll always get a good parking space.

What I can promise you is this: If you are diligent about this work, if you are consistent and alert and apply yourself, when you are finished with this book you will have more time on your hands than you ever thought possible. You will have less, you will do less, and you will accomplish more, faster.

You will always be able to find anything—in your home or office, kitchen or car—within 30 seconds. You will never be late because you misplaced your car keys. (You may be late because of traffic, but we can't control everything.) You will finally have the time to do the things you love to do. Or to discover the things you love. Or to rediscover them.

If you don't have to waste another minute looking for something you were certain you just saw but now can't seem to find, that's one more minute you have to write a love letter or the great American novel, to bake some brownies or bathe your baby, to visit your mother or solve global warming. Now imagine those minutes adding up and then picture what you can do with another hour, day, or week. Exactly.

I can't tell you what to do with that time once you get it. That's covered in another of my books—*Calling BS on Busy*. What I can do here is guide you through a precise process that will enable you to unstuff your life of everything that doesn't serve you and shine a light on everything that does. How's that sound?

Now, so we don't waste another minute discussing theories or waxing philosophical, let's get you cracking on this new way of life. I want to launch you into the rest of the book with whatever messy mix of enthusiasm and skepticism, inertia and hope you're currently brewing and, from there, help you change your life.

Deep breath. And here we go.

2

KEYS · WALLET · BAG · MAIL

Beware of the door with too many keys.

–PORTUGUESE PROVERB

WHAT WE'RE GOING TO COVER IN THIS CHAPTER

* Day One of Physical Unstuffing
* One Home for Everything and Like with Like
* A Home for Your Keys
* A Home for Your Wallet or Bag
* A Home for Your Mail
* Establishing a Mail Routine
* Processing Historic Mail
* Living the Work and Maintaining the System

THIS CHAPTER, as with each chapter that follows, is best read in one sitting. Additionally, to lay a proper foundation, to build new habits, and to anchor them well into your life, I strongly urge you to read the previous chapter and complete the initial exercises within the first two days of starting this book. Remember, we're trying to establish new habits, and we need to allow enough time for these new behaviors to hatch into habits.

Once you complete the exercises, you may reread the chapter as often as you need or want to. But the first reading and the exercises should be done within the first two days for maximum impact.

You are also encouraged to write in this book. Whether you're using the companion workbook or not, consider this book an additional place for notes. It's a fun read, I hope, but it is intended to be a guide, so don't be shy about claiming it as a tool. Underline, highlight, or flag key phrases and paragraphs that grab your attention so you can easily find them later.

DAY ONE OF PHYSICAL UNSTUFFING

Congratulations are now in order. By this point, you've successfully navigated several large conversations and explorations. You've investigated and charted (I like thinking of this process in a concrete way as a clear journey, so I often use map-related language) where you begin and your stuff ends. I hope you have a slightly lighter grip on your belongings and can feel a shift in how you relate to your physical environment and the things that surround you.

You might now be asking yourself questions when you interact with your possessions, really looking at what you are attached to, what your relationship with an object is, and what function it serves rather than clutching things unconsciously and chasing elusive comfort. Hopefully, you are now no longer living in a fantasy land of "someday" where a currently useless item will suddenly spring into useful purpose.

In the Introduction and in Chapter 1, I made no distinction between clutter at home and clutter at the office—possessions are possessions. As the lines between where we live and work continue to shift and blur, I'm primarily going to address residential spaces. For those of you whose homes may be in great shape but whose commercial offices are drowning in paper or other clutter and disorganization, take the principles I'm discussing and apply them to your situation.

The same goes for renters versus homeowners. Some of my suggestions will require more permanent additions or modifications to your home. If you're renting and you have a good relationship with your landlord, it's always a good idea to ask if they would be willing to share the costs for some improvements, particularly if those improvements will stay in place when you move. Any smart landlord should appreciate a tenant who takes initiative to improve the quality of the home when it also improves the value of the landlord's investment.

So regardless of whether you want to unstuff your commercial space or residential space or whether you rent or own, focus on the instructions, outlines, and solutions offered for each thing—as that information supersedes location. For example, your keys will have their spot in either a home or an office, or in a home and an office. The guiding principles behind the first two legs of The Organizational Triangle—One Home for Everything and Like with Like—know no boundaries and are not site-specific.

ONE HOME FOR EVERYTHING AND LIKE WITH LIKE

Let's talk about coming and going. You are on your way out of your space. Maybe you are late or maybe you are not. Perhaps you know where your keys are or perhaps you do not. They might be in your bag, they might be lying on a surface somewhere, or they might be in the pocket of the last garment you were wearing. They might still be dangling from the lock of the front door. Most likely, they are not in their "home." And that is where the problem begins.

One Home for Everything and Like with Like are the keys, no (bad) pun intended, to the entire process of getting organized. The third leg of the triangle—Something In, Something Out—is how you'll stay organized.

In its simplest form, this means that you'll maintain organization and prevent future clutter by letting something go when something new comes in. If that freaks you out at all, it's okay. Just recognize you're worrying about something that hasn't happened yet and isn't guaranteed to happen, and that should help you relax a bit.

Either way, set the third leg aside for now and know that we'll explore it in depth later in the book. For now, focus on the first two legs as they are the foundation and the only two rules you need to know and use right now.

Using One Home for Everything and Like with Like, almost anyone can improve their relationship with stuff. If you do nothing more than determine where each item lives and group similar items together, you will greatly improve your current situation. I strive for excellence, so "good enough" is not good enough for me. But it may be for you. I won't judge you. If you can always put your hands on the letter opener or the scissors, if you never misplace your keys again, I'll consider you a success. If, however, you want more out of life than crumbs—please keep reading.

Everything has a home. You have a home. Your friends have
homes. Your books have a home. And most certainly your keys and
your wallet or bag have homes. If everything you own has one home
and only one home, it can only ever be in one of two places: out being
used or back in its home awaiting its next use. This is so simple a concept that it's easy to see why many people might overlook it or dismiss
its significance in the process of getting organized.

Your wallet may have a different home in your house than my wallet does in mine. There is no universal home for each object, such as
the top-right drawer of the dresser in the bedroom. You might not
have a dresser (or a bedroom). But every item needs a home based on
how, when, and where you use it. Wherever it makes the most sense
for each object to "live" is its home.

Now, I'm aware that keys and other inanimate objects don't actually breathe, so technically they don't "live" anywhere. Indulge me.
This is an essential piece of language that will shift how you interact
with every single object that crosses your path going forward. Resist
the urge to feel morally superior to me and my silly word choices

because once you accept that everything has a home and lives only in that one place, you will always be able to find it in its home.

A HOME FOR YOUR KEYS

Find the home for your keys. Mine live in a rice bowl on a console table near my front door. The first thing I do when I walk in the front door is empty my pockets and drop my keys in their bowl. The first thing.

I may set down some heavy packages right inside the front door, but I don't walk into the kitchen or some other room, unload the packages, and then return to the front door. That's not how you build a consistent new behavior. Perhaps in several months you *could* rush to the bathroom and then return to the front door and hang up your keys. But for now, practice walking through the door and immediately placing the keys in their home. This needs to become second nature to you.

What if the phone is ringing? What if it's an emergency? I don't want to miss the call because I had to stop and hang up my stupid keys!

Excellent questions—that is, if you're looking for an excuse and a way out of new behavior. This line of thinking and these types of questions are attempts to undermine you and prevent you from changing. They are natural. Counterproductive but natural. Don't fear them. They can't hurt you.

For any number of reasons, we each resist change. It's okay; it seems to be part of the human condition. It's worth noting that as creatures of habit, we often prefer ineffective familiarity to efficient unfamiliarity if it means not having to change, even if that change is for the better.

Accept that you're probably going to want to argue with me, hunt for a loophole, and resist changing your behavior *even* when that change is beneficial and desirable. It's almost absurd, isn't it? You want to know where your keys are, but you also don't want to change the habit of just dropping them wherever you feel like it without paying attention. Welcome to human frailty.

So argue with me. I can take it. I've done this countless times. You are not unique, and you are not the exception. Take some comfort from that. I'm not a bully, and I'm pretty certain I'm right about this, so I can wait for you to run through your excuses and then flop exhaustedly into agreement. Or at least acquiescence. I'll settle for compliance if not enthusiasm. See? I'm easy.

Go find the home for your keys. Whether it's a hook next to your front door or a decorative bowl or container on a table just inside your front door, it needs to be one of these kinds of places. They need to live on a hook or in a container—not just on top of the table but in a vessel that is now identified as the proper home for your keys.

If you want the home for your keys to be in a bag or purse, you can't just drop them in the bag—they need to be attached to a hook or clip within the bag. That way, they have a specific home and you will always be able to find them in the bag rather than feeling around in the bottom of the bag, searching for them.

Specificity is very important here. The vagueness of just setting the keys down *near* the front door won't work. Vague is not your friend in these matters. So select something. It can be a cereal bowl; it doesn't need to be a precious artifact. Don't get hung up on the container. Get hung up on the location.

When I visit my mom's house, I actually use a cereal bowl. I set it on her kitchen counter, just inside the front door, and that's where I deposit my keys. It's not that pretty, but it works. You, of course, can have pretty *and* functional; pretty is just not that important to me at my mom's house as I'm only visiting. At home, I have that antique rice bowl from India as I mentioned earlier—there, pretty *is* important to me.

Perhaps the most important points in all this are for this new home to be

1. someplace visible,
2. someplace you can easily get to, and
3. someplace *near* the door but not visible from outside your home.

That way, the keys will always be the last things you pick up on your way out and also the first things to find their home when you enter your house.

I'll wait here while you go and find your keys and establish their new home. Go. Now.

Great. Keys have a home. Write down where your keys' new home is in your companion workbook, notebook, and/or below.

Keys live here: _____

A HOME FOR YOUR WALLET OR BAG

Now for the wallet and whichever kind of bag you use. I'm using the word *bag* to refer to anything you load up and carry around on a regular basis. So that could be a backpack, book bag, canvas tote, briefcase, designer purse, or any other carryall container. And if you carry your wallet in your bag, focus on the instructions for the bag's location only—we'll assume that your wallet's home will be inside your bag.

When you walk in the front door, you'll put your keys in their home. Now, what are you going to do with your bag? Where is the best place for it to live? We don't want it following you around the house like a lost puppy. So think about what makes sense for you.

Back to my all-purpose rice bowl. Along with my keys, the entire contents of my pockets are emptied into it. I don't like carrying a bag with me when I'm out—but I appreciate that you might. For me, cash money, my wallet, lip balm, and keys are what I always have with me and what gets dumped into the rice bowl when I get home. (My mobile phone is still in my pocket at this time.)

I separate out any cash receipts (I don't bring home credit/debit card receipts anymore—I'll explain why in Chapter 4) and anything else that's found its way into my pockets during the day—business cards, flyers, random notes. Any trash—gum wrappers and things like that—immediately gets tossed. There's no need to carry trash any farther into the house.

Once the money, wallet, keys, etc. are in their dish, I leave the entryway. If I have business cards or similar items, I'll head into my home office and deposit these things into a basket there. Then I leave that room, unless I planned to spend some time in there anyway.

In each room, I have a dedicated dish or pad for my mobile phone. So as I move from room to room, I put the phone in its home. For health reasons, I don't keep it on my body.

So that's a useful pattern for those who have functional pockets and carry things in them. For those who carry a bag, there are still these questions: Where does it live? Where will you always be able to find the bag (visible), and where can it live so that it isn't distracting or unsightly or constantly underfoot? Is there a chair in your entryway that no one ever sits in, even to put on or take off shoes? Is there a hook or shelf inside the coat closet that makes sense? What about a small table or chair in your bedroom? Do you have a small desk-like surface in the kitchen? This would not be my favorite choice, but it might be yours.

So let's figure this out. What makes sense to you? Where will you always know where your wallet or bag is? Walk through the house and find that spot. Commit to it as much as you can in this moment. I'll be right here.

Great. So this is now where your wallet or bag lives. Write it below or in your companion workbook or notebook.

Wallet or bag lives here: _____

If you need to move your wallet or bag for some reason, just return it to its proper home when that task is complete. Don't say to yourself, *Oh, I know where its home is now; I'll put it back there* later.

"Later" is a junior version of "someday." If you want to know where the wallet or bag is at all times, take the time to put it back in its home every time. It's surprisingly simple, but just note how insidious that voice is when it tries to seduce you into not following through. That voice is *not* your friend. It promises a secret cache of time that you'll have by not returning your wallet or bag to its home. That's a lie. You'll spend all that secret cache of time—and then some—searching for your wallet or bag if you succumb to the voice's siren call.

I've witnessed this over and over again:

[A friend calls.]

Friend: Hey, do you have so-and-so's number?

You: I do; it's in my address book in my bag. I'll go get it.

[You set the phone down, fetch your bag, and return.]

You: I've got it. You want the cell or work number?

Friend: Give me both.

[You do.]

Friend: Great, thanks.

You: You're welcome. Hey, how's the—

Friend: Fine. Sorry, I don't mean to be short, but I've gotta run. I need to call so-and-so and then get to the store before they close. I'll call you later.

You: Sure. Talk with you later. Bye-bye.

Friend: Bye.

And now you may be thinking about the call or about so-and-so whom your friend is phoning right now with the number you just gave her. Or maybe you've moved on to thinking about picking up the dry cleaning. That's fine. Just think about these things as you're returning your bag to its home. Don't get up from the conversation and wander away, leaving the bag behind. Complete the task—which was fetching the bag, retrieving the number, sharing it, and returning the bag to its home.

Think of every task having a beginning and an end, and don't walk away until you're finished. This will prove handy in other circumstances as well.

So now the keys and your wallet or bag have homes. Excellent.

NOTABLE NOTE

Because cell phones are now every bit as universal as keys and wallets and bags, I suggest you do as I do and establish one home for your phone in *every room*. It could be a decorative dish or a felt pad or a charging source. As you move through your spaces, get in the habit of putting your phone in its home as soon as you enter each room and returning it to its home after every use. It may seem tedious at first, but I promise, once this becomes a habit, you will never misplace your phone again.

Chances are you've already experienced trying to locate your misplaced phone by having someone call it—which only works if the phone is charged and the ringer is on or set to vibrate. If it's in airplane mode or out of juice, you'll waste time and likely grow increasingly frustrated as you search for it. Then you'll grumble that this could have been avoided had you only put your phone back in its home in the first place. That grumbling reinforces a negative mindset that "proves" you are somehow destined to never get organized, which is, of course, hogwash and simply another one of those 200 lies.

A Clarification about Bags

We have only *one* bag going at a time. That bag is your primary bag—your purse, book bag, backpack, briefcase, etc. You may also have a dedicated gym bag with your workout clothes or yoga mat inside, or a diaper bag or other specialized bag that you occasionally carry with you. If you convert one of these kinds of bags into an all-purpose bag for a particular outing, remember to empty it of all extra items, such as your cell phone, wallet, keys, or whatever, when you get home. It should once again contain only its dedicated items.

Likewise, if you carry different purses for different occasions, you'll want to *completely* empty your purse out when you swap it for a different one. You may want a container in which to store the surplus contents of your bag if you're swapping out from a large tote-like bag to an evening clutch. These items no longer traveling with you will need a home, too. Enter a decorative bowl. Or basket. Or shoe box. Again, don't get hung up on aesthetics. I'm all for pretty. It's just that function needs to lead the way with pretty picking up the slack.

The point is, if you have a standard set of things that leave your house with you most days, keep them all together so you can easily load back up before heading out for the day. You don't want to be frantically searching for your lip balm any more than you want to be looking for your keys. Ditto for your address book or business cards. So keep them all together somewhere that is visible and discreet and that makes sense to you, someplace where you will always know to look for these items. One Home for Everything.

So, for those of you who do swap bags, find a container for your daily items, and then find this container a home. Now.

Bag-contents container lives here: _____

Now, along with your keys and your bag, your daily items for your bag also have a home. Perfect.

A HOME FOR YOUR MAIL

When you bring the mail in, you guessed it, it needs a home until you're ready to sort and process the mail. Bowl, basket, box, bag—it doesn't matter. Just be consistent. It's a good idea to keep this container either just inside the front door or inside your home office. If that space can be located only in your kitchen, then you really need to consider where this container will live. We don't want to surrender useful counter space to a basket of mail.

Where is the mail's home? Think carefully—where does it make the most sense for the mail to live? Ideally, this location will have trash and recycle bins nearby and accessible. Where do you typically pay bills and answer correspondence?

If that has been the kitchen or dining-room table, unless you also have a hutch or other piece of furniture in the same room in which you can store *out of sight* the incoming and processed mail along with the mail supplies (stamps, envelopes, etc.), I invite you to reconsider this. That table is not where your mail (or Christmas presents or recycling) should live. It's where you should be eating dinner.

If you have a dining room in your house that contains an actual dining-room table, and you live alone or don't ever entertain, you are an exception to this. You may place a basket in the center of the table and deposit the mail into it.

For everyone else, find the mail's home now. That's not rhetorical—I'm serious.

Consider where you want the mail to live in your home; set the book down and go to this new home for the mail. Pick out whatever vessel you'll use to hold the mail until you're ready to open it, and once that's in *its* home, head out into the house in search of any stacks of mail currently lying around. Bring them all together and deposit them into the mail's new home.

Don't dawdle, and don't get distracted. Don't stop for a snack—there'll be time for that later. This is simply a search-and-rescue mission. We are not concerned with what's *in* the mail right now; we're merely gathering it. So do not start sorting through it—just don't. In a bit, we will discuss how to sort and process the mail in an efficient and expedient way. For now, we just want all the mail to finally be together in perfect Like-with-Like harmony.

This rule, Like with Like, is the second cornerstone in kicking the clutter habit and ensuring that you'll always be able to find anything in an instant. If you take nothing else away from this book, these two rules or tools—One Home for Everything and Like with Like—will transform your relationship with objects. But for Like with Like to work, you have to apply it completely. That means, in this case, you can't just gather most of the mail—you have to gather *all* of it.

So go and gather the mail now, please. When you've completed this task, please return to the book.

Excellent.

Mail lives here: _____

Now the mail is all together in its home. Good. Finally, those random piles of envelopes, catalogs, magazines, and solicitations are reunited in one location. It's kind of like their farewell tour because there will never again be this volume of unopened mail scattered around your house. That's got to feel like a bit of a relief. Savor this moment. You've just done something quite significant.

Moment's over.

ESTABLISHING A MAIL ROUTINE

This is how you will handle new mail starting tomorrow: you will bring the mail into the house and immediately take it to its home. What you won't do is drop it on a random surface, and you also won't dig through it, hunting for fun things, and then toss the leftovers into the mail's home for later. If you do not have the time to sort through *all* of the mail when you bring it in, just put it in its home until you are ready to sort it and then keep walking.

This will help with at least two things. First, you'll stay focused on other tasks by putting the mail in its home and continuing on with those tasks. Second, when you do process the mail, you'll quickly learn how much time you need to budget for this task so you can complete the task in one sitting.

PROCESSING HISTORIC MAIL

Now that you know how you'll handle new mail going forward, let's address all the existing mail that you've corralled together. To start, you'll want a basket/bin/container for each of the following categories along with a shredder and a recycling bin:

- Bills and Asks (finance-related)
- Invitations and Events (time-sensitive)
- Read and File (including personal correspondence)
- Action Items (finite tasks)

If you read magazines and periodicals, they're going to need a home, too. You may prefer a magazine rack or basket for them. Likewise, catalogs. They could be added to the magazine rack or just recycled with the other junk mail.

We're now going to sort and process your historic accumulation of mail into those four primary categories. This is the same procedure you'll follow each and every time you open the mail. You will, I'm confident, never have the volume of mail that you are about to sort through, and that's another thing to celebrate.

This is not the time to pout or feel sorry for yourself or tell yourself that you're stupid or anything else that's negative about having to sort the mail in such a deliberate and mechanical way. Who cares? All we need and want is a consistent and replicable way of handling the mail from now on. Why it's never been done like this before or what that means about your character is just noise. There's no need to get lost in a nasty conversation. Today we're building a new skill. Focus on that.

Now, take a deep breath and begin sorting the mail into its corresponding baskets.

Catalogs

Let's start with the biggest items first. Find and pull out every single catalog and, unless you are currently shopping for something specific, toss them directly into the recycling bin. If you want to get off any mailing lists, rip off the last page containing your address label and customer code/ID and hopefully their toll-free number as well, and drop those pages in the Action Items basket.

If you are shopping for something, keep those catalogs only. These few catalogs can be placed in your magazine rack or on the coffee table—wherever the home for magazines will be.

Never keep more than the most current issue of any vendor's catalog. Each catalog has an issue number or name, such as Late Summer, so find the most current issue and recycle the rest. If you've flagged a particular item for purchase in an earlier catalog, make sure that item is still available in the new issue, then recycle the older one.

Magazines and Periodicals

These are also oversized and should be easy to pull out of the pile. We're looking only for printed material that you've subscribed to or that arrives on a regular schedule.

Going forward, after you've sorted the mail each day or week, you should drop off any magazines or periodicals in their home. So where should that home be? Think about it. Besides the bathroom, where else do you like to read? In the den? In the bed? Where are you likely to settle in for a little reading time?

If you commute to work on public transportation and that's when you catch up on reading, perhaps a basket or rack near your coats (or bag) would be a great place to keep the magazines, so you see them and are reminded to grab one on your way out the door.

So decide where the home for the magazines will be. When choosing that home, it should be someplace where you'll see them but not trip over them and where they won't create clutter by spilling over onto a table or the floor.

Magazines live here: _____

Great. The magazines (and catalogs) have a home. All is almost right with the world. Now we just need to address the backlog in this stack.

Magazines, like catalogs, come with some frequency and regularity. Be honest about how much back reading you can and will do. Unless there is a very specific article you've flagged in a back issue, a good rule of thumb is to keep only three back issues, and that doesn't change whether it's a weekly or monthly title. So if you've got issues going back further than that, unless you're housebound and recovering from surgery (God forbid), chances are you'll never be able to get caught up.

If you're feeling any resistance to letting go of back issues because of how much money you've spent on those subscriptions, here are two things to do:

1. Get honest with yourself. You've probably blown more money on something else with fewer good intentions. Forgiveness is useful here. There's no benefit to shaming or blaming yourself for past decisions—accept the choices made and let the rest of the conversation go.

2. Suspend your subscription or donate the balance of it to a local hospital or somewhere that has a waiting room in need of reading material. You could drop off all your back issues there, too.

If what you're stuck on is the time lie, this fantasy that time will mysteriously appear during which you can read those back issues, it's time (no pun intended) to release that story, too. You don't have a time machine—you're living within the same 24 hours we all are. You can barely make it through your day with all the current things there are to do; when is "someday" finally going to arrive? The answer is, of course, never. Today is it.

And any magazine that you don't read at all should be discontinued immediately. Regardless of why you began subscribing to it in the first place, it's now time to cancel.

Great. On to junk mail.

Junk Mail

This process is the same. Sort through the historic stack and remove every single piece of unsolicited mail. Credit card offers and anything that could potentially be used to steal your identity get shredded. The rest gets tossed or recycled. Shred and toss now. I'll wait.

Good. (Note that we haven't actually opened a single piece of mail yet. This will prove a significant time-saver when you're sorting on a regular basis and not working through an accumulated stack of mail.)

What's left is specific mail you have some relationship to. Before opening any of it, let's sort what remains.

Types of Useful Mail

Bills: We know what those are. You've requested a service or created a financial commitment and are now being asked to pay for that. Seems fair.

Asks: You support various charitable organizations and/or friends of yours do, and they've sent you a request for a contribution. Bills and Asks can live in the same basket.

Invitations and Events: Little Ashley's bat mitzvah, Ralph and Sabina's 25th wedding anniversary, Susan and Becky's commitment ceremony, and so on.

Read and File: Letters from friends, greeting cards, diplomas, etc.

Action Items: Time-sensitive requests that need your response and participation for them to be complete (for example, the field-trip notice requiring your signature for your kid's trip to Washington, D.C., or a request from the insurance company for clarification on a pending claim).

Now that we've identified the different types of mail, we're going to sort yours into these categories. (Note that the mail still remains unopened.) Let's attend to Bills first.

BILLS

Open each envelope now. Discard the envelope the bill arrived in. Don't open the mail and then reinsert the opened mail back into the envelope. That is a waste of time. Likewise, toss any stuffing or junk that comes in the envelope besides the bill (or invoice) itself and the return envelope. (If you pay bills electronically, you may also toss the return envelope.)

Any invitations for "gifts" or other offers go immediately into the trash or recycling. If your bill has multiple pages, please staple those pages together in the upper left-hand corner.

When this category is complete, you should have a neat stack of bills, either without the return envelopes attached to them or with the return envelopes' flaps enclosing the bills and secured with a paper clip. We'll turn our attention to Asks next.

ASKS

We do the same thing here. Open the mail and toss everything that isn't necessary. If the ask includes a personal note on the letter, retain the letter as a tickler. If not, toss everything besides the donation slip and the return envelope.

The carefully crafted plea for support is unnecessary. You're either going to support this group or not based on your relationship with this group or with someone affiliated with this group. You don't need to spend time having your heartstrings tugged if you're already prepared to support them (apologies to development directors everywhere).

Do you have a giving plan? I do. I have a group of charities that I support annually, and once a year I sit down, review the list, and write out those checks. You'll find a copy of my Giving Schedule Template in your companion workbook or at unstuffbook.com/paper.

I always instruct charities I support to suppress mailings to me—I don't want my contribution used to solicit a donation I'm already committed to giving. That's just wasteful and redundant. Therefore, there are very few asks that make it into my financial basket. The only exceptions are any asks from people I know who are soliciting support for causes that are important to them. Depending on the person and the cause, I consider these as they arrive. Until I write a check, they will remain in this basket.

INVITATIONS AND EVENTS

Let's start by stating that you don't have to attend any event you don't want to attend. You may choose to be a sport and accept an invitation you'd otherwise decline because it's hosted by a close friend or family member who has attended one of yours—that choice is yours.

If you do plan to attend, save the invitation, directions, and RSVP card/envelope, and toss any tissue paper, glitter hearts, etc. Do not stick the invitation back in the envelope it came in. That should go into the recycle bin.

If you need the return address for your address book, tear that flap off and put it in a basket for contacts. That is a basket (or other container) where you will deposit business cards, return addresses, and other contact information you want to save to update your contact list or address book. We'll discuss this in greater detail in Chapter 4. For now, if you don't already have something like this, grab a container and drop into it any addresses you want to save.

The Invitations and Events basket is not where we keep the reminder cards from the dentist, the doctor, the vet, and so on—those go into the Action Items basket. The difference between Invitations and Events and Action Items is that the first types are optional—the second are not. If you are required to show up at a particular date and time, it's an action item.

READ AND FILE

These are items that you need or want to save. They include bank statements after you've reconciled the accounts, receipts or other documentation of any capital improvements you make to your home (if you own your own home), insurance policies, and love letters. At unstuffbook.com/paper, you'll find a comprehensive list of which kinds of documents to keep and for how long.

Contrary to what some people may think, I can be quite sentimental. I have love letters in my files that are older than your children. What I don't have are birthday or holiday cards that were sent to me with nothing more personal inside than

Happy Birthday!

XO

Bobby

While I appreciate Bobby's thoughtfulness in all seriousness, I got the message, and that's what the card was sent to do: communicate a thought or a feeling. Think about it. If we held on to every thought or feeling that came our way, we'd be drowning in them. Look around. Are you drowning in thoughts or feelings right now?

If Bobby wrote me a heartfelt message or letter, then that might be something worth saving to look back on in my golden years. But a preprinted holiday card from my accountant accomplished its mission—it let me know that he was thinking of me at a particular time of the year. Got it. Acknowledged it. Recycled it.

You're not a bad person for releasing these kinds of items. You're not. And it's not uncommon or unusual to throw these kinds of things away. You might be the best baker this side of the Mississippi or a crack sudoku player, but you are not exceptional in discarding these things—most of us do it.

You might also want to examine at this time if you have expectations about greeting cards you've sent to others. Do you grow resentful if other folks toss your greeting cards? Are you holding them hostage over a birthday card they threw away? If you can let them off the hook, it will be that much easier to let yourself off the hook as well.

One thing to consider in all this is the popularity of e-cards and electronic invitations, both as a sender and receiver. As a sender, you can customize your cards to your heart's content. As a recipient, you're off the hook, unless you feel compelled to print the e-card and save it. Please don't.

We'll talk in greater length about sentimental objects and their hold on us in Chapter 8.

ACTION ITEMS

If you are someone who procrastinates—and if you are, please don't berate yourself for it—this basket is going to be very useful to you. Everything that has a deadline for completion besides bills belongs in this basket. As mentioned, the permission slip that you need to sign off on, the tax return that needs to be mailed, the reminder for your dental cleaning—these are the things that belong here. Any task or problem that won't be completed or solved without you doing something belongs here.

Those catalogs you want to stop receiving—their back pages go here since you won't get off their lists until you notify them. The possibly fraudulent charge on your recent credit card statement—that lives here, too, until you contact the card issuer and get your dispute started. Health insurance or other reimbursement forms wait here to be sent in for payment.

The difference between an Action Item and an Invitation or Event item is as stated earlier: invitations and events are voluntary—they'll still happen whether you show up or not; action items will not be resolved without your active participation.

For example, a wedding or concert (invitation) will still happen if you are not in attendance (unless, of course, it's *your* wedding). But your child will not board the bus for Washington *unless* and *until* you have signed that permission slip and returned it to her teacher (action item). Now, you might think that if you miss a medical appointment, the doctor will just see another patient sooner, and that's partly true. But I wouldn't classify healthcare as voluntary or optional—certainly not in the same way as seeing a movie or a play. So those are the distinctions.

There's no harm in having a lot of things in your Action Item basket. The only risk is that you will load it up with so many tasks that you become overwhelmed by the volume of pending things to do. If that should happen, increase the time allotted for processing the mail to address more action items.

Particularly now, when first processing a large volume of mail, you may discover a lot of items needing your attention. Once you've moved through this historic glut, the number of action items should resume a more manageable flow. If you are unsure of how to categorize a piece of mail, err on the side of placing it in the Action Items basket. That way, it'll get addressed sooner than later. Just think of how productive you're about to become!

Mail Sorting and Processing

When you bring in the mail tomorrow and each day after, you now know where it lives. Its container will always hold all the unopened mail, with possibly the back pages of several catalogs (awaiting transfer to the Action Items container), until you're ready to sort the mail.

It's possible that with very little mail arriving each day, sorting will not require much time. Even so, you might want to use a stopwatch when you sort the mail the first few times to gauge how long it takes. Likewise, if you're returning from a trip or the mail has otherwise been accumulating—it's useful to know how long this can take.

We want to start thinking in terms of a time budget, just like a money budget. The less guessing we do, the better. Numbers can't hurt us. By extension, we can't have too much information about how long things take to accomplish since we don't want to create time debt. Remember "someday"?

So keep track of how long it takes you to sort the mail.

Then, celebrate that with each step the mail is ceasing to be a messy pile of things that only wants something from you and offers little in return. Also celebrate that you're learning how long tasks take. Excellent.

Now we need to figure out when exactly you'll interact with the mail—meaning complete the action items, respond to the invitations and events, and pay the bills. This can be done every few days or once a week. I do this once a week, but that might be too long for you to wait at this early stage in your development.

Find the time in your schedule every three days to have a 15-to-20-minute mail appointment, and add it to your calendar. Now, I mean. Get your calendar and commit to these 15-to-20-minute sessions. It's best to stagger them between daytime and evenings since some action items may need to be accomplished during business hours.

When you are finished, you should have a series of appointments with yourself scheduled for the next 30 days. No need to go out any further than that at this time because once you get going, you may discover that you've allowed for more time than you need. Or it may not be enough.

If the former is true, if you're blowing through this phase of the mail, then adjust your calendar to reflect the need for less time. Don't just do it mentally. Return to your scheduled mail appointments and alter them manually.

If the latter is true, if you're finding that after 20 minutes you still have tons to do, you either need to increase your budgeted time allotted for these tasks, or you may want to enlist help, either paid or provided by another family member or friend. If you're running a home-based business, it may be time to get some part-time assistance or a volunteer or an intern.

In either case, pay attention. Refer back to your log. How long is it taking you to sort the mail before you even begin to respond to it? Also note that in the beginning, as you're possibly playing catch-up on a larger-than-average pile of mail, everything will take longer. For many folks, once a pattern is established, these durations for sorting and processing the mail will decrease.

Track how long it takes you to process the mail. Use your companion workbook or notebook to keep track of these times, and add any notes to further clarify your process. For example, if it takes you only a few minutes to write out checks and pay bills but much longer to attack your action items, make a note so that the next time you're doing action items, you can adjust your schedule accordingly.

LIVING THE WORK AND MAINTAINING THE SYSTEM

This is what the next 30 days will look like:

- You will come and go from your house, placing your keys and your wallet or bag in their proper homes.
- You will swap the full contents of your bag every time you change bags.
- You will deposit the mail into its home until you're ready to sort it.

- You'll deliver any new magazines to their home, recycling the oldest issue.
- You will sort the mail.
- You will track your mail sorting and processing times.
- You will keep your appointments to sort and process the mail, adjusting them according to how long it takes you.

And that's it. That's all you have to do for this chapter. Obviously, life goes on—you'll continue going to work and meeting your other obligations. But you are not to start digging into the junk drawer in the kitchen after a few days of success. You are not to attempt to clean out the garage with all your enthusiastic fierceness. There will be time for all of that.

Right now, focus on the tasks at hand. Do them consistently, and do them to the best of your ability. Don't judge them, and don't negotiate with them. No corner cutting, no creative juggling, and no procrastinating. If you tell yourself you'll do it tomorrow, gently and firmly remind yourself that you have a commitment to do it today. The conversation doesn't need to be any longer than that. No convoluted schemes or grandiose promises.

Ditto for trying to impress the teacher with your deep understanding of this process. Remember, this isn't nuclear fission, it's the mail. I'm impressed if you're impressed. And it should take only 30 days of consistent behavior to really see what you are capable of. Good luck!

3

KITCHEN • PANTRY

In department stores, so much kitchen equipment is bought indiscriminately by people who just come in for men's underwear.
–JULIA CHILD

If you can organize your kitchen, you can organize your life.
–LOUIS PARRISH

WHAT WE'RE GOING TO COVER IN THIS CHAPTER

- What a Kitchen Is and Isn't
- What's Happening in Your Kitchen?
- One Home for Everything and Like with Like
- Breathing and Visualization
- Structural Elements of a Kitchen
- Work Zones or Stations
- Sorting, Purging, and (Re)Arranging
- Reloading the Storage
- Appliances
- Maintaining the System

WOW! By now you've gotten control over the mail, and you haven't misplaced your keys once since working through the last chapter. You rock!

Before we dig into the kitchen, let's remember our ground rule laid out in the last chapter—this chapter's initial read should ideally be completed in one day.

When you begin working, you'll find that some of the exercises in this chapter may take more than one day to complete. But none of them should take more than two days, and I'm confident that you will find two days in a row to dedicate to completing them.

It is important that you choose two consecutive days—for both practical and psychological reasons. Once you begin the process of emptying cupboards and drawers and start sorting, there will be substantial piles of things lying around. It gets bigger before it gets better. Navigating the space around these piles may be awkward physically, and living with these piles any longer than necessary may sap your energy and enthusiasm for finishing the project.

The good news is that after you've completed these exercises you likely won't have to repeat them for a long time to come, perhaps ever.

WHAT A KITCHEN IS AND ISN'T

Kitchen (noun): A room equipped for preparing and cooking food; any room used for the storage and preparation of foods and containing the following equipment: sink or other device for dish washing, stove or other device for cooking, refrigerator or other device for cold storage of food, cabinets or shelves for storage of equipment and utensils, and counter or table for food preparation

So, in turning our attention to the kitchen, I'd like you to think like you're in a food shop, as in a wood shop but with different tools. This is a room to prepare food—unless you don't prepare food. We'll address that separately. Assuming you do prepare food, is your kitchen currently set up to easily and efficiently support that activity?

If not, when you're finished with this chapter, you'll possess a functional, accessible kitchen where any kind of food preparation and cooking is easy and as fun as you find cooking to be.

Do you think of your kitchen as the hub of your home? And by that I mean a gathering place, a return to the hearth, and a warm place to visit while food is prepared. The kitchen is not the hub of the house if you're thinking instead of *war room* or *command central* or *Houston, we have a problem.*

The kitchen is a workroom. This doesn't mean it's devoid of character or drab or uninspired. Your kitchen can reflect as much of you as you desire—as long as it first functions well and serves its purpose without clutter or unnecessary complications.

WHAT'S HAPPENING IN YOUR KITCHEN?

Get your companion workbook or wherever you're taking notes, and take a few minutes to write down the different activities you currently perform in the kitchen.

Great. Of the activities you just wrote down, how many would you do in another place if you had other functional spaces in your home? Circle them. We'll come back to these later and find you more appropriate locations for them to be accomplished. For now, we want to remove them from the kitchen so we can streamline the kitchen's contents and purpose.

That leaves us with which remaining activities? Review them now.

These are the things that your kitchen needs to accommodate. This may change over time, but for now let's be mindful of what you want to do in the kitchen and how the kitchen can be arranged and organized to best support these activities.

To reiterate, the kitchen is the room where food, supplies, and tools are stored specifically for the preparation of tasty, nutritious meals. Even if all you ever do is hire caterers or assemble meals from delis or kits of prepared foods, it is still a room that is dedicated to food and its preparation and serving.

I think it's great if your kids are nearby doing homework while you cook. Or if your partner/spouse/roommate is paying bills from the bar as you slice and dice (or microwave a frozen meal). Or if you're watching the Food Network and incorporating tips and recipes into your meal plans. All good.

But the homework doesn't *live* in the kitchen. Neither does the checkbook. And unless you have a surplus of counter space, it would be a shame to have a chunk of it dominated by a television, even a super-thin, flat-panel LCD.

ONE HOME FOR EVERYTHING AND LIKE WITH LIKE

As we move through the home, knowing where things live (One Home for Everything) and having them living with all their brothers and sisters (Like with Like) is going to simplify your life significantly. We're about to unstuff your kitchen, so remembering these governing principles is going to be useful when you start to reassemble your drawers and cabinets.

Over and over again, I've seen cabinets and drawers previously exploding with things suddenly become more-than-adequate storage simply by applying these two basic concepts. So before you lament your particular lack of storage, wait and see what One Home for Everything and Like with Like can do to solve your storage challenges.

BREATHING AND VISUALIZATION

Before we launch into unstuffing your kitchen, I want to pause to address what might be starting to happen at this point. Your heart might be racing now. You may be muttering under your breath or out loud to yourself that this is impossible or pointless or exhausting, or that you think I'm too demanding and this is fine for a perfectionist like me but too much work or too intense for someone like you.

I get it. It's okay. Breathe. Although this is a potentially challenging project or series of projects, we're not attempting to solve world hunger or some incurable disease. No one is holding a loved one hostage, threatening to hurt her if you don't do this or if you do it poorly or bail on it halfway through. So you can soften your shoulders right now, breathe, and release the tension in them. They are never really supposed to be up around your ears. Let them fall.

Some of us, along with breathing shallowly, may also retreat to home improvement magazines or reality TV shows where the renovation and cleanup have already occurred. With a touch of envy, we fantasize about these other kitchens where other people get to live. Then we tell ourselves that it's fine for someone else, but we'll never have that kind of kitchen. And then we start to list the reasons why.

We're done with those negative lists. That's what the exercises in this book offer you. There are no *good* reasons for your kitchen to be anything *other* than the room you want it to be. So stop the lists. You aren't exceptional or unique—at least not in this case—no matter how hard you try to convince yourself that only *you* can't put things away or only *you* have to live with X, Y, or Z. It's a lie.

Stop making excuses for yourself, and stop letting yourself wiggle out of responsibility for the way things look. There may be circumstances operating in your life beyond your control, but it is the rare individual indeed who can't put the can opener back into a drawer when they are through with it.

And—I'm completely serious now—if your life *is* so threatened or compromised that putting the can opener away creates some sort of dangerous situation for you, put this book down right now, get out of the house, and get some help. Call the police, get to a friend's house, get to a shelter, go somewhere. You have bigger problems than clutter. I mean it—*go*!

For everyone else, reading this book will not magically grant you granite countertops and gleaming stainless steel appliances and exotic wood cabinets. For you to accomplish what you want in the kitchen, none of those things are necessary. Pretty, sure. But necessary? Not for a minute. Your kitchen just needs to be neat and orderly and clean. And that is not beyond anyone!

It's also possible to increase feeling calm and peaceful in your kitchen by simply removing anything that causes mental or emotional friction when you see it or interact with it. If you've got a story that insists something live in the kitchen that agitates you or stresses you out, try to quiet that story down or just dismiss it. Then remove the item. You deserve a kitchen that functions as a place for nourishment and self-care—physically and spiritually. So, from appliances and tools to decorations or general clutter, remove anything that disturbs you as you unstuff this room.

If you're like most people, food is a way that others have shown you love, and it is probably one of the ways you demonstrate *your* love for family and friends. Your kitchen can become a room where you consistently express your love for yourself and others through food in a simple, direct, and sustainable way. And just as easily it can be cleared of any obstacle to achieving that goal.

Without getting too woo-woo, take this time to hold that vision gently in your hands. Let it rest in your outstretched palms. There's no need to grab or clutch it, just let it lie there, content.

Think of the kitchen in the film *Babette's Feast* but on a scale that works for you. If you're ambitious and accomplished in the kitchen, you can prepare complicated, multiple-course meals. But if you're satisfied with tasty and nourishing fare that's less complex, your kitchen can support you in that effort as well. Whether you're inspired by the culinary encyclopedia *Larousse Gastronomique* or an Eggo toaster waffle, your kitchen can be the room that makes it possible.

Now sit down for a minute and really breathe. You'll find several focused breathing exercises in your companion workbook that can help with this. Think about your dream kitchen. Think about the meals you'd make for those you love. Think about waking up in the morning, walking into the kitchen, and pouring or making yourself a delicious cup of tea or coffee or a glass of juice.

It's peaceful in this room. Things are put away, and there's space to breathe. Space to plan and space to spread out. Your knives are sharp, your dishes clean. You know where everything is. You have the tools you need. You don't have to get clutter out of your way every time you want to prepare something; you have just what you need, just where you need it. The broken appliances and the tools with missing or incomplete parts are gone.

Your kitchen is a model of efficiency for *you*; it's been organized by you to serve you. You are strong and capable and efficient and effective when you are in the kitchen preparing food. You move through the kitchen easily. It is a pleasure to be in this room, even if it's just to heat up a bag of microwave popcorn. You're smiling. Imagine how it would feel to have this room be the kitchen of your dreams.

Good. Now let's create this room for you.

STRUCTURAL ELEMENTS OF A KITCHEN

Countertops

These are probably the largest surfaces in your kitchen, possibly larger or longer than your kitchen table, if you even have room inside your kitchen for a table. Countertops exist as shining, gleaming potential in every kitchen. For example, a large expanse of uninterrupted countertop is essential for rolling out pastry dough. Imagine how difficult that would be if there were obstacles strewn in your path.

I currently have a galley kitchen, and the only things that live on my left countertop are: to the left of the sink, dish soap, hand soap, and a small Nespresso machine (this actually comes and goes depending on whether I'm currently drinking coffee); to the right of the sink, a basket of supplements. On the right countertop is a marble turntable, one or two crocks or baskets filled with fresh produce, a cutting board, and a sentimental (yet functional) spoon rest. Visit unstuffbook.com/kitchen to see pictures of my kitchen.

I've compiled a list of things frequently found on people's counters that you can use as a checklist when deciding which of these items in your own home you want to relocate or release. It's included in the companion workbook and can also be downloaded at unstuffbook.com/kitchen. If you have more items on your countertops than I do on mine, that's fine. For today.

Let's go into the kitchen now. Bring a pen, your companion workbook or notebook, and your phone (or camera) with you. Before you touch anything, take pictures of the kitchen as it currently is. Do not move a thing.

When you're done taking pictures, pick up your pen and begin writing down everything, all the items currently living on your countertops. You don't need to record that there are five wooden spoons or 37 pens in or out of a vessel—*wooden spoons* or *pens* plural will suffice as a single item.

Since I'm not there to support and police you, we must employ the honor system. *Do not* omit anything, even if you're telling yourself right now, *Oh, well, that was just on its way to the linen closet,* or *I'm taking that back to the store on my way to class in the morning. I just can't find the receipt right now.*

This is the insidious nature of denial. We minimize the things that contradict our established view of ourselves either by promising (again) to finally complete a long-delayed task or by glossing over anything that might make us look "bad" in someone's eyes *if* they knew the whole truth.

No one is judging you—well, they may be, but who cares? If that really mattered to you, you'd have made different choices by now anyway. It's worth noting that we often only care what people think of us just enough to punish ourselves with it, not enough to actually do anything about it.

So tell the truth, at least to yourself. If there are piles of papers or other things you consider "in process" that are currently lying on your counter, note them. You can't develop new habits until you cop to the old ones. What would there be to change if you were already doing everything efficiently?

Finish writing down the things that are currently living on your counters. If there are more than 20 things living on your countertops, pay attention. Don't abuse yourself, just note it—you have a lot of things on your countertops.

Now I'd like you to study these things, really look at them, and think about the last time you used each of them. Can you remember the last time? Do you make toast often? Are you a daily smoothie drinker? Do you take your vitamins regularly? Set a timer for three minutes to explore the counters' contents and their frequency of use. Go.

NOTABLE NOTE

Purchases still in bags (either coming in or going out) should not be sitting on your counters. If the kitchen is their final destination, the items should be integrated into the appropriate drawer or cupboard. If they are destined for some other room, how did they end up in the kitchen?

Likewise, if they're awaiting a return to their store of origin, there needs to be an established location, ideally near an exit door, where all returns gather until loaded back into a vehicle for transport. Of course, make sure you include the correct store receipt!

Great. Now let's address two things. First, what have you not been able to do because there is clutter on your countertops? What are the tasks you defer doing because clearing space seems like too big of a hassle? Write down the things you would do if you had the room.

Second, what do you *really* need to have on the countertops? Forget about storage space right now—let's pretend that whatever you didn't want on your counters could find a home inside a cupboard. What do you use every day that you would not want to have to get out of a cabinet, not out of laziness but practically speaking? Some items, like a plant, would obviously not fare well behind a closed door.

Refer back to your list of countertop items and circle the essential items—things you feel you must have on your countertops. Are there things not on this list that you would like to have on your countertops if there were room? Add them to your list.

Excellent. Now physically gather these essential items together and set them aside. When we're done, these are the only things that will live on your counters. Everything else that didn't make the cut should also be gathered together into a separate group.

Congratulations! In completing these two actions, you have just successfully sorted something.

The items in the group that will no longer be living on your counters fall into one of the following categories:

1. Things that are leaving your house
2. Things that need new homes in other rooms
3. Things that need new homes behind closed cabinet doors in the kitchen

Since we're on a roll, let's sort them into one of these three groups. First, get yourself a large container, such as a box or a basket or a tub— something with stiff sides and a sturdy bottom. Right now.

Great. Now identify everything that you're done with, that's leaving the house, and put each of these things into this container—this has just become your thrift-store donation container. You can keep this nearby while you work, but ultimately you'll want to find a permanent home for this container (or containers) as some version of it is going to remain in your home. At any time on any given day, you may decide that something needs to leave your home for good, and until it does its new home will be this container. I find that either just inside the garage or just near a doorway to the outside is a great place to permanently locate the donation container.

Now collect everything that is headed for another room and place those items at the entrance of the kitchen, so you can take them to their new homes the next time you exit the room. If they are heading to a new home in the kitchen, just set them aside. They will join their sisters and brothers very soon.

Cabinets

Besides countertops, the other major structural element of most kitchens is the cabinets. These come in as many different configurations as there are kitchens. You may have any combination of drawers, bins, shelves, doors, and cubbies. You may hate your cabinets, love your cabinets, or be indifferent to your cabinets. They may be laid out in the most organic, flowy, smartest way possible, or they may be seemingly plopped into place by an absentminded contractor who had never boiled water in his life.

Short of renovating your kitchen (which is another book), we're going to stretch and utilize your current cabinet configuration to provide you with the most useful and clever storage possible without having to do anything besides shift what's contained in each of them. Because in the kitchen getting organized is an inside job!

NOTABLE NOTE

If you have an older kitchen and/or an awkward floor plan, think creatively to solve these challenges. Will rearranging any of the appliances help the flow? Maybe the fridge and range could be swapped? Are there any cabinets that block your view or impede access to other areas of the kitchen? Could these could be relocated or removed with little finishing work required?

Would a cart on wheels or a freestanding cabinet or hutch provide additional storage? Is there an adjacent room that could become a pantry or easily house seldom-used appliances or serving pieces? Zoom out far enough to shift your perspective, and these design "flaws" will cease to be insurmountable problems—from this new vantage point, you will find workable solutions for many of them.

WORK ZONES OR STATIONS

For those of you who have never had the privilege of working in food service, this may be a new way of thinking about how to organize and arrange your kitchen. For those of you who have worked in food service before, this may be a somewhat nostalgic trip down memory lane. It may also be something that made sense in a professional kitchen but that you never thought to apply on a smaller scale to your home kitchen.

In every commercial kitchen, there are dedicated work zones or stations. While the specificity of stations in a commercial kitchen would be overkill in most residential kitchens (i.e., individual stations for salads, desserts, sauces, grilling, deep-frying, etc.), the general concept is useful as a guide.

Don't be misled, either, if you're a big fan of the Food Network or other channels' cooking shows. When you're inside Carla Hall's, Giada De Laurentiis's, or Ina Garten's "home" kitchen, you are in a kitchen large enough to comfortably fit a film crew, in addition to the professional chef who is filming television in their home. They have more space than most of us and, perhaps even more significantly, they have prep and cleanup staff. So, enjoy the food-based entertainment but don't spend any time comparing their kitchens to yours.

Instead, let's focus on the main zones you'll want to consider in your own kitchen:

- Preparation
- Cooking and Baking
- Beverages
- Food Storage and Pantry
- Tableware
- Cleanup (Including Storage)

It doesn't matter how large or small your kitchen is, some variation of these zones is possible in any space. If you're thinking, *There's no way to distinguish these kinds of zones in my little space,* you may want to explore why, inside your tiny apartment where you seldom cook, you still feel compelled to keep things you'll never use.

All kidding aside, if you have a kitchenette or even a tiny galley kitchen, these rules can still be applied to your spaces. Just reduce everything. If you entertain a lot, first of all, hats off to you—it's no small feat to pull that off when your space is so limited! The thing to work out is where everything will live.

Maybe the space is so small that all tableware needs to be relocated to a bureau or buffet wherever you eat—the dining room or dining/living room. That can include plates and cups and glasses as well as silverware and napkins and place mats.

This also applies to seasonal serving items or appliances. See if there's room in a coat closet or somewhere else to relocate items you use maybe once or twice a year. Doing this frees up more space for actual cooking tools and supplies in the kitchen.

Let's say you're moving to a new home, and it's temporary but longer-term temporary, meaning you won't move for at least a year. You might be thinking, *I'll just put everything I don't need right now into storage!* But this means you're going to pay $100 a month to store an old toaster, some pots and pans, a few wooden spoons, a torn sofa, and some sheets and towels. If you end up staying in the temporary home for two years, this is what you will pay to keep those items: $24 \times \$100 = \$2,400$.

So if by the time you're ready to move again, you could actually replace everything in storage for that amount of money (you may have already been planning to replace that torn sofa), you may be better off giving the items to friends or donating them to a charity, taking whatever tax deduction is available, putting $2,400 into a savings account, and going shopping when you take possession of your new living quarters.

Whenever possible, in small kitchens, consider all of the vertical space available. If you're tall, this might be something you already do; if not, look around. Can you hang a pot rack from a wall or the ceiling? How about a utility bar for utensils across a backsplash wall or on the face of the exhaust hood? What about a magnetic strip for your knives mounted to the wall or the side of a cabinet? Likewise, can you add a hanger for your paper or cloth towels to the underside of a cupboard?

Without creating a chaotic jumble of things, think of how you might keep everything you need organized and within reach. In small spaces particularly, a lot of things stuck all over the walls can blur into a visually noisy mess, so choose carefully. Take adequate time to reflect on how you cook, the tools you use often, and where you use them to determine what goes where. And if you look around the room and still can't find anything because your eyes won't focus for all the visual activity, consider how you can edit what is out in the open and what could live behind doors or within drawers.

Preparation

- Knives, scissors, other cutting or chopping tools
- Steels, stones, other sharpening devices
- Graters, zesters, peelers, rasps
- Spoons, spatulas, scrapers, other mixing utensils
- Cutting boards
- Graded measuring devices
- Mixing bowls
- Strainers, colanders, cheesecloth
- Herbs, spices (or with Cooking and Baking)
- Small and handheld appliances
- Squeeze bottles for sauces
- Cookbooks, recipes

This is the work zone where you'll prepare foods and most likely where you'll spend the bulk of your time, so this should be the largest dedicated space. I consider prep to be everything right up until you apply some form of heat or refrigeration to the food or arrange it for serving. So chopping and slicing, peeling and seasoning all take place here.

It's important to make sure that all the tools and ingredients you'd need for prep work are in or near this area. Ideally, this area is built around an ample bit of clear surface. I'd recommend at least 36 inches of uninterrupted countertop space and would prefer 42 inches whenever possible.

The storage below or near this area should include your knives and other cutting/coring/chopping tools, mixing bowls, ramekins or other vessels for your mise en place (pronounced MEEZ-ahn-plahs and literally translates as "putting in place"), spices and marinades, cutting boards, etc. This workstation is where these items need to live.

Ramekins will live in your Cooking and Baking zone but are very useful to borrow for mise en place.

In my kitchen, I have a four-drawer base cabinet directly below this surface area. And this is how the drawers break down.

Top Drawer: This is dedicated to cutting tools—all the knives, graters, scissors, and cleavers live here. I have an in-the-drawer knife block that holds the bulk of them, with the fine-toothed Microplane (my favorite tool!) and other graters alongside the block. I put these things in the top drawer because they are the tools I use most frequently.

NOTABLE NOTE

Learn to sharpen your knives or find someplace that will sharpen them for you. Whether you use a manual sharpener like a knife steel or whetstone, or a sharpening machine, a sharp knife is a happy knife. And a happy knife is a happy cook.

Second Drawer: The drawer directly below the cutting drawer houses additional prep tools—everything from a mushroom brush, sushi rollers, small spatulas and spreaders, a nutcracker, and a garlic press to melon ballers, basters, zesters, peelers, and funnels.

Third Drawer: This drawer is the baking drawer. It contains cheesecloth, cookie cutters, graded measuring cups and spoons (the larger measuring cups have their own space on a shelf opposite this area), pastry knife, pastry brushes, pastry bag and tips, and pie weights.

Bottom Drawer: This drawer contains wax papers, aluminum foil, plastic wraps, and plastic storage bags in assorted sizes.

Diagonally opposite this base cabinet is a six-foot-long stainless-steel counter unit from a retired diner—I got two of them at a local auction. They flank my range. On the upper shelf are all my small appliances—the food processor, blender, hand mixer, and immersion blender, and all their exchangeable parts corralled inside one basket. This is also where the rolling pin lives. And the slow cooker.

The lower shelf houses all the mixing bowls (stainless, copper, ceramic, glass, plastic), measuring cups, strainers, and colanders that I use. Kitty-corner to these two cabinets is a bookcase where I store my cookbooks.

Cookbooks are a slight exception to the rule of Like with Like. These are books that don't necessarily have to live with other books, but they do all live together. That way you still only have to look in one place to find any cookbook you want. These can be organized by celebrity chef (alphabetical order), genre (desserts, baking, slow cookers), or cuisine (ethnic, seasonal).

I suggest you find a cupboard shelf, bookcase, or some area that you can dedicate to the storing of your cookbooks. Like everything else we're discussing, do not romanticize your cookbooks. If you have some that you have never used, it's fine to release them. The internet is a wonderful resource when it comes to recipes, so you can let them go knowing that if you really need to find that recipe for lemongrass crème brûlée, it's probably only a few clicks away.

For pictures of my kitchen, you can visit unstuffbook.com/kitchen—that way you can get a visual sense of what I've been describing here.

Cooking and Baking

- Pots and pans, griddles, woks
- Utensils (for turning, stirring, and mixing ingredients)
- Pot holders
- Oils, vinegars
- Herbs, spices (or with Preparation)
- Cookie sheets, cooling racks
- Pie weights, pastry bags
- Cake pans, muffin pans, pie plates, ramekins

This workstation is where heat enters. You've done your prep work, and now the fire happens. It's nice, whenever possible, to have adequate surface area around the heat source. Most kitchen designers agree that 18 inches on either side is the minimum. See what you can do to clear that much surface on at least one side of your range or cooktop. That way you can have all your mise en place containers on one side and a landing place for any hot dishes or utensils you're using as well.

As I mentioned, there are only a few things on my countertops. The left countertop in my galley kitchen contains the sink. The right countertop is divided by the range. That marble turntable I mentioned is home to oils, vinegars, and salt and pepper mills and lives directly to the left of the range. My dad's spoon rest is directly on the right. Farther down on the right are the crocks or baskets of fresh produce and the cutting board.

About that spoon rest—it makes me smile whenever I see it and use it. I would never have bought it for myself. My dad got it when he lived in Santa Fe. It's decorated with red chili peppers. So for me, it's a perfect combination of sentiment and function in one object. I get to have my dad in my kitchen with me (sentiment), and it fills a consistent need—I rest spoons and other tools on it every time I cook (function).

Whenever possible, I store pots and pans to the left of the range. I'm a lefty, which is significant only in that I have laid out my kitchen for my convenience. So should you. If you're always reaching for the tongs with your left hand, as I am, it makes sense to store them to your left so they'll be easy to get when you want them. This sounds simple, but few people consider how to use and organize their kitchen based on comfort and convenience rather than on what fits or looks good.

You're not most likely living in a show house, so it doesn't make any sense to live as if you're on display or constantly expecting to be judged by guests. Friends and family love to cook in my kitchen because it's easy to find everything, and it's easy to work in the space. It's also easy to clean as you don't need to move a bunch of stuff out of the way to wipe down surfaces or put things away.

I store skillets and frying pans together, pots together, and the roasting pan and griddle together, and the Dutch oven lives next to the cast-iron stockpot. Cookie sheets, cake pans, and pie plates are stored together. Covered casserole dishes are kept with the uncovered casserole dishes. Like with Like.

I've lived in homes with almost no storage and a few with plenty of storage. Either way, I've adapted so that I keep stacking things to a minimum, which makes getting things in and out easier. Simply by keeping pots with pots and pans with pans, and avoiding stacking whenever possible, you'll make finding the right-size vessel easier, and you'll spend less time unpacking drawers or cabinets as you reach for what you need.

It would be good to have all the cooking oils, sauces, and spices used for cooking nearby as well, either in drawers or on a turntable inside a cabinet. It is not a good idea to store herbs and spices near heat as that weakens their potency, so avoid stacking them on a ledge behind your range, in an upper cabinet directly next to the exhaust fan, or over the range or cooktop.

Utensils used to mix and move the food around over the fire should also be nearby—again, in a crock on the counter, hanging from the range hood, or in an adjacent drawer. Likewise, keep hot pads and insulated gloves close to heat sources. And if you use a cookbook holder, moving it from the prep area to the cooking area should be accounted for as well.

NOTABLE NOTE

I find drawers to be the best use of space in a kitchen. It's simpler to just pull open a drawer rather than having to open one or two doors and then possibly get down on your hands and knees to start rooting around for something. I realize we're not redesigning your kitchen, but if you are planning a remodel soon, consider base cabinets with drawers.

The next best thing to drawers are pull-out shelves inside base cabinets with doors. If you are not planning a remodel and can afford to retrofit your kitchen, consider this option. While you'll lose a bit of interior space to the new hardware, the convenience of having everything roll out more than makes up for the inches lost. Many companies offer after-market versions that make conversion very easy regardless of who originally made your cabinets.

Beverages

- Wine, beer, liquor, mixers, soft drinks, juices
- Teas, teapots, tea cozies, tea balls, strainers
- Coffee, coffee grinder and maker, filters
- Corkscrew, bottle opener, corks
- Ice buckets, coolers, tongs
- Specialized stemware, glasses, mugs
- Cocktail shakers, strainers, stirrers
- Cocktail napkins, coasters

Regardless of whether you have a bar in your home, you can still have an area dedicated specifically to storing and serving beverages. If you are a serious collector of wine, you have special needs around controlling temperature, light exposure, and other factors, so I'll trust that you have arranged for your investment to be properly stored. If you have a cellar or elaborate wine room where you invite people to taste your wines, then you would store all related wine items together there.

If you are a casual consumer of wine, keeping it stored with the other beverages is fine. Just keep it out of direct light, as cool as possible (not stored on the top of a fridge or other appliance or near a vent), on its side (keeping the cork moist to minimize premature exposure to oxygen), and not exposed to unnecessary vibration. Ideally, some form of wine rack (of any design or price point) or even speed racks (found in commercial bars for storing bottles) will keep your wines neat and condensed within your beverage area. Speed racks are excellent alternatives as well for storing other beverages, from hard alcohol to shaved-ice syrup.

All other bulk beverages, from mineral waters to mixers, should be stored here. If you have an under-the-counter fridge or refrigerated drawers, the best place to create a beverage center would be near these appliances. Conversely, if you have the room, you might consider installing a small fridge near where you already store beverages to keep them chilled and ready to serve.

All beverage-related tools will live here, too—stirrers, shakers, corkscrews, wine keys, bottle openers. Bar napkins, swizzle sticks, and specific glassware for cocktails or wine also could be stored here—or with other glasses in the kitchen proper. Likewise, store mugs here or with other glasses and cups stored elsewhere in the kitchen. Either option is acceptable; available space and convenience can inform this choice. Coasters could also go here—or they could live on the surfaces you're interested in protecting.

Food Storage and Pantry

- Pastas, cereals, grains
- Canned vegetables, dried vegetables, beans
- Canned fruits, dried fruits
- Canned meats and fish—tuna, ham, chicken, smoked seafood
- Prepared sauces, marinades, stocks
- Prepared soups
- Boxed meals (mac and cheese, Tuna/Hamburger Helper)
- Bulk ingredients
- Snacks, chips, crackers

This zone is where dry goods, canned goods, and packaged goods all live. Keep them organized by subtype as well: pastas and grains, cereals, canned vegetables, canned fruits, canned meats, prepared sauces and marinades, and so on. It's much easier to cook if the rice is in the same place each time you want it and not crammed between the tomato sauce and canned pineapple. Likewise, dried fruit all lives in the same area—raisins, currants, cherries, cranberries, figs, dates, etc.

It's best to store flours in the fridge to keep them fresher longer. Keep seeds and nuts in the freezer for the same reason; the oils in them will get rancid faster when exposed to fluctuating temperatures.

Tableware

- Flatware
- Dishes, glasses
- Serving pieces (platters, bowls, plates, gravy boats, specialty pieces)
- Serving utensils (salad tongs, carving knives)
- Napkins
- Place mats, tablecloths, trivets
- Candlesticks, vases, decorative items for the table

Like with Like informs your choices here, too. You're leaving the kitchen (at least the cooking area) and are heading to the eating area, so everything you use to serve food should be located here together, including serving utensils, large platters, and dishes. That way you can select the appropriate vessels, then fill them and bring them to the table.

Additionally, this will be where you store the textiles and other things you use to dress up and protect your table, such as napkins, place mats and tablecloths, vases, and decorative trivets.

Cleanup (Including Storage)

- Plastic ziplock bags (assorted sizes)
- Plastic, paper, and foil wrap

- Resealable and other storage containers
- Vacuum sealer and supplies
- Jars with lids
- Soaps, sponges, brushes
- Trash can and trash bags
- Recycling
- Composting

NOTABLE NOTE

Several manufacturers offer "nostalgic" dishes for storing food that don't provide an airtight seal. Air is the enemy of freshness when it comes to food, so as cute as these dishes may be, resist bringing them home. You'll just end up with more food heading to the trash sooner.

The meal is finished, and it's time to clean up. We're recycling what we can, composting vegetable and other degradable waste, discarding trash, and storing leftovers for a later date, either in the fridge or in the freezer. We want to have each item we need for this task near one another, sort of like a mise en place in reverse. As we disassemble the foods and store them, it is much easier to have all the possible containers close by rather than having to leave the room in search of a stray bowl and its lid.

SORTING, PURGING, AND (RE)ARRANGING

We have covered a tremendous amount of theoretical ground in this chapter. We even did a little sorting of our countertop items—all excellent as a foundation. And so the real work begins.

Now that we've mapped out how you might arrange your kitchen into specific zones that allow for the simple and logical grouping of like items and tools, let's start to put this into practice. If you're not currently in the kitchen, pick up your book and head into the kitchen.

Earlier in the chapter, we eliminated everything from the countertops that wasn't kitchen-related. Those items are in a container destined for a new home, either in your house or in someone else's home. What remains on your counters right now is everything you believe still belongs in your kitchen.

Now clear these items off, too. Clear every surface in your kitchen, just for now. If you need to have your toaster on the counter, we'll replace it when we're finished. You have several options in doing this—you may use your kitchen or dining-room table, you may set up a card or banquet table, or you may use the floor.

As you're doing this, if you haven't already, separate out *anything* that is broken that you have not repaired in six months. If you haven't replaced it, it is clear that you don't need it, because you've gone half a year without it. Place it either in the trash or in the recycling bin now.

Please do not debate with me, silently or otherwise, about this. Trust me, you don't need it. You haven't used it, and you haven't missed it. Or if you have missed it, you've found some working alternative, so it's still no longer necessary.

The items that still work and that you still use should be grouped according to your zones:

- Preparation
- Cooking and Baking
- Beverages
- Food Storage and Pantry
- Tableware
- Cleanup (Including Storage)

This is the basis for what's coming next.

Now open your cabinets, start to gather like items with one another, and group them with the items that you've already sorted. Pay attention and keep your eyes open for redundancy and duplication.

We'll come back to this in fuller detail in a few minutes; for now it's enough to recognize overlap and excess.

Gather all the cookbooks and recipe files and scraps of paper and put them all together. We'll find a proper home for these in a bit.

I know this is going to look chaotic and scary—it gets bigger before it gets better. It's fine. It's the first step in identifying what you own, what you need, what really makes sense for you, and where you'll end up storing it so you can easily put your hands on it when you need or want it. And given all the places we've yet to travel to in your home, the kitchen should be relatively painless when it comes to this kind of sorting.

As you empty cupboards and drawers, you may discover things that don't belong in your kitchen at all, just like you did when sorting the countertop contents. Whenever you come across one of these items, place it near the exit or the door of the kitchen so you can take it "home" the next time you head out into the rest of the house. If you're uncertain where its home may be, set it aside in another large container, and as we move to other parts of your house, we'll discover its proper home.

The Sad, the Lonely, and the Mismatched

Isolate broken, mismatched, and orphaned things immediately—pots with missing handles, storage containers without lids or lids without bottoms, hand mixers missing a blade, damaged plastic utensils, etc. The same goes for tools that you have *never* used—like the pineapple corer that Secret Santa gave you three Christmases ago.

Any broken tools, sad melted spoons, ice-cream scoops missing the swipey part that forces out the ice cream—anything that is missing a part or damaged beyond full use is now to be discarded. Broken things do not get sent to the thrift store; they end up in the trash, unfortunately. A broken wooden spoon will not be useful for someone else if it's so damaged that you can no longer use it, either. In this one example, if you have a fireplace or woodstove, you could burn the spoon as kindling. Otherwise, what you're looking at is trash.

Don't torture yourself about this. You're not wasteful or a bad environmentalist for discarding broken items responsibly. Anything that *does* still have life in it should of course be repurposed by you or a friend or through someplace such as a local thrift store. But garbage is garbage. Calling yourself names for something ending up in the land-fill as you navigate this process is not serving anyone. Chances are, the result of that kind of shaming talk will have you either clinging to things that serve no purpose in your life or resenting yourself for trashing the planet.

I realize that the costs of waste are significant, so we must be as responsible as we can. But I also think it's important to forgive our-selves for past mistakes. Growth occurs when we start to make dif-ferent choices about accumulating and hoarding things rather than feeling crappy about ourselves while doing *nothing* to change our behavior. If you don't want to eventually throw something away when it breaks, don't bring it home in the first place. That is the simplest way to resolve this dilemma.

Ultimately, what I hope you will take away from this experience is an awareness that once you bring something home, whether a stray dog, a lover, or a spatula, you are now its steward. So, going forward, choose wisely and be a conscious steward.

Now, continue sorting. Place each pot with the other pots. All the lids for these pots should be with the pots as well. If the pot is sup-posed to have a lid, find it now. Put the wine keys and corkscrews together. All the small appliances. All the mixing bowls. All the dish towels. The oven mitts and hot pads. All the wraps and bags. All the food items—canned veggies with canned veggies, canned fish with canned fish, dried beans and grains—ditto.

Do the same thing with all the drawers—open each one and empty its contents into the growing piles of things surrounding you.

Like with Like. That's all this exercise is about. It's like a giant three-dimensional game of Concentration.

When all this is done, when every space inside a drawer or cabinet is empty, take stock. This is what you own, what you are the steward of, what you've accumulated. How does that feel? Are you feeling abundant, as though you have enough of everything? Do you feel wasteful, as though you have too much stuff and don't understand where it all came from? Do you feel sad or disappointed that you actually have less than you thought and are surprised at how so little could take up so much space?

Set the timer for two minutes and sit with whatever you feel for these few minutes. Don't judge or question what you feel, just let the feelings come and go, or come and stay.

When the timer goes off and before you begin the next step, take a deep breath and acknowledge your feelings. Know that whatever you're feeling, it's all okay. And whatever you *are* feeling, good or bad, can be used to inform your decisions as you go forward. Feeling good and want more of the same kinds of feelings? Make similar choices. Feeling less enthusiastic? Make different choices as you proceed and you're likely to feel better about your results.

Either way, once you've reviewed them, you can release them and let them go. And now, you can get back to work.

Start moving deliberately and slowly through each area, from pots and pans to bakeware and serving dishes, and pull out everything that you are certain you don't need, haven't used, or don't know what it's used for, and add it to the thrift-store container. (There might be more than one container by now!) These items are leaving your life.

Resist the urge to set things aside for specific people. If there are a few items you could give away—perhaps a friend just mentioned needing to replace her blender and you have three of them—then, sure, earmark those and set them aside. But as a rule this practice of "saving this or that for so-and-so" will trick you into feeling that you're being a good friend/neighbor/steward while you're actually procrastinating. Be clear: the beginning of the task is the identification of something obsolete; the end of the task is when it's no longer in your possession. So remember that right now, it doesn't matter how you feel about any of this—it matters only that you finish.

NOTABLE NOTE

Staying hydrated, snacking, and taking little breaks during this sorting process is acceptable and often helpful in remaining focused and on track. If you're going crazy looking for the stray pot lid, break it up by gathering all the mugs together. If you haven't eaten and your energy is crashing, make a sandwich or grab some protein. This is hard work, and you want to stay alert and attentive from beginning to end. If you feel yourself slipping or getting distracted, regroup, refuel, and forge on.

Now is also the time to get serious about how much storage you have and the volume of things you need to store. You can't keep three sets of pots and pans in a modest kitchen. Who needs three sets of pots and pans anyway? Even if you keep kosher, that's only two. Choose your favorites and let the others go. Continue using this process of elimination as you sift through items in each area.

NOTABLE NOTE

Let's not have a junk drawer that contains all sorts of random things, some of which are clearly trash. For example, I used to have a dedicated folder containing all my delivery menus— now I use an app to order things online. If you order online, too, paper menus can now be recycled. Resist the urge to shove useless receipts in here, or spent batteries, leftover Ikea hardware, the one earring that's missing its mate, or a commemorative key chain.

This drawer should not be a catchall for everything you can't figure out what to do with. If an item is that confusing to identify, it probably is junk and belongs in the trash. If it's not, you most likely have similar items elsewhere. Find them and store them all together. Matches, a pen or pencil, some Post-its, a pad of paper, batteries for the timer—none of these are junk, so go ahead and place them together in a drawer. If you use rubber bands and twist ties, keep them neatly organized in snack-size ziplock bags rather than scattered throughout the drawer.

If you inherited your grandmother's china and you don't like the pattern or you already have dishes, it's okay to let them go. It doesn't make you a bad child or ungrateful or heartless. Really, it doesn't. They are only dishes, ultimately, regardless of what you or anyone else tells you. If you have duplicates of certain items, select the better one or your favorite one, and let the others go.

If you feel stymied and need a way into this process, ask yourself the following questions:

- Is this something I currently and/or frequently use?
- Is it beautiful? Do I enjoy looking at it?
- Does it serve a practical purpose in my kitchen?

If you can answer no to any of these questions, the item can leave. I realize it may be difficult to accept what I'm about to say: you are not living for posterity. Having a pizza stone is useless if you don't eat carbs, no matter how cool you might think it is. Likewise, keeping a food processor you never use just so someone will think you've got skills when they visit is not a good enough reason to hold on to it. This is particularly true if the food processor is hogging valuable space that could be used for another appliance.

You're not doing this for me; you're doing this for yourself. Really be honest with yourself about how you live, how you want to live, and how you don't want to live. If you're tired of living in a fantasy of "someday" and are ready to live your life as it actually is or, more importantly, how you want it to be, chuck the stuff that's holding you back. Letting these things go can't possibly affect your life negatively since some of them have never seen the light of day. How can you miss something you've never used?

Practically speaking, toss out all herbs and spices that have expired, but keep a list of all of them so you can easily replace them at the store. That said, think this phase all the way through. If you cooked Indian food only once and you just tossed out the cardamom seeds, you probably don't need to replace them until you're ready to make *aloo gobi* again.

Likewise, oils—they get rancid after awhile. Examine the label and see what you can find out about the current life expectancy of your oils, nuts, and seeds. Things that contain fats will go bad eventually. That time may have already come and gone.

Be informed and thoughtful about ingredients you need to have on hand, and what you may need to pick up when an infrequently used recipe calls for it.

RELOADING THE STORAGE

So now we've purged. What remains all works. Pots and pans have lids as do food-storage containers. Appliances have all their parts. Their wires are intact and not frayed. Groceries are organized into their categories as well. We have everything laid out in groupings according to our zones:

- Preparation
- Cooking and Baking
- Beverages
- Food Storage and Pantry
- Tableware
- Cleanup (Including Storage)

Before putting a single item away, wash and wipe down the interiors of every cabinet and drawer.

Really.

Now, as we start to put things away, we're going to load the zones with all the tools necessary for the tasks of each zone. Concentrate items near where they will be used. Store heavier objects down low where getting them out will be easier. Store pots and pans in a base cabinet near the range or cooktop. Likewise, if you bake often, put all your cookie sheets and muffin pans together and near the oven.

Dishes go together as do glasses—typically near the sink or dishwasher so that putting them away is convenient after they've been cleaned. When putting food back in the cupboards or pantry, load unopened packages in the rear and opened packages in the front for easy access. Group all the spices together, snacks together, juices together, breakfast cereals together, pastas together, and so on.

When you begin loading things back into the cupboards, pay attention to the space each family of items takes up. If you find that you have too many boxes of instant pudding to put next to the boxes of tea, reconsider which cabinet you're using. This is your kitchen—bend it to serve you.

If there is a larger cupboard that would easily house all your dishes but it's not exactly next to the sink, it's more important to have everything living together according to type rather than spread out across several locations. Always use Like with Like to guide you when confronted with situations like this.

Using the blanks below or your companion workbook or notebook, record where each zone will be located in your kitchen. List the cabinets and other structural elements within each area so that you'll end up with a comprehensive list of where to find each kind of item without hunting for it.

Preparation lives here: _____

Cooking and Baking lives here: _____

Beverages live here: _____

Food Storage and Pantry lives here: _____

Tableware lives here: _____

Cleanup (Including Storage) lives here: _____

Whenever possible, do not stack things on top of one another inside cupboards. Bowls that naturally nest inside one another are one thing, but stacking all the pots inside one another when the bottom stockpot is the one you use every day doesn't make much sense. Make choices based on accessibility and convenience as you arrange the contents of each zone within your kitchen. Reload the drawers and shelves to support you in efficiently preparing whatever it is you're cooking, whether it's a pot of chili or a five-course meal.

Once you're finished and everything is back in a cupboard or a drawer, look around at what's left. The only things remaining out and unaccounted for should be the things you still want living on your countertops.

With the doors and drawers all still open, scan each space to see if there is anywhere you might store any of the items that are still out and destined for the countertop. Could the vitamins live near the sink in an upper cabinet or in a drawer by the fridge? Do you really make toast every day, or could the toaster live on the top shelf in the base cabinet next to the sink?

Don't do it just to please me—do it because it makes sense to you. And if it doesn't, if having the vitamins on a staggered tower on the counter is where you want them, then that's where they should live.

Now, with all the drawers and doors still open, take some pictures so you'll have a visual record of where everything now lives. Then close the doors and drawers and take a few more as a record of a job well done. The first set of pictures can be used as a guide any time things start to drift or accumulate. The second set of pictures can be part of your "clutter warrior" self-esteem toolkit any time you start to doubt your progress or ability.

APPLIANCES

Refrigerator, Freezer, and Wine Cooler

Even I have a few things on my fridge door, such as magnets and a few photos—nothing that prohibits me from opening or closing the door, however. And all are secured well enough so that opening and closing the door doesn't cause them to shift. Consider that when decorating your refrigerator.

Turning our attention to the interior of your fridge and freezer, you should arrange it in the same way we've arranged your food storage and pantry. Keep all the condiments, jams, eggs and dairy, beverages, meats and cold cuts, and flours together. I have a few shelves dedicated to leftovers only, enabling anyone to find what they need with a minimum of fuss. Maybe it's because I was always yelled at as a child to keep the fridge door closed, but I find it's helpful to know what I'm looking for before I open the door. It's much easier to do that when each shelf or bin has its own category.

My grandmother used to keep a red pencil near her freezer, and she would carefully label everything that went in with its name (chuck roast, chicken breasts) and its date. That way, she could always use the oldest items first. If you're buying in bulk, portioning things out, and then vacuum-sealing them, a label maker or a permanent marker works just as well.

Stove, Range, Oven, and Microwave

My late Aunt Sylvia never—and this is not hyperbole—never used her oven. It was stuffed—again, not hyperbole—with baked goods made by the Keebler elves, Sara Lee, and Little Debbie. If you wanted a sugary snack, the oven was the place to look.

I think a few things were going on for her there. One, it was a minor act of defiance that not only was she uninterested in cooking, but she rendered the act of cooking impossible by the sheer volume of packages. Two, she didn't have a pantry and had limited cabinet space. And three, she had a tremendous sweet tooth.

I'm all for repurposing things, even appliances. If you don't cook and find you're short on cupboard space, go ahead and use the oven or microwave. Of course, I'd suggest you disconnect any source of power to the appliance so you don't end up with flammable wrappers so close to a source of ignition.

Other than that, I think having adequate heat for cooking is what a range is all about. Whether that's induction, gas, or conventional electric is a matter of personal taste and budget. If yours is active, do not clutter the range with anything that might be combustible.

MAINTAINING THE SYSTEM

So we've sorted through everything in the kitchen, gotten rid of a bunch of stuff, and found smarter places to store what remained. Excellent.

Now, how will you maintain this? By remembering that everything has only one home (refer to your photos if you need a reminder). And now that you've successfully identified a home for everything in the kitchen, anything you take out and use will either be in your hand, in the sink or dishwasher, or back in its home. It is that simple. Put things back where you found them and they will always be there when you look for them.

This system begins to unravel the minute you defer returning something to its home in favor of doing it later. Bad habits die hard, and this is one of the most stubborn. The seductive, insidious voice you'll hear that suggests you could just set something down on the counter and get back to it in a bit is going to win if you do not remain vigilant.

Alternatively, if you're neurodiverse and staying focused long enough to consistently complete a task is your issue, I've had great success for myself and some clients with visual cues as reminders to finish something before moving on to the next event or task. A Post-it on a cabinet door in the kitchen that says, "Empty the dishwasher before bed," is sometimes just the prompt needed.

In all cases, take comfort in knowing that if you are diligent and deliberate about your efforts, after 30 or so days of consistently putting things away when you are done with them, it will naturally start to seem wrong to leave something lying around. And that's the best kind of freedom—free your mind and the rest will follow.

If you have family and they participated in the kitchen organization process, great. If they didn't, you'll want to fill them in now. Everyone needs to know what you know—where each item lives. You may want to label each door or drawer for a while so everyone can easily find what they are looking for.

What you'll begin to understand as you do this work is that much of the result is now alive in your muscle memory. You've had the process of touching every vegetable peeler, every food container, and every cookie sheet, so you have a commitment to returning things to where you found them.

Others don't have that memory—they just have the pleasure of working in a functional and orderly room. So either get those who also use this room to do this work with you, or help them out with some labels or other shortcuts to bring them up to speed. What you don't want to do is assume that they'll figure out your new system by themselves.

Inform them explicitly so they can find what they want when they want it. Otherwise, they are likely to tear through the pantry, looking for a bag of chips, and leave a trail of smoked almonds, crackers, and sardines in their wake. If that should happen, don't pick a fight or shame them; part of the cause of the mess was your lack of communication and assumptions.

So, rather than insisting that you're right and they are wrong because they didn't successfully intuit where things now live, choose to be stress free and happy instead. Take the high road, apologize for your omission or assumptions, and show them all the changes you've implemented. That should restore some harmony to your relationship and go a long way toward keeping your house organized and stress free.

Finally, let's turn our attention back to those tasks you've been doing in the kitchen that you'd choose to do elsewhere if there were room. Refer back to your list and take a few minutes to figure out where they would best be performed. Laundry room? Home office? Living room?

It's okay if there still isn't room for these activities to take place in these preferred spaces. That will be a goal—to clear those spaces as well. Hiding out in clean and organized spaces will not bring you any closer to transforming the holdout spaces, so keep this list alive until every task has been properly relocated.

Likewise, let's grab whatever you set aside that didn't belong in the kitchen. It's now time to redistribute those items around the house. Using Like with Like to guide you, begin walking these things to their new homes. Clothes are destined for a closet or a drawer. If you know that some of the items belong in the home office, since we haven't gotten there yet see if you can figure out what they would live alongside; what other items are they like? If that baffles you, keep them in a container near their future home, and we'll get to them in the upcoming chapters.

Do this for each item. Even if you have to move things one or two more times until you find the best home for everything, each trip brings you that much closer to mastery of The Organizational Triangle.

4

OFFICE ·
HOME OFFICE ·
PAPERWORK

What the world really needs is more love and
less paperwork.
–PEARL BAILEY

WHAT WE'RE GOING TO COVER IN THIS CHAPTER

- What an Office Is and Isn't
- One Home for Everything and Like with Like
- What's Happening in Your Office?
- Office and Container-Supply Stores Are Not the Answer
- Filing Is the Answer
- Superior Filing Tools
- Designing and Practicing the Right Way to File
- Transitioning from an Outside Office to a Home Office
- Structural Elements of an Office
- How to Set Up Your Office
- Client-Friendly Space
- A Time to Gather
- Sorting, Purging, and (Re)Arranging
- When Space Is Limited
- Those Other Activities
- How Long Do I Have to Keep This?
- To Shred or Not to Shred?
- Maintaining the System

YABBA DABBA DOO! You now enter and exit your home and office with your keys always within reach. The mail is under control. You've seen how the kitchen can look and function without clutter. How great is that?

Now you're ready for the first real foray into Paperland. Here we'll learn how to deal with bills and the other mail we began sorting in Chapter 2. We'll also tackle office supplies, setting up a computer and printer (organizing files and other information stored on your computer will be covered in Chapter 10), owner's manuals and instructions, catalogs—all the tools and equipment that are supposed to make running our lives and our homes simpler and more manageable.

For the sake of convenience, I'm going to speak about this office space as if it were a room with four walls and a door. If you have an open-floor-plan space or a landing, adjust any references to layout accordingly. And if something is not easily translatable in the moment, keep reading because chances are it soon will be.

For those of you with less space than a full room, just do the same thing you did in the kitchen—adjust my words to match your space. If I'm calling for a cabinet for office supplies and you only have a small desk in the corner of your dining room, perhaps the adjustment would be to get a small basket or box or an old trunk or suitcase to substitute as a corral for your office supplies. Work with me to get beyond the limitations of the page by adapting these tips and information to your particular situation. That way, you'll get real results from this work.

So whether you have a dedicated room or simply a desk, you can still have order and manage the flow of paper. I've converted tiny closets to home offices for clients. I've even set up desks in out-of-the-way hallways or in corners of other rooms. There are many ways to isolate paper in your home and gain control of it, so please don't allow limited space to deny you a healthy relationship with paper, mail, and technology.

Whatever the confines of your office space, this is big stuff. And remember, this can't hurt you—your biggest risk is getting a paper cut. So let's take a deep breath. Really.

Pause, breathe, and acknowledge what you've accomplished and what you're about to embark upon. Close your eyes, inhale as you count to five, and exhale as you count to five. Repeat twice.

Excellent.

If you haven't already done so, grab your companion workbook or notebook and travel to your work space or the place where you *would* do paperwork if you didn't leave it in a pile or in a shoebox or under the bed. At least the mail is no longer a part of those piles, right?

Now that you're in this space, what will you do here? How do you envision using this space if you could be here without clutter? Do you imagine writing the great American novel? Maybe scrapbooking or assembling photo albums? How about paying bills, researching your family tree, writing holiday cards, helping your child with a research paper, or downloading music? If you build it, they will come.

NOTABLE NOTE

Paperwork is emotionally charged for so many people. Observe yourself. Every time you try to dodge something, seeking a loophole in how this particular instruction or piece of information does not apply to you, note it. It's a common reaction. Recognizing it is key to shifting your attitude toward paper.

If you find yourself saying something along the lines of *Well, that's great for so-and-so but could never work for me*, that should tip you off that you might be about to cheat yourself out of an experience. Allow yourself to try the exercise or task as described—the worst that could happen is that not all of it is applicable. I'm confident that at least some part of it will ring like a bell and make perfect sense once you've attempted it.

WHAT AN OFFICE IS AND ISN'T

Office (noun): A place of business where professional or clerical duties and activities are performed

Home office (noun): A room in a person's home equipped as an office so that the person may work from home

If a kitchen is a food shop, think of your office—at home or otherwise—as a paper and technology shop. This is where you run the business of your business or the business of your life and your family's lives. It's a serious kind of place, although that doesn't mean glum or drab or without levity. But in some ways the crispness that we're called upon to achieve here is as close to perfection as we will probably see in any other room.

If that makes your heart race, think of it this way: Math is one of those disciplines that doesn't function in an "almost" or "approximate" way. We know that two plus two equals four all of the time, not just occasionally. When it comes to bill paying and filing, let's stretch our math metaphor to encourage precision and care, ensuring our equations always add up. The consequences of a misplaced lid in the kitchen are much less dire than misfiling your insurance policy or bouncing several checks.

So if you have a tendency or desire to fudge the corners or aim for "pretty good," I'm going to really encourage you to dig in and shoot for excellence here. To tame the paper tiger, you'll be best served if you call on all your innate fierceness.

This isn't to scare you; at this point, I believe you are completely capable of this kind of clarity and accuracy when it comes to organizing a room. Rather, I'm making the point that once this room is in shape, the real work of the room comes alive. And that work invites rigorous consistency.

ONE HOME FOR EVERYTHING AND LIKE WITH LIKE

One Home for Everything and Like with Like are essential in keeping up with the flow of documents and equipment that inevitably travel through this space. Bills with bills, statements with statements, warranties with warranties. Same with cables, printer paper, folders, paper clips, staples, and pens and pencils. Evaluate what you need to store, find adequate and appropriate storage space, and establish each thing's home.

Even if most of your banking is done online, we aren't a completely paperless society yet. There will be paper, and without taking the time to identify and institute One Home for Everything and Like with Like, you will create additional work and delays for yourself. As the one-two punch of organization, One Home for Everything and Like with Like will ensure that loose papers will never be lying around unfiled for long and that each kind of document will be easy to find among its siblings.

That said, it's still best to reduce the number of physical documents whenever possible. For example, these days I don't bring home credit or debit card receipts, only cash receipts. I review my credit and debit card transactions on a weekly basis so I stay current with my purchases. As a result, any suspicious or fraudulent charges are easy to find and easy to dispute. This habit keeps me on top of my spending and is another way I reduce paper entering my home.

WHAT'S HAPPENING IN YOUR OFFICE?

Let's start by writing down in your companion workbook or notebook the different activities that are currently performed in the office.

Good. Of the activities you just listed, how many would you do elsewhere if you had other functional spaces in your home? Let's identify them now by circling them. We'll find you more appropriate locations for them to be accomplished a little later. For now, we want to isolate and remove them from the office so we can streamline the office's contents and purpose.

Now you've determined the tasks that actually belong in your office. Copy all the non-office tasks to their own list, and then copy all the tasks staying in the office to their own list as well. These are the things that your office needs to accommodate. Not that this can't change, but for now, let's be mindful of what you want to do in the office and how the office can be arranged and organized to best support these activities.

To reiterate, an office is a room where the administration of your life happens. If you have someone handling your personal finances for you on-site, if you have staff, or if you are the designated manager of all things business, this is the room that should house the documents and machines that facilitate that work.

I think it's swell if this is the only multipurpose space in the house, and as such it doubles as the den, the library, the dining room, the craft room, or the exercise room. Together, we can create a system for all of those activities (and more) to coexist. But to do so, we must ensure that there is adequate storage for papers, supplies, and tools before we begin loading in the sewing machine and treadmill.

OFFICE AND CONTAINER-SUPPLY STORES ARE NOT THE ANSWER

Getting organized, and managing paper in particular, is not an outside job. Shopping for file trays, pretty bins, decorative folders, or playful labels will not bring you any closer to actually being able to put your hands on a document when you need it or want it.

You can, of course, use colored folders for specific categories or types of documents. You could have all the files relating to money be green, for example. Or you could use randomly colored folders simply because you'd rather look at colored file folders instead of manila ones.

The point is that any of these choices can make it more fun or pretty to be disorganized, but they won't deliver what I think you ultimately want: a filing system that is easy to use and easy to maintain. The next fad or latest trend in office supplies will not fix what ails you.

That's not to say that innovations won't make office work easier—good ones always will. But the answer to managing paper more efficiently and effectively lies in less rather than more. Remove every single thing that is nonessential from your relationship with paper, and you'll gain control over paper. Anything—any tool, any technique, any methodology—you put between you and filing is what will keep you from immediate access to any document.

I realize that may be disappointing to hear. Or even upsetting. Few people like filing. I don't. It's tedious and repetitive. I could dress it up in clown folders and zany labels, and it would still be a drag for me. I'm not particularly fond of taking out the trash or flossing, either, but I sure like having a house that doesn't stink and healthy gums.

If you feel the same way, the sooner you get over any frustration or disappointment, the sooner you can settle into acceptance and get down to work. What we both want is the result of a good filing system. We want to know where everything is, and we want to put our hands on it quickly. So that's what we should focus on.

FILING IS THE ANSWER

So what does a good filing system look like, and how simple can you make it so you'll actually use it?

Filing is not a mysterious thing. Just like sorting in the kitchen, we begin with categories. Then from the categories, we come up with any subcategories that apply, and within those subcategories, we gather together all the documents that belong to each. The difference is that instead of workstations and cupboards and drawers, here we have filing cabinets and desks and drawers. Otherwise, it's the same process of sorting and organizing.

Start with the filing cabinet's or desk's drawers—if you have a lot of paper in a particular category, you can assign that category its own drawer. Any subcategories will have their own folder within that drawer. And inside each folder will live the documents that belong to that particular subcategory.

Once you have this system defined and mapped out, label your drawers with their categories. Then create a series of folders that are also clearly labeled, and put the corresponding documents into those folders in chronological order with the oldest documents in the back and the most recent documents in the front.

Folders within each drawer should be arranged in alphabetical order, and here's where you can jazz it up a bit. You can decide whether you want your drawers to go from *A* to *Z* or from *Z* to *A*, left to right or front to back. How's that for fun? Beyond that, it couldn't be simpler.

The more drawers you have, the more you can isolate certain kinds of documents from one another. Here's a generic outline of the contents of each drawer within a filing cabinet:

Drawer
   → Category 1
      → Folder (Subcategory)
         → Document (Oldest)
         → Document
         → Document (Newest)

And here's a general breakdown of some common categories:
- Administrative: Personal
- Administrative: Business/Work
- Capital and Home Improvements
- Client Files I (A to M)
- Client Files II (N to Z)
- Research: Personal
- Research: Professional

Administrative: Personal

This contains everything related to the administration of your life, including medical records, mortgage documents, deeds or leases, bills and statements, tax returns, insurance policies, résumés, and so on. If it is about you personally and not your business or work product, this is where it lives.

Travel folders could live under here, too, including any trips you've taken with particular itineraries you want to refer back to. If you have frequent guests or tenants and have a folder with house rules, that could also live here.

Administrative: Business/Work

This is where everything about your business or work product lives. Blank forms for client contracts, informational handouts and flyers, press clippings, trademarks and patents, client folders (including your copies of client contracts), contracts with outside vendors—these all live here. Bills for business expenses live here, too. Personnel files are also in here.

Capital and Home Improvements

Major and minor renovations live here. All receipts and documentation of repairs, improvements, and additions live here. Keeping a corresponding spreadsheet and/or recording these expenses as they occur in bookkeeping software will be a great time-saver when you need these figures for capital gain filing.

Do not keep monthly bills for services here; those are filed under Administrative: Personal. Include just billing for specific improvements to any property.

Client Files

If you have clients and generate paperwork on their behalf, those documents belong here. Likewise, if you manage or track their finances, any bank or credit card statements, receipts, tax returns, and correspondence between them (or you on their behalf) and their vendors or creditors, place all that material in the client's folders. If you have their copy of your contract, it would live here.

Research: Personal

This drawer contains articles and documents that interest you personally. Don't get too excited. While you can certainly store information and articles about everything from home improvement projects and gardening to health and fitness, this is a category that often has way more coming in than going out.

The key to maintaining this category is acknowledging that these are things that interest you but have no transactional relationship to you—nothing in this category has actually happened yet and may never happen—and as such, you need to be diligent about going through this category at least once a year. This is not a clip-it-and-forget-it category. Each time you look through this drawer, it should be with an eye specifically to purge obsolete items.

Research: Professional

This drawer contains articles and documents that interest you professionally. Information about your work or business, which could include public speaking, business development, marketing techniques, new products, ways of scaling or growing your business—all that and more lives here.

You will likely be in this category much more frequently than you are in the personal research category. I schedule a few hours every month to look through the things I've saved here to spark my imagination and creative thinking. If I don't make an actual appointment with myself—if it doesn't make it onto my calendar—it won't happen. So if I want to be proactive about building my business and exploring ways to increase my and my team's efficiency, our enjoyment, and our clients' and customers' success, too, I need to set aside dedicated time to revisit my professional research.

Like the personal research category, this needs to get purged of obsolete items at least once a year. At the rate with which business practices evolve, a year is the minimum for culling this category.

You'll see that organizing documents is not difficult to do, it just takes time. If you have a business and staff, an assistant, or even trustworthy, responsible children of a certain age, you can enlist them to do this with you or for you. Whoever does it just has to be careful and reliable.

The *worst* thing that can happen regarding filing is having someone file who is not careful. Once a document is misfiled, it becomes a major hassle to locate again. You or the person filing can try to retrace your steps, but you may end up having to look through every folder or else wait until you stumble across it when looking for something else.

Filing may not be thrilling, but it is about as simple a task as can be—and just requires focus and attention to detail to complete it without error. Remember, you can visit unstuffbook.com/paper for examples of my files and a template you can use to create your own filing system.

SUPERIOR FILING TOOLS

I lied a bit earlier when I said I didn't like filing. I sometimes find it calming to put on some instrumental music and work my way through the To-Be-Filed basket until everything's been put away. Who knows, you might find it strangely relaxing, too.

I recommend two-hole punches and classification or fastener folders for all filing. Each document is punched at the top and secured inside a folder with metal fasteners at the top of each page or divider. You'll recognize these as the folders you've seen in doctors' or attorneys' offices with your records in them, although those typically are end tab folders, and for our purposes, we'll want top tab folders.

They come in a variety of colors, and as classification folders, they are available with one, two, or three interior partitions or dividers. They are called fastener folders when they have no interior dividers, just fasteners on the inside of the front and back covers. Classification folders allow you to organize the contents into subcategories within each folder, using each divider to further isolate different types of documents from each other. Based on the number of subcategories, you can determine how many dividers (or pages) you'll need.

For example, let's say you have five different credit card accounts, and you still get paper statements for all five. By using one classification folder with two internal partitions (six possible pages) to file all these statements, each individual account can have its own page within one folder. The folder would look like this:

Credit Cards 20XX (File Folder)
> American Express 2100 (Page One)
>> January bill, February bill, March bill, etc.
> Bank of America 4339 (Page Two)
>> January bill, February bill, March bill, etc.
> Bank of America 7828 (Page Three)
>> January bill, February bill, March bill, etc.
> Chase 4399 (Page Four)
>> January bill, February bill, March bill, etc.
> Discover 6004 (Page Five)
>> January bill, February bill, March bill, etc.

Each individual page is home to one particular account, and that account's statements are arranged in chronological order from the oldest on the bottom to the newest on the top. Now, instead of interacting with one of five folders anytime you need to check a credit card statement, you just have to get one folder out of the drawer and all five accounts are there in one neat folder. Perfection. To see an example of a classification folder in use, visit unstuffbook.com/paper.

DESIGNING AND PRACTICING THE RIGHT WAY TO FILE

It's now time to design your filing system. At unstuffbook.com/paper, you'll find a template for creating your own filing system as well as a list of my files. Using the template, list the names of categories you need for your files. You can reference my list for guidance. In the companion workbook, you'll find additional bonus filing guides created exclusively for my private clients—these will help you level up your filing system.

Now, for each of your categories, begin to list the folders (or subcategories) that you'll group under them. Don't worry about keeping this list in any order, alphabetical or otherwise—for now just get them all down in one place. When you create the actual folders, you'll load them into the drawers in alphabetical order at that time.

This exercise is not busywork. It may seem remedial, but it will focus your thinking and help you to design a useful and manageable filing system you'll actually use. It's also a chance to explore different ways of naming and organizing folders *without* wasting time and money renaming and reprinting labels and folders.

If you currently have some sort of filing system, refer to the folders you already have as you make your list. Are your existing folders specific enough? Too specific? Now's the time to shed any old bad habits and develop new ones that support using and maintaining a new system.

While there's no perfect way to name files, these tips should help hone your efforts:

1. **Look for what is common and what is unique about the contents of each folder.** Like with Like tells you that all the insurance folders should live together, but each policy is

distinct. So you could label them Auto Insurance and Health Insurance and Homeowner's Insurance, but what they all have in common is that they are insurance policies. Using what's common unifies them while what's unique distinguishes each from the other:

Insurance: Auto
Insurance: Health
Insurance: Homeowner's

This way, you know they all are filed under *I* for Insurance and then arranged in alphabetical order from *A* to *Z*.

2. **Keep folder names simple and structured:** category, year or date (if applicable), subcategory, any additional information. The fewer the words and the more specific they are, the better.

So, rather than this:

Our Trip to the Grand Canyon with Bob and Sally 20XX

Try this:

Travel: 20XX, Grand Canyon (Bob and Sally)

We begin with the category, Travel, then the year or date, 20XX, and then the destination, Grand Canyon. Finally, we list any additional information—here, the companions Bob and Sally.

3. **Look for ways to combine Like with Like documents together into one folder.** Rather than a series of individual folders labeled Utilities: 20XX: Cable; Utilities: 20XX: Gas and Electric; Utilities: 20XX: Phone; Utilities: 20XX: Water and Sewer, use a classification folder that is labeled Utilities: 20XX with internal pages for each separate entity.

Once you feel confident that you have a system that makes sense to you and follows the practices I've laid out, leave this page and enter the actual filing cabinet to create or rearrange and rename the folders you currently have.

If using fastener folders and a two-hole punch seems tedious or overly involved for you, it may be. Consider, though, that with this system, you will never again drop a folder and have its contents scatter across the floor. The one document you swore you had put into the X folder will never actually be discovered in the Y folder.

I have saved clients thousands of dollars and hours of time because I always insist on fastener folders. Nothing can be lost, and the little bit of extra time involved in the actual filing guarantees that you will never inadvertently drop a document in the wrong folder.

If you're still not convinced, then simply use regular file folders and be *very careful* when filing. Filing is not an activity that should ever be multitasked. As repetitive as it may be, it requires your complete attention to avoid the simplest of mistakes. It will give me no pleasure to tell you "I told you so" should the inevitable result of distracted filing occur.

TRANSITIONING FROM AN OUTSIDE OFFICE TO A HOME OFFICE

If you're currently working remotely, whether you're a digital nomad, a traditional corporate worker, an entrepreneur, or some hybrid of these, it's important to make your transitions from outside workspaces to home workspaces as frictionless as possible. No matter where you're working, you still want work to be done in a timely, efficient, and professional manner, right?

If you've got staff or a team somewhere else, how do you get them important information? Are you sharing files on the cloud? Are you scanning things? If so, what do you do with the originals once you've digitized them?

If working virtually is relatively new to you, here's a tip from those of us who have been virtual for a while. While it may be fun at first to be at work in your pajamas or even naked, studies show that dressing for work improves productivity and focus. You can be casually dressed—shorts and a T-shirt—but anything more than boxers or your birthday suit helps.

If you've recently left an external office and brought home boxes of files, office supplies, and personal artifacts, you'll want to be thorough and attentive as you integrate them into your home. Things like duplicate framed photos of significant people in your life or redundant office supplies should be passed along to others. If you do most of your work online and seldom print documents, how many pens or cases of paper do you really need, even if they were free?

STRUCTURAL ELEMENTS OF AN OFFICE

You'll find a thorough list of all the things that one might have in an office in your companion workbook and by visiting unstuffbook.com/paper. You likely won't need everything on the list, but you may find a few things that are nice to have, if not essential.

Look around your office now. Using the list as a guide for things you would use but don't have, have but don't use (these you may release—put them directly in the thrift-store container), and have and use, check off each item that belongs in *your* office. Then use this list and Like with Like to determine where each item or group of items will live.

HOW TO SET UP YOUR OFFICE

Furniture

The largest and most-used piece of furniture in the office is most likely a desk. So let's place or arrange that first. It's nice not to have your back to the door of the room. It's not imperative, but if you can avoid it, please do. Do you have a standing desk? That may also influence placement. You can see my current office setup at unstuffbook.com/paper.

You'll want a comfortable desk chair with adequate back and wrist support, ideally one that adjusts up and down—particularly if you spend lots of hours at your desk. If you use a credenza or a filing cabinet and are in and out of your files often throughout the day, then it's probably a good idea to keep this piece nearby.

If there's room, could you use some shelving? For storing reference books and office supplies as well as displaying personal items, adequate shelving is crucial. If there's little floor space for freestanding bookcases, consider wall-mounted shelving.

Electronics

Make sure that you have enough electrical outlets for all your equipment. Make sure that you have surge protectors as well. Anything that can be plugged into a surge protector should be—the fewer things directly plugged into the wall, the fewer the opportunities for power surges to short out your equipment, even just blowing light bulbs in lamps.

For space-saving reasons alone, choose a multifunction printer (printing, copying, scanning, faxing) whenever possible. While they may have a larger footprint than a regular printer, a single machine takes up less space than individual machines that do only one thing.

If color printing is not important to you, a black-and-white laser machine is faster, and the cost per page is lower than a color inkjet machine. If color is important and cost is also a factor, then inkjet it must be. And while more expensive than either previous option, color laser machines offer the widest range of features, including double-sided printing and scanning to name just a few.

When it comes to computers, get the largest, highest resolution monitor you can afford, and max out the built-in RAM on your desktop or laptop. Additional RAM is relatively cheap when configuring your computer purchase and essential when running several applications at the same time. Unless you're playing a lot of games or editing video, some minor variations on processor speed will probably not be that noticeable. But inadequate RAM will slow you down and frustrate you again and again. Don't be penny-wise but pound-foolish in this instance.

All computer equipment should call the office area home. If you use your tablet or laptop in other rooms during the day, I suggest you "put them to bed" back in the office at the end of the day. Likewise, calculators, printers, shredders, etc.—if it's considered an office machine, it should live in the office. All of these machines' supplies— toner or ink, paper, shredder lubrication sheets—should live here as well. These supplies could be stored with general office supplies in a closet or cabinet, but group anything electronic together in one area for easy access.

You'll find lots of information online about a proper ergonomic tasking setup. Utilize it. Make sure that using your computer and other electronic devices does no harm to your health, both in the short-term and long-term.

Refrain from sticking notes and other reminders (or decorations) on your monitor or other equipment, other than maybe the number of your tech wiz or IT person. Learn to create reminder notes either on your computer or, even better, write or enter them directly onto your calendar as tasks so they actually get done. After a few days, Post-its or other sticky notes blend into the background and just become clutter.

SOFTWARE

Most software is now downloadable, but a few things may still be on a disk, and those should all be stored together. As you gather any software disks from around the house, make sure you toss any old disks for any machines or programs that are obsolete, no longer in your possession, or no longer being used.

DATA CDS, DVDS, AND FLOPPY DISKS

If you still have any of these kinds of obsolete formats, it's now time to harvest their contents. Gather any disks together and review them. Compare data on disks against data on your computer to see if any files you need or want from these disks are already on your computer. If so, destroy the disk, or if you don't care who may have access to the contents, toss them. If the disks contain any personal information, the easiest way to destroy them is by shredding them or snapping them into pieces. Wear protective gloves as CDs and DVDs can be sharp when broken.

We'll discuss digital files in detail in Chapter 10, but for now, any files you are importing from disks should go into a new folder you create just for this task. That way, you'll avoid confusion or redundancies. Create the folder in your Documents folder and label it 20XX Files Import.

You can also mount any backup disks, if they aren't already up and running, and create a new backup that includes the files imported from your disks. Then, if you have multiple external drives, those can be stored together. While you can almost never be too backed up (just ask anyone whose computer has crashed!), multiple copies of multiple copies become redundant and confusing when you need to restore data from one of these backups.

Lighting

The right lighting is key. You'll want a desk lamp for task lighting and secondary lamps and/or overhead lighting fixtures for general lighting. If you shoot video, you'll also want lighting specific to that. A guideline for good lighting is that there should be enough light available anywhere someone might be sitting and reading. Three-way bulbs and dimmers can certainly create a softer mood when you're not working, but there's no reason to struggle with inadequate lighting when you're trying to get some work done.

Filing

A place to store documents and folders on their way into a filing cabinet is essential, as is a scheduled time each day or week when filing takes place. I don't think there's a need to distinguish between never-filed and previously filed documents. If a project requires you to frequently return to a particular folder or two, keeping it handy at your work area may be a better choice than filing and refiling the folder throughout the day. Either way, there should be a bin or basket established for all documents that are ready to be filed but haven't been yet.

Mail Revisited

We're now going to return to the mail. If you remember, we talked about sorting the mail into the following major categories:

- Bills and Asks (finance-related)
- Invitations and Events (time-sensitive)
- Read and File (including personal correspondence)
- Action Items (finite tasks)

I'm assuming that you have been managing the mail as detailed in Chapter 2, right? If the office is *not* where you have been processing the mail, this may be the time to now make the office the home for the mail. Given that much of what will need to be filed probably arrives through the mail, it makes sense that the mail should be sorted and processed in this space.

I have a preference for wire-mesh bins/baskets that are stackable, but if you prefer wicker or lined or unlined, go for it. What I'm most concerned with is that the mail is processed consistently. And if you have adequate room, setting up homes for the bins that do not need to be moved or altered on a daily basis will save you time and effort and reinforce your new habits more quickly.

Office Supplies

Like with Like means all office supplies live together. It means all active and backup supplies live together, ideally corralled into containers and clearly labeled. I have a stapler, a Post-it dispenser, two round coasters, one felt pad for my mobile phone, and a bell on my desktop. My standing desk has a small cubby that stores my eyeglass-cleaning cloth and a few pens.

I go into my closet to get anything else I might need during the day. That includes scissors, paper clips, and binder clips. Things are neatly arranged on shelves, Like with Like, so anyone can come from anywhere in the house, and they only have to look in one place to find whatever they need.

In my world, there may be a pair of scissors in multiple rooms—I have one in the office and one in the kitchen, for example. But I wouldn't suggest squirreling away random supplies in random closets or rooms. Scattered tools means you're more likely to misplace something, run out of or overbuy supplies, and waste time. It only *seems* more convenient to have things everywhere.

Owner's Manuals

If you're going to keep physical owner's manuals, they should be gathered together and stored in either a clear plastic envelope or an accordion folder or two (as volume dictates). Start by collecting them from every drawer or cubby or surface where they might currently be. Once you have them all together, immediately purge any for equipment that you no longer own. Throw those in the recycling bin.

Of the ones that remain, you can either alphabetize them by manufacturer or group them according to subcategories, such as small kitchen appliances, large appliances, office machines, etc. Or you could do what I do: go online, download the PDF version, and toss the paper out. I can literally count on one hand how many times I've opened a physical *or* digital owner's manual—and giving up drawer space and time to store these seems like a waste. Just make sure whenever you bring a new piece of equipment into the house, you add its manual to the others. Likewise, any time a piece of equipment leaves, find its manual and let it go.

Contacts Container

In Chapter 2, we established a container of contacts for any return addresses we harvested from incoming mail along with random business cards, matchbooks, and any scraps of paper with phone numbers scribbled on them. Once a week (or at some other regularly scheduled interval), make it a point to enter at least some of these details into your contacts, whether you still keep an address book or use an app.

Whenever you bring home a business card or exchange contact information with others, add some identifying notes to the back of the card or in the note section of the digital entry to remind you of when, where, and why you now have this contact in your records. Don't over-think this and keep it simple. Something like this works well:

Sally Smith

Met Christmas 20XX

Works w/ Steve at Troyan's Construction

Partner: Ruby

Any time you attend a conference or other event where you're networking, take a ziplock bag with you and drop all the cards you collect into it when you're back in your room. Label the bag with the event name and date to help refresh your memory when you start entering the cards into your address book or app.

Over the years, I've come across many stacks of random cards at clients' homes and offices from people they don't remember. They've been holding on to them thinking someday they'll remember who the person is and make contact then. Objectively, that is never going to happen. So if this kind of thinking sounds familiar, change your behavior going forward, and for now, forgive yourself for the piles of potentially missed opportunities. Just toss those old cards into the recycle bin.

CLIENT-FRIENDLY SPACE

If you meet with clients in your home, depending on your work and your relationship with your clients, it may be important to maintain a professional appearance for your workspace. Food wrappers, kids' toys, lunch's leftovers, and other signs of your personal life should probably be removed before the client arrives.

It's also important that you can easily put your hands on any files that belong to the client or any forms you may need for your work together. This only reinforces the imperative that you develop a filing system that is easy to use and easy to maintain—and that you do in fact use it.

A TIME TO GATHER

You've already done a junior version of this exercise with the owner's manuals. Now travel around the house and gather all remaining documents that you think belong in your office area. The mail is already accounted for, but there are bound to be other papers lying around. Let's corral them all together into a container of some sort, not worrying too much about their order. Step one is to find them. Step two will be to sort them.

SORTING, PURGING, AND (RE)ARRANGING

Things to Keep, Things to Toss

Now that we've gotten every stray piece of paper together from the various corners of the house, it's time to sort through them. Go to your companion workbook or to unstuffbook.com/paper for a list of documents you can toss out immediately. You don't need to wonder or fret about anything on that list, I promise.

After you've tossed out everything on that list, what remains needs to be sorted and filed. Like with Like makes filing go faster, especially when there is a stockpile of things to file. So begin by grouping like things together—all your utility bills, bank statements, credit card statements, and so on. Then, further sort them by account number whenever there are multiple accounts with the same vendor. This way, when you start to pull out or create folders, all of a certain kind of document is already together, ready to be filed at the same time.

Always create the folder and handwrite its label before committing yourself to a printed label. You may determine that you need a larger or smaller folder or that the nature of the contents has shifted enough to warrant a change in label.

Continue filing until everything has a home inside a folder, one of the mail bins, or the recycling bin. If you need a reminder about the how-to of filing, please refer back to the filing sections on pages 106–110.

When you are finished, there should no longer be any loose documents around the house, all owner's manuals should be in one place, and your paperwork should be accurately labeled and smartly filed.

WHEN SPACE IS LIMITED

As I mentioned earlier, there are almost no instances when some sort of space to house and manage paperwork can't be found in a home. So don't give up hope. Don't let limited space convince you that disorganization, missed appointments, or even late payments are your destiny. I disagree, and I support you in drowning out any internal denial conversation you might be having right now.

With that in mind, explore your home to see where you could reasonably establish a workplace that is large enough to contain all you need to store and accommodate the kind of work you'll do there. Is there a corner in the basement or an odd-shaped closet under the stairs you could use?

If it's large enough for a chair and a work surface, you can have a fully functioning, if snug, office of your own. And once you've picked a spot, be creative in utilizing every inch of usable space. Consider installing shelves right up to the ceiling. Hang your monitor on the wall. Even your printer can be supported on brackets, taking away no space from your desktop.

Whatever you choose, keep things to scale for both furniture and supplies. Oversized furniture will quickly crowd you out of a smaller space, and stocking up on too many supplies will leave you without much breathing room. You don't want to frequently run out of supplies, but you also don't have the space to store tons of extras. Find the right balance, and you will have a crisp and tidy space to call your own.

THOSE OTHER ACTIVITIES

Now that you have a functional workspace, it's time to consider those other activities that you isolated at the beginning of the chapter. In this new configuration, what do you have room for? And what would still be better relocated to some other part of the home?

Consider each activity to find the strongest match. If the office is still the best fit, then carve out enough space to house whatever equipment and supplies belong to the activity. If instead the den, family room, or basement would be better, take the grouping of things to its new home. If these items are already contained in a cabinet or basket or bin, that's great. If not, guesstimate the volume of things, get them an appropriately sized container, and label it. Do this for each activity that you're moving out of your office.

When you get to the new space, don't just dump everything in a corner—find whatever you've brought with you a proper home. Use Like with Like liberally in identifying these new homes. Even if the rest of the room is a shambles, create a distinct and orderly location for this one activity and its requisite parts. This one action will lay the foundation for when you return to this space to tidy up the rest of it. Make it a priority that the next time you visit this space, you will set your timer and dedicate some time to bring it into alignment with your new crisp and defined area.

HOW LONG DO I HAVE TO KEEP THIS?

This is one of the questions I'm asked most often: "Is it okay to get rid of XYZ?" "Do I still have to hold on to ABC?" Not knowing what to keep and what to let go stops more people in their tracks than almost anything else when it comes to paper.

Rather than go into excruciating detail here, I've created a handy list in the companion workbook, which can also be downloaded at unstuffbook.com/paper. Refer to it whenever you have a question.

And given that rules and laws vary from jurisdiction to jurisdiction, *always* check with a tax or legal professional if there's even a hint of doubt. It's always better to err on the side of caution before shredding your last copy of something important.

The one thing I will state here definitively is to *never* get rid of your tax returns. Your tax adviser will counsel you on when you can dispose of supporting materials, but never, never, *never* discard the actual filed return. You can scan it, and once you've confirmed you have a digital version of every page, you can destroy the paper version. But you should *always* retain a copy of every tax return. Seriously.

TO SHRED OR NOT TO SHRED?

Identity theft is a big deal when it happens to you. Until then, it may be easy to write off as a vague threat. But believe me, if you find out someone's been using your ID to do their Christmas shopping or to purchase a condo in Miami, tracking down and repairing the breach may be a colossal pain in the butt, requiring stamina and many tedious hours. And, like other forms of trauma, the impact identity theft can have on your mindset and ability to trust may continue for years after the situation is resolved.

I wish I could say that shredding your documents guarantees you protection from this most personal intrusion and violation, but it doesn't. It helps with prevention, but criminals are always looking for new ways to beat the system, and we have to do our best to keep up with them. In the meantime, anything, *anything*, that has your name, address, and any account number, suggestion of an account number, or an offer to establish an account number should be run through a crosscut shredder.

Remember Oliver North and Iran-Contra? The cheapest shredders simply cut your papers into thin strips that can be taped back together to recreate the original document. Crosscut shredders turn your paper into a version of confetti that is virtually impossible to piece back together. This is not a time to cut corners or to save a few bucks when weighing the difference between these two types of machines. Pick up some shredder lubrication sheets as well to keep your blades sharp and unclogged. This will protect your investment and prevent the gears from seizing up.

Likewise, any other media that may have confidential information on them—credit cards, for example—need to be destroyed as well. Either shred, smash, cut, or break these things until they are unreadable. Cut old credit cards through the magnetic strip on the back and across any account numbers. Also, these kinds of materials are not recyclable—once destroyed, they go in the trash.

MAINTAINING THE SYSTEM

I'm a proud member of the clean-desk club, and I'd like to sponsor you for membership as well. If possible, never leave your office with papers lying on your desk, the one exception being a current project that you'll immediately resume working on in the morning. Even if you're working on a few projects simultaneously, you can only start working on one project first, so that should be the only thing left out.

Otherwise, at the end of the day, clean your work surface. You don't have to file everything each night before leaving, but every document you're finished with should be placed in the To-Be-Filed basket. Any documents that arrived in the mail should be in their baskets as well. Any cables or electronic devices should find their way home, too.

At the end of the day, even if you're just walking down the hall, you want to go home for the night. So does everything else you've used throughout the day. Put things back where they came from, establish a proper home for anything that came in from the outside during the day, and dispatch to the donation container, trash, or recycling anything that is now leaving your home because it's no longer useful. Ten to fifteen minutes at the end of the day should be enough time to ensure that everything is back where it belongs.

And certainly, if you pulled out something during the day for a finite activity, there's no reason to wait until the end of the day to send it home. Build the habit of returning things to their home as soon as you're finished with them, and maintaining order will actually take care of itself.

5

CLOTHES · CLOSETS

Women usually love what they buy, yet hate two-thirds of what's in their closets.
–MIGNON MCLAUGHLIN

I base most of my fashion sense on what doesn't itch.
–GILDA RADNER

WHAT WE'RE GOING TO COVER IN THIS CHAPTER

- What a Closet Is and Isn't
- Kinds of Closets and Their Contents
- Structural Elements of a Clothes Closet
- Clothes and Proper Storage I
- Clothes and Proper Storage II
- Presorting and Purging
- Emptying the Closet(s)
- Sorting and Purging
- Reloading the Closet
- Drawers (Mini Closets on Their Sides)
- Overbuying and Buyer's Remorse
- Shoes
- Maintaining the Clothes Closet
- Other Kinds of Closets
- Dirty Laundry
- Maintaining the System

SO WE'VE CONQUERED, or at least survived, the workspace. We now have a system set up in a dedicated area for paying bills; we know how to deal with the mail when it comes in; we have a handle on our magazines, catalogs, and other periodicals; and there are no longer piles of paper scattered in other areas of our home.

Now it gets personal. We're going to tackle closets—in particular, those used for clothing.

I've heard this countless times: "I've got a ton of clothes and nothing to wear." Maybe you feel that way, too. You've got "fat" clothes, "skinny" clothes, torn clothes, worn clothes, red clothes, blue clothes, and even with all that, you can never find that cashmere sweater that makes you look and feel like a million bucks when you want it. Well, that is about to change.

Let's start with a simple but powerful suggestion (or rule, if you respond better to rules): if you don't like wearing it, if you can't wear it, or if you haven't worn it in two years or more, it's time to shed it. When we get to sorting, we'll dismantle once and for all those stubborn arguments you may have for why this suggestion applies in almost every situation *except* yours. But for now, keep this suggestion in mind as you read this chapter.

Things You Will Need for This Work

- A good friend
- Seven containers/areas defined on the floor for sorting:
  - » Keep
  - » Someplace Else
  - » Donate
  - » Sentimentaland
  - » Sell
  - » The Fence
  - » Trash
- Good lighting
- A full-length mirror

WHAT A CLOSET IS AND ISN'T

Closet (noun): A small and enclosed space, a cabinet, or a cupboard in a house or building used for general storage or for hanging clothes

Since we're focusing on the hanging-clothes part, let's first agree that there will be no general storage in our clothes closets except when clearly labeled and absolutely necessary because of space constraints.

A closet is never a hidden room where you can barely open the door and where, to avoid an avalanche of oddities tumbling onto your head, you frantically insert another random object and slam the door, narrowly escaping disaster.

That is *not* a closet. That is your next project.

The goal of this chapter is simple: for you to organize your closets so that within 30 seconds of opening the closet door, you can successfully put your hands on whatever you're looking for.

KINDS OF CLOSETS AND THEIR CONTENTS

Clothes: Clothing, shoes, adornment, and accessories.

Linen: Towels, bed linens, surplus bathroom supplies, sewing kit.

Guest Room(s): Linens, towels, etc. that a guest would use when staying in this room.

Utility: Household maintenance items, cleaning supplies, tools.

Coat/Entry and Mudrooms: Outerwear, foul-weather gear, sporting goods and equipment, pet items.

Travel: Suitcases, travel laundry bag, travel pouches, shoe bags, packing cubes, toiletry case, refillable carry-on bottles.

Gifts/Presents: Gifts gathered throughout the year to be given to others, wrapping paper, bows, ribbon.

Party: Supplies for parties and entertaining, decorations, children's party games.

Seasonal Decor: Decorations sorted, containerized, and stored by specific holiday or season.

In your home, identify the types and locations of the closets you have. You'll find a template for this in the companion workbook, or in your notebook you can make a simple list of them following the format below.

Type of closet: _____

Location in the home: _____

Contents: _____

We'll use this list later when it comes time to sort and purge items and then reload closets.

STRUCTURAL ELEMENTS OF A CLOTHES CLOSET

Below are the things I'd like to find in any clothes closet. You'll find this list in your companion workbook, and you can also download it at unstuffbook.com/closets. It's a helpful checklist as you start to organize your clothes closets:

- Good, bright, and plentiful lighting
- An ample supply of wood, padded, or other good-quality hangers (preferably uniform in size and type)
- Sturdy rods and shelves that don't bow under weight
- Hooks or a hooked hanger for belts
- Hooks for robes
- Racks or hooked hangers for neckties
- Shoe racks/shelves/cubbies that are expandable or already sized for your shoes
- A valet hook or pullout rod
- Containers, baskets, or bins for small or odd-shaped items
- Containers, baskets, or bins for small handbags (purses, clutches, etc.)
- Clear shoe boxes for special-occasion shoes

The following are things I wouldn't like to find in any clothes closet:

- Dry-cleaning bags discarded and lying on the floor
- Old food or food containers
- The one remaining shoe of a former pair
- Random piles of dirty laundry or baskets of clean, unfolded laundry
- Discarded or obsolete telephone equipment
- Expired animals—pets or pests

You get the idea.

CLOTHES AND PROPER STORAGE I

If space allows, this is how you will organize your closets:

- Items are sorted by type—all slacks together, shirts together, coats together, etc.

- Within each type, items are further sorted by color and style—long-sleeved or short-sleeved, business or casual, winter or summer, etc.
- All two-piece and three-piece outfits go together and stay together.
- All hanging clothes are kept on uniform hangers so everything hangs at the same level.
- Robes and nightwear hang on hooks nearest to the door.
- Handbags and decorative hats go on shelves (cold-weather hats belong with outerwear in coat closets).
- Smaller handbags (purses, clutches) are stored in baskets or bins.
- Small or odd-shaped items are corralled in baskets.
- Scarves are folded and placed in baskets.
- Belts belong on hooks or hangers with hooks.
- Neckties go on racks or hooked hangers.
- Seasonal shoes go on the floor (snow boots are stored with outerwear in a coat closet).
- Clear shoe boxes on shelves are for special-occasion or fancy shoes.

If adequate space for your entire wardrobe is unavailable in one contiguous space, your closets should only contain clothes for the current season. Twice a year—and it may be worth adding reminders to your calendar (in the U.S., you can use daylight saving time changes as guides)—rotate your wardrobe to a storage closet or a hanging rack so the current season's clothes are always front and center.

Current Sizes

For sorting, purging, and storing clothes, it's best to start with the correct sizes of everyone in your household. It's also good information to have when you're shopping for these people or they're shopping for you.

Go to your companion workbook or unstuffbook.com/closets for a form you can use to capture this information for you and anyone else you typically shop for.

Clothes That Don't Fit or Work and the People Who Love Them

Remember shouting, "I am not my stuff!" back in Chapter 1? Well, this might be even harder to say convincingly: "I am not my clothes!"

Sure, clothing can be a form of self-expression, and fashion as wearable art takes that concept even further. But there is nothing artistic about closets overflowing with clothes that are worn out, don't fit, or that you don't even like any more.

And whether the chaos is caused by inertia or a less-than-healthy attachment to our clothing, the result is the same—wasted time and wasted space, along with lots of frustration and unnecessary stress.

Over the years, I've recognized a few archetypes when it comes to clothing. See if any of them resonate with you. As always, these are both playful and serious—and useful when it comes to developing the right mindset for unstuffing your clothes closets.

THE BARGAIN HUNTER

My client—we'll call her Doris—used to be a size 6, and she wore a size 7½ shoe. Then she had her sons, Jesse and Claude. She's now a size 10 to 12, and her foot will never see this side of an 8 again. She has plenty of clothes that fit her.

But occasionally she'll see a great Gucci loafer on sale in size 7½, and she can't seem to help herself. Sometimes they even come home with her in different colors because they were "such a bargain." She'll tell me, "You don't understand, it's a woman thing," but I think I do understand. I love a bargain as much as the next person, but it's not a bargain if you can't fit into it. It's a bargain for the woman behind you who still wears a 7½.

THE SIZE KING/QUEEN

If you've struggled with your weight, body image, or eating disorders, and your size has fluctuated, you may have several wardrobes competing for your (possibly) limited closet and storage space.

Take a deep breath. Now let's speak frankly. When was the last time you actually wore that skirt? Or those trousers? If any article of clothing is more than two sizes away from your current size, it's time to say good-bye.

I have a client, we'll call her Claire, and she has struggled with her size for years. She's been up and down, and she has a wardrobe that reflects this. When I first met her, she had already worked with another organizer who had redesigned her closet with expensive hardware that actually reduced the amount of clothing that could be stored in it. While it was lovely in the way it displayed her clothing, in a Manhattan apartment with limited closets it was also a huge waste of prime real estate.

On top of dealing with limited space, there was also Claire's frustration with her unsuccessful attempts to lose weight and a stockpile of clothes in many sizes. Currently, she was stuck somewhere between her heaviest and her ideal weight.

I encouraged her to tell me the story of her most recent attempt. After her tearful and heartfelt recounting, we climbed into the story together. I helped Claire to see which parts of the story were factual and which parts were just stock phrases that she was not aware she was even repeating—that's how ingrained they were in her way of thinking about herself and her size.

Phrases such as "I'm fat; no one's ever going to love me" or "I'll always be alone" or "I can't do anything right" were automatic responses to any discomfort she was feeling.

After a few minutes of playful, direct dissection, we were both giggling at the blatantly false and sometimes absurd ways she viewed herself. Several times she'd start to say something self-deprecating, only to catch and correct herself and then burst out laughing.

Wiping tears from her face, this time from joy, she marched over to the closet and began tossing out clothes she had been saving just in case she woke up 40 pounds heavier. Overnight. The freedom in her voice and laughter as she gathered these plus-sized stretch pants and flowing, drapey tops was inspiring. No longer waiting for something "inevitably awful" to happen, Claire was now free to use her closets for her life today.

We also curated her "skinny" clothes, keeping some timeless pieces and letting go of the rest. Most of the things she was holding on to for her descent in size were too random, and while the sizes might have been right, some of the styles were way out of date, even for a retro or artsy look.

We kept the best pieces and made peace with the fact that if or when Claire gets down in size and needs more clothes, that would be a legitimate reason to shop. In the meantime, her closet was an accurate reflection of her current size, with room for some movement north or south in the size department.

William, too, had clothes that he just couldn't fit into any longer. In sorting through his closets, we repeatedly came across another pair of "skinny" jeans or a favorite pair of shorts from college. These discoveries were always qualified with "God, I really need to get back to the gym," or "I had those on a few weeks ago, and I could almost button them all the way up!" When pushed, William admitted that his gym membership had lapsed seven months ago and that the "few weeks ago" he was referring to was actually a year and a half past.

I'm aware that you may be holding on to clothes in smaller sizes with the hope that you will once again fit into them. And I support you in accomplishing your goal. But like Claire and William, you need to be honest with yourself about how diligently you're working on slimming down. And if you are more than two sizes away from those jeans, how likely is it that you'll be back in them before the styles change? Only you can answer that.

I will say that if you're keeping them as any form of negative reinforcement or as some other shame-based motivational tool, you need to get rid of them immediately. Any victory achieved at that cost is too expensive. If they are providing positive motivation, though, I still suggest selecting the best examples and strongest styles and letting faded or quirky pieces go. Read on for more on this topic.

THE RETRO GOD/GODDESS

Clothes that are out of style should not be difficult to spot. And unless you're a famous artist, fashionista, or other public figure, chances are that you will not be leading a trend by reclaiming some iconic era-specific design. Let them go. If, in 20 years, you need to wear elephant bell-bottom, hip-hugger jeans again, you'll line up to buy them like everyone else.

ALWAYS A BRIDESMAID

Bridesmaid dresses, mother-of-the-bride outfits, and other themed clothes are what I like to call "specialty" clothes. These are often the easiest to release because, while you may have enjoyed the event, you may not have even liked wearing the outfits in the first place. I know that they may not have been cheap, but that's the price of love and friendship. And you can always get revenge when *you* get married, if you're so inclined. Meanwhile, make a drag queen happy. Get those dresses out of here now.

THE ONLY-IN-YOUR-DREAMS OUTFIT

I fell in love with a pair of electric-cobalt-blue brushed-cotton Cacharel jeans when I was 18. I wore them out of the house exactly once. There is no doubt they were beautiful and fit me well, but I was so self-conscious in them that I couldn't relax the entire day. It's not an exaggeration to say that when I walked into a room, everyone looked at me. You couldn't *not* look, that's how bright and shiny they were. I didn't want that much attention. They weren't me. Even though I wanted them to be. I'm sure they eventually found a happy home in some aspiring rock star's closet.

If you have a similar item, it's time to pass it along. You can celebrate your sense of style and your willingness to break out of your comfort zone as you add it to the going-away pile without regret. Also celebrate being realistic and practical by accepting that your clothing experiment didn't pan out. The decision to let a garment (or more) go doesn't need to be any more fraught than that.

There's value in knowing what you feel comfortable in and what you don't. An added bonus is that by putting something back into circulation, you're letting someone else unleash their inner diva, goth, or cowboy.

THE NEW ENGLAND "OLD MONEY" LOOK

Even if you take excellent care of your clothes, your favorite shirt will become worn at the cuffs or collar, heels will wear unevenly, or a back pocket may get snagged on an exposed nail. It's okay—clothes wear out and get damaged. If you wear them enough, eventually something will happen. And when they become stretched out, shrunk, faded or damaged, it's game over.

Other than serving as a bizarre badge of Yankee pride, clothes that have worn thin or have holes in them are best relegated to yard work, cleaning the garage, painting, or community service work, such as planting spring bulbs with your neighborhood gardening society. But you need only a few of these items. You don't need 14 sweatshirts with grease stains and holes—even if they used to be your favorites. Three or four will suffice. The rest become rags, chew toys for a pet, or end up in the textile recycling pile.

Clothes That Do Fit and Simplify Your Life

Given that we gravitate towards our "greatest hits" garments over and over, why not lean into that and reduce your wardrobe to only the clothes that you actually wear? Even better when they are all flattering, fit well, and make you feel confident—if not glamorous—every time you step into them.

These are a few easy guides for simplifying your choices without compromising on style or quality.

THE UNIFORM

I'm not advocating a homogeneous style or look for everyone. You know what you look good in or at least what you feel comfortable wearing. When working away from home, I wear button-down, collared shirts with either short or long sleeves, dressy black or blue jeans, and a good pair of shoes. The shirts are all either stripes or checks. It simplifies things for me, and it's very easy to get dressed in the morning.

If I'm speaking somewhere, I either add a sports coat to this outfit or replace all of it with a suit. Otherwise, I'm in shorts and a T-shirt. It's a uniform of sorts, and one that I'm very comfortable in.

For daily wear, a tailored, somewhat limited wardrobe can make getting out of the house that much easier and quicker. If you're looking for a way to trim down the amount of clothing in your closet, creating a few uniforms is a great solution.

THE CAPSULE WARDROBE

A clever cousin of the uniform is a capsule wardrobe. A capsule wardrobe contains tops, bottoms, dresses, outerwear, shoes, and accessories that can be easily mixed and matched together. You should build your capsule wardrobe with the highest quality items you can afford, and everything in it should be classic and timeless so everything will still look good years from now.

By limiting your items to a certain number, say 33, you select garments that work well together and because they mix so well, they create the appearance of a much larger wardrobe. You can find a breakdown of a typical 33-piece capsule wardrobe in your companion workbook.

There are several reasons why a capsule wardrobe could be a good choice for you.

The most obvious benefits are saving money and time since once you settle on your capsule wardrobe, you don't need to shop again until something wears out.

Another benefit is reducing stress and decision fatigue. With a capsule wardrobe, getting dressed every day is fast and easy because while your choices are somewhat limited, you also love and look great in everything you own.

Brain science says that people only have the bandwidth for a certain number of decisions each day. Why waste any of them standing in front of your closet when you could just grab any top and bottom and get on with the day?

Postcards from the Edge

There are clothes that are special because of where we got them, who gave them to us, who they belonged to, or what we were doing when we wore them. This always makes me think of the play *The Woolgatherer* by William Mastrosimone. I think the title says it all. It doesn't matter whether the sweater was from an old flame, your grandfather, an outlet mall, or Bergdorf's, sweaters with holes in them go to someone who can mend them, meaning reweave them, not just sew a patch on them. Likewise, suits and other dressy clothes should be repaired if possible and discarded if not. They are not souvenirs. They are clothes.

If you absolutely cannot let a particular piece of clothing go but you also cannot wear it, place it in a separate pile that will join its brothers and sisters in a place I call Sentimentaland. More on this later.

A Cautionary Tale from the Interweb

Perhaps you've read the story that has traveled around the internet maybe 100 million times by now about a brother who is cleaning out his sister's dresser after her funeral and discovers a silk teddy or some fancy lingerie. The story goes that she was saving it for some special day, and he implores us to recognize that today is that special day. He wants us to cherish the moment, live the day fully, and be here now because we don't know what tomorrow holds for us—or, for that matter, if we even get a tomorrow.

While the story is fake, the sentiment behind it is real—"someday" is a fiction. So take the sad man's advice and dig in today. Besides, you certainly don't want someone writing about *you* on the internet after you're dead, using your mistakes as teachable moments. So, wear the teddy. And when it gets frayed, get a new teddy. Don't get 47 new teddies. Because you can wear only one at a time.

CLOTHES AND PROPER STORAGE II

Before we take everything out of the closet, open the door and take a few pictures. While the door is open, pull up a chair, sit down, and study the closet. Does it have everything you need or want it to have? The more time you spend planning now before we begin the big sort, the less time and money you'll spend later in either physical labor or correcting mistakes.

Now, take some measurements. Evaluate the space:

- Do you have adequate shelving?
- Are the shelves sturdy and stable?
- How about the rods—are they well secured to the walls? Do they bow in the middle?
- Were all your clothes bunched up with no room around them, or was there adequate space between the items?
- How about shoes? Do you have cubbies for them or a shoe rack? A slanted shelf or two down low? Or are they all just jumbled in a big pile on the floor?

Get out your companion workbook or begin a new page in your notebook labeled Closets, and write down your observations, notes, and ideas. Is there anything that you would redesign? Search online for closet design ideas to spark your creativity. Dream big from a design point of view—we're less focused on finishes right now. Solid walnut or white melamine—these decisions don't matter as much as having the right hardware and configuration for everything you want to store in the closet in front of you. There'll be plenty of time to dress it up; let's make sure right now it works as a *closet*.

If you do want to make improvements, are they simple fixes that you can do by yourself or with a friend, or do they require a contractor's help? Before we start sorting, you should make sure that the space you'll return everything into is a space that works for you. There's no point in sorting and purging if, when it's time to put everything back, the closet still doesn't work for you.

For tenants and other people who may not be allowed to physically alter the layout or location of the closet, think about what you can do to improve the space to better serve you. Are there freestanding pieces you can use to transform the closet's interior? Are there too many shelves, and if so, could some be stored elsewhere or doubled up to create more depth between shelves? Work with whatever structural limits exist to creatively transform an awkward closet into a more useful closet.

In thinking about the physical layout and construction of your closet, if you determine that restructuring or replacing components is necessary, draw yourself a plan and start to create a shopping list. If this is a DIY project, make sure you have all of the proper tools and new/improved components on-site *before* you go any further.

Keep in mind that the finished project will look cleaner and crisper if the products, hardware, materials, and appointments go together well. Personal preference and budget may influence whether the look is more utilitarian or decorative, but standard and uniform finishes and design provide a good foundation—simple lines keep the focus on the clothing and quiet any visual jumble.

Equally important is not to fall prey to propaganda. There is no end to the new and "innovative" products and gadgets that promise *they'll* get you organized. Here's the truth: no product will magically produce the same results that you will as you work your way through this book. Don't be seduced or confused by advertising that claims a product will transform your disorganized closet (or office or life) from bad to good for only $19.95. There is no magic device, and you don't need to be rescued.

Carefully consider what you *do* need when it comes to clothing storage, and then search the marketplace for the smartest and best products. You may not need to spend a lot of money to get useful and well-constructed components. As with many things, a moderate approach often yields the best results, even in closet transformation.

PRESORTING AND PURGING

You're ready for this next phase after you've gathered all the supplies, tools, and hardware needed to restructure your closet yourself. If you're doing a closet makeover and using a company to supply materials and labor, your appointment should be scheduled for today. That way, you can unload the closet for the work crew and take the entire contents into another room to sort and purge while they transform your closet for you. Either way, you should be prepared to complete any construction as soon as the closet is empty of its contents.

Things to have on hand as you begin:

A Good Friend

Ask a friend for help only if they are objective, committed to the process, and not easily distracted—otherwise, you're better off on your own.

Seven Containers or Areas Defined on the Floor for Sorting

Keep: These are items that you really love, not items that you loved many years ago or wish to love in the years to come. These are items that fit and flatter you today. These will be laundered, folded or hung up, and put away.

Donate: These are things you are clearly done with and willing to give away, because they either don't fit or no longer match your style.

Sell: These are things you are clearly done with that are heading to a local consignment shop or being sold online because they either don't fit or no longer match your style. If you're going the online route, either you or someone you hire will need to handle this, so be sure to budget extra time to post photos, respond to inquiries, and ship your sales.

Trash: These are the unfortunate things you've kept long beyond repair or use, and they now need to be discarded. If you can find someplace locally that recycles textiles, please send these items there.

Someplace Else: These are the things that should have never been in your closet to begin with, the "general storage" items I mentioned at the top of the chapter. When you're finished with everything else, you'll containerize and label them, and find them appropriate homes.

Sentimentaland: As its name suggests, this is a mythical land defined by clear plastic tubs containing objects of dubious monetary value but that are ultimately priceless to you. These clothes can be further sorted by type—baby, maternity, etc.—or just placed in tubs along with other objects that you don't necessarily use but that are too significant to let go of.

The Fence: This category refers to being on the fence or unable to make a decision. It is to be used with hypervigilance and only in cases of extreme uncertainty. It is never to be used as a mask for procrastination or regret but only in cases of true confoundment. This is not a get-out-of-jail-free card—use it only as a last resort!

Good Lighting

This is not a date, and there's nothing romantic about to happen. You need to be able to see and see clearly. We're looking for rips, holes, stains, and, most importantly, fit. If the overhead light is out, replace the bulb. If you have only indirect lighting, remove the lampshades from the lamps. Even better, hang up a clip light or two, and turn the place into *Close Encounters of the Third Kind*. When you can actually see what's going on, you'll be more likely to act on it and remain decisive.

A Full-Length Mirror

Be sure you can see yourself from your head to your toes.

EMPTYING THE CLOSET

This is the moment of truth. As we've done before in other spaces, begin by removing everything from the closet. This is an exercise in trust (for me) and in liberation (for you). To create a little emotional space, perhaps you can think of this as an inexpensive and exhaustive shopping trip to a store you have always heard about but have never been to. You're about to discover old treasures, fashion mistakes, and everything in between without ever leaving your home.

Resist the urge to make too many decisions as you remove things, exceptions being those things you already know are trash or are being donated. It's important to empty the closet quickly, so you don't want to get distracted by sorting when you're really just unloading.

Once everything is out of the closet, now is the time to do any rebuilding, repairing, or restructuring. If the basic structure of your closet is completely satisfactory, then all you want to do right now is clean it. Take this time to wipe down everything—every surface, every piece of trim—and finish by sweeping, mopping, or vacuuming the floor.

Now that that's done, we can start sorting in earnest.

SORTING AND PURGING

Clothing with holes you can't/won't repair or stains that can't be removed get tossed. Resist the urge to turn every piece of clothing that is torn or stained into a rag. The moth-eaten cashmere sweater is sad, but it's not a chamois for you to polish your car with. Throw it away.

Clothes that don't fit, including shoes—even really expensive, sexy shoes—go away. If they're in great shape and worth some cash, resell them. Otherwise, a local charity gets them.

Clothing that is ripped in unfashionable or inappropriately revealing ways may be something you'll change the oil in or wear as a costume, but it doesn't belong in your closet anymore. Feel free to start a costume bin to store the things you wear only on Halloween or at Burning Man or on "play night." But they don't deserve prime closet real estate unless your daily work *requires* specific costumes.

These designations should allow you to move quickly through the worn, the torn, and the obsolete. Anytime you come to a piece of clothing that you're on the fence about, set it aside, and we'll return to it in a bit.

Everything else is subject to the following six questions. If the answer to questions one or two is no, let it go. If any answer to questions three through six is yes, let it go.

1. Have I worn this item in the last year or two?
    Yes. Go to the next question.
    No. This item is no longer in your current wardrobe. You may be saving it for any number of reasons, but to wear it isn't one of them. Let it go. The exception is formalwear that *still fits*.

2. Does this go with anything else I own?

    Yes. Go to the next question.

    No. Although you may have spent decent money on it, you're not going to build a wardrobe around it. Different from a costume, this is something that is terminally unique. Let it go.

3. Has this item lost its shape (stretched or shrunk), or has the color faded?

    No. Go to the next question.

    Yes. Of all the questions, this one has the least interpretive wiggle room. While the item itself may have evoked some sentimental tug, it's clearly past use. Let it go.

4. Am I waiting for this trend to come back before I wear it again?

    No. Go to the next question.

    Yes. It's not coming back. Not in this form. With the exception of haute couture, when something returns as a style contemporary designers typically interpret the classic fashion elements and either offer the new piece as an homage or as an ironic take on the past. Either way, your item will just look dated. Let it go.

5. Am I waiting to lose or gain weight before I can fit into this item again?

    No. Go to the next question.

    Yes. How many sizes away are you right now? If more than two, again, let it go. You can bargain all you want with yourself, but I'm pretty immovable on this point. When all else fails, remember the stories of Claire and William at the beginning of this chapter. If you're struggling with your weight, it might not be clothing that's providing the best motivation.

    Consult your therapist or other health professional on how to move deliberately and consistently forward to your preferred size and weight. No need to create opportunities to feel bad about yourself in the closet you use every day. Let it go.

6. Am I keeping this item because it was an expensive impulse purchase?

No. Depending on your answers to the other questions, you should now know which of the seven containers or areas defined on the floor that this item belongs in.

Yes. This is often one of the more difficult conversations I have with clients. The shame and remorse most people experience when confronted with these impulse purchases often freezes them in place. This is how the conversation often goes:

Andrew Mellen: Are we done with this jacket yet?

Client: I don't know.

AM: What's the debate?

Client: It was expensive.

AM: I can see that. [pausing] Do you ever wear it?

Client: Of course not. Never.

AM: How do you feel when you see it?

Client: Stupid. Angry. Stupid.

AM: That can't be fun.

Client: Yeah, it sucks.

AM: Okay. Tell me about your last relationship.

Client: That jerk?

AM: Okay. So you didn't hang onto him because he was expensive, did you?

Client: [laughing] Of course not.

AM: So why keep this hanging around just to give yourself something to feel bad about? Let it go.

Client: [with attitude] Fine.

AM: Look, don't do it just to make me happy. Do it because it makes sense to you. I don't have to live with it, you do. And it's taking space away from clothes you actually wear.

Client: No, you're right. I just hate it. I hate that I bought it, and I hate that I can't let it go.

AM: I get it. It's okay. It's fortunately, I hope, not the biggest or most expensive mistake you've ever made, so all things considered, it's not such a big deal.

Client: I hear what you're saying, but it still does feel like a big deal.

AM: All right. Then feel it as a big deal and still make the choice to let it go. Give yourself room for the things you love—don't let them be crowded out by the things you feel regret and remorse over.

Client: Oh, this is so hard. [pausing] Why is this so hard? [pausing] Good grief, where's the container for the consignment shop? Put this in it. It's ridiculous, I know. I'm just . . . I'm done, just get it out of here. Oh my God. I need help!

AM: [holding up another garment] How about this? Are you ready to let go of this?

How do you feel right now? Do you identify with this client? Are you agitated just reading this?

Study this feeling so you can remember it the next time you're shopping and looking at something you love but don't know what you'd do with it once you actually own it. That's when this feeling comes in handy. You can appreciate the item—shoes, slacks, belt, whatever—as a beautiful thing. You can appreciate it in the store or online and then just keep moving. Then you don't have to feel this way again. Try it the next time you're shopping. Leaving the lovely item behind likely won't feel worse than the sense of remorse does; chances are it'll feel a whole lot better.

For me, this is not about winning an argument. It's about advocating for the part of the client they seem less inclined to stand up for in those moments. The part that wants to be on the other side of the struggle, to relax, release, and be done. Unfortunately, like most of us, there's that other part of them that's really committed to protecting some sense of being right, that they must have been right to buy it in the first place because no one would knowingly do something so wrong or make such a costly mistake.

It's humbling to recognize that, despite our best efforts, we all do some things that are costly and don't serve us. If we've survived this long, we can take some comfort from knowing that it didn't kill us. It's just a piece of fabric—maybe with pick stitching and from a very exclusive goat, but it's still just fabric. We can let it go.

Once more, if the item has significant value, you can always return it to the store you purchased it from. If too much time has lapsed, then place it in the Sell container and resell it. It's one way to turn lemons into lemonade.

Using these six questions, don't stop until each item has been sorted into one of the seven piles. Well, except for bathroom breaks— definitely stop for those.

The Fence

At this point, everything should have been touched once and a decision about it made. For the few items you were uncertain about, which you've placed in The Fence pile, now it's do-or-die. Try them on one at a time. Look yourself over. Flattering? Or clingy in any number of wrong ways? Soft? Or itchy? Anything that doesn't flatter, doesn't fit well, or feels uncomfortable should leave.

For some things, the answer will be immediately visible. For any that look good *and* you're still on the fence about, ask yourself the six questions again. Nothing will remain a mystery after both a fitting and the gauntlet of questions a second time around.

Clothes-Swapping Parties: An Alternative to Thrift Stores

Although women are more likely to arrange something like this (Men—what a missed opportunity!), I often hear of clients or friends attending clothes-swapping parties. This is the basic idea: A bunch of friends and/or coworkers get together. Food and drink are always welcome components. Everyone brings the clothes they're done with and tosses them into the middle of the room. Each person takes a turn selecting an article of clothing, going around the room until everyone's had a chance to pick something. Repeat until either all the clothes are spoken for or no one wants the items that remain. These are then bagged and donated to a local charity.

Beyond this basic structure, the rules of the game are wide open to alteration. I've heard of swaps that resemble holiday grab bags where the last to draw has the right to swap with anyone prior or where cross-negotiations for coveted items are brokered. The key is to have fun and come home with new clothing that you'll actually wear while eliminating items you are done with.

RELOADING THE CLOSET

Once you've cleaned the closet, repaired or improved anything structural that wasn't up to snuff, and determined which clothes you are going to keep, you're now ready to put them back into your closet.

Remember, the simplest system for finding and keeping clothes organized is to arrange them by category and within each category by color. For example, on the clothing rod, keep all your jackets together, shirts together, pants together, dresses together, skirts together, and so on. You can clearly delineate categories with labeled rod-divider disks if you get confused by where the trousers end and the blouses begin.

When arranging the clothes within each category, hang clothes by color from either light to dark, starting with white, or corresponding with the order of colors in a rainbow: white, pink, red, orange, yellow, green, blue, purple, and black.

Also match your hangers to your clothes. Pants should have pant hangers, skirts skirt hangers, jackets and shirts sturdy wooden or padded hangers, and strappy dresses or lingerie notched hangers.

If your closet has built-in storage (drawers, shelves, or cubbies) or you are corralling things into baskets or other containers, these, too, should each be assigned a specific category (e.g., T-shirts, pajamas, workout clothes, etc.).

I've learned from several female clients that the best way to store pantyhose is to roll them up to prevent runs, and never store them in wicker or rough baskets without liners.

DRAWERS (MINI CLOSETS ON THEIR SIDES)

Like your closets, your drawers should be organized by type of clothing stored—ideally one kind of item per drawer. Like with Like rules the day here. So store socks with socks and, if space allows, sport socks and shorty socks isolated together and heavier wool socks or wintry socks living together. Stockings can live alone or be combined with one of the sock categories.

Keep T-shirts with T-shirts. If you have a category of dressy T-shirts, those would live distinctly from nondressy T-shirts; likewise, you may want to separate long-sleeved T-shirts from short-sleeved or cutoff T-shirts.

Organize sweaters with sweaters. These, too, can be subdivided further into bulky wool sweaters distinct from lighter cotton sweaters, cardigans separated from crewnecks separated from V-necks, etc. Keep underwear with underwear and, if space allows, bottoms (panties or boxers or briefs) with bottoms and tops (undershirts or bras) with tops. Shorts go with shorts, swimwear goes with swimwear . . . You should have the picture by now.

If space is limited, think about what can be logically combined. Underwear can be combined together with tops and bottoms in the same drawer, for instance. I wouldn't merge sweaters with shorts, however, since sweaters are cold-weather wear and shorts are for warmer weather. Shorts would do better with trousers/jeans since they're both bottom clothes.

The most important result of organizing your drawers is that you should be able to see the entire contents of each drawer easily as soon as you open it. A drawer should not be a crammed and jumbled mess of clothing needing to be compressed just to get the drawer to close. Items that can be folded should be folded neatly. Items that want to be rolled up should be—again, neatly. You want to be able to find exactly what you're looking for in a drawer the same way you can find things inside your closet. It may help to label each drawer (temporarily) with a Post-it or some other signage until you can remember the contents of each drawer.

I tend to load drawers whenever possible from head to toe in descending order, meaning things that go on the top of the body tend to go toward the top drawers of the dresser while socks are usually in the lowest bottom drawer. I find it easier for folks to remember the contents this way.

You do want to take the dimensions of the drawer and the volume of the clothes into consideration as well. So if you have larger drawers on top and not so many bras, you might want to adjust your storage to match the drawer capacity, forgoing the head-to-toe strategy. For a peek inside my dresser drawers, visit unstuffbook.com/closets.

OVERBUYING AND BUYER'S REMORSE

These two concepts are related to each other through our relationship with time. The first involves a deferred decision at checkout: we've gathered multiple items in our physical or virtual cart, such as the same pants in several sizes or colors or similar tops in different fabrics, figuring we'll buy them all now and sort through them or try them on in the privacy of our home, and then just return the ones that we don't like or that don't fit later. I cannot count how many times I've come across clothing in clients' homes with tags attached, the sad story told to me about misplaced receipts or too much time elapsing before they managed to return them.

In all seriousness, this is an advanced shopping technique not to be casually employed by anyone who has trouble keeping track of paper, time, or stuff. In the novice's hands, this is likely to result in more store credits they'll need to keep track of, possibly frequent trips to return items to a third-party shipper, and/or a closet filled with unnecessary and unwanted merchandise.

Buyer's remorse is a different experience. You were in love with the item when you saw it and had no doubt that you two were destined for each other when you swept it into your cart. Now that it's home with you, maybe you're thinking about a commitment you made to yourself or a partner or spouse about your spending, and this is now intruding on your shopping buzz. You're having second, possibly even third, thoughts.

Whether you've fallen victim to overbuying, buyer's remorse, or both, you need to have someplace *outside* of your closet where these items can land, preferably a hook or rod where they can hang in plain sight. I suggest stuffing the receipt into a prominent pocket or pinning it through a buttonhole so it stays with the garment. This way, you can see it each day until you're sure it's staying or you've decided to return it. If you put this kind of item away, chances are the conversation's over—it's staying put, which pretty much guarantees some unhappy feelings when the piece surfaces again, never worn.

SHOES

If you remove your shoes at the entrance to your house, provide some sort of shelving or rack for their storage so the entryway remains neat and stray shoes do not become a hazard for anyone entering or exiting with their view obscured.

If you wear your shoes in your house, the proper place to store them is on the floor and down low in your closet. Keep the pairs mated, and arrange them in a similar fashion to your hanging clothes—sandals together, athletic shoes together, dress shoes together, high heels together, boots together. Shoe racks are available everywhere these days. You could also build yourself a few low slanted shoe shelves or repurpose some cubby shelves and turn them into an impromptu shoe center.

It may go without saying, but I'm saying it anyway: Unless you only have one foot, don't keep only one shoe of a pair. And if you do have only one foot, only keep the shoe that fits that foot. Either way, if after a thorough search, you still cannot find a lone shoe's mate, it's time to say so long to the steadfast holdout. No matter how much you loved them as a pair, the solo shoe hits the road for the last time.

MAINTAINING THE CLOTHES CLOSET

Once you've done a complete reorganization, if you've been thorough and diligent—even if it takes you awhile to complete—you won't ever have to do this again. Hanging clothes in the closet becomes a fun game of Concentration—simply match the incoming items using Like with Like, and you'll maintain it without even exerting yourself.

If you're happy with your clothes now, another way to maintain the integrity of your closet and wardrobe is to keep the balance in place, what I call "stuff equilibrium." When you buy something new, have it replace something old. Now that you've bought those new boiled-wool slippers, do you really need those scuzzy old plastic ones you still have from college?

If you can't help shopping for new clothes, be sure to keep your existing wardrobe in mind. Buy things that will coordinate with as many of your current clothes as possible. That's the best way to avoid ending up with another lone-wolf or only-in-your-dreams piece.

It's also important to have a system for managing clothes in purgatory—the ones that aren't quite dirty but not quite clean, either. You'd wear them again to run to the market or hop on a Zoom call but maybe not for lunch with your mother-in-law. Designate an area, hook, or chair where you can place these items that keeps them from ending up in a pile. This way, you avoid doing more laundry than you need to, and you won't grab slightly wrinkled khakis when you're late for casual Fridays.

Finally, rather than having them taking up space in the back of your closet, take your wire hangers back to the dry cleaner to recycle. If you care to and aesthetics matter to you, make it a habit to transfer your clothes from the cleaner's hangers to your own hangers when you first bring the clothes home.

OTHER KINDS OF CLOSETS

Linen Closets

As we've discovered already, there are few places "someday" is more evident than in our closets. Closets seem to be temples to "someday." And curiously, people seem to stockpile sheets, pillowcases, and towels even more than clothing, as if someday they will be descended on by hordes of out-of-town guests all in need of a hot shower and a comfy place to rest their heads.

If this includes you, the good news is that, of the many projects outlined in this book, organizing the linen closet is remarkably manageable and easily accomplished, even for the most disorganized among us. And this is partly because it's one space with ideally only one kind of item—linens. Whether towels, sheets and pillowcases, duvets, pillows, or blankets, it's all just linens.

And for the frugal among us, it's also a project that requires few, if any, new purchases. This project should take you, at most, only a few hours, with the results being significant and lasting. Like the clothes closet before this, we'll begin by emptying out the linen closet.

Go do that now.

Great. Now clean and wipe down the shelves, the walls, the trim, and the baseboards. Vacuum or sweep the floor. If your shelves are adjustable, now is the time to move them if needed. Likewise, consider installing extra shelves if called for.

Now sort everything into Like with Like piles, and match linens with their siblings so that the pillowcases and top and bottom sheets of a set are reunited. Do the same thing for suites of towels—if you have bath towels, hand towels, and washcloths that match, they should be gathered into groupings as well. If you have surplus pillow protectors, those, too, should all be gathered together. Any stray items should all be laid out as well—not to make them feel bad, but so you can really take stock of what there is and whether you'll be keeping them or not.

If you're saving the Speed Racer sheets from your college-aged son's first bed, now is the time to either let them go (ideally) or, if you can't bear that thought, at least send them to the container now known as Sentimentaland. It's possible that you'll need more than one tub or box for Sentimentaland before we're done with your entire house. That's okay. These items all need to live together, and we need to ensure that their contents are consistent. Do not mix general items seeking a home into these meaningful touchstones of life's important moments. Like with Like.

Next, subdivide by room: primary bedroom, kids' bedrooms, guest bedroom, primary bathroom, kids' bathroom, guest bathroom, and so on. You might also want to color-code your linens to help keep everything organized. In other words, assign different colored linens to different rooms of the house—patterns for the kids' rooms, white or ivory for the primary bedroom and bath, and a distinctly different color, like sage or graphite, for each guest room.

Think of threadbare towels as retired soldiers. If budget dictates that they cannot be replaced at present, you can still assess all of the towels you own to find the ones that have passed their usefulness for absorbing anything more than a few drops of water on the floor. Let those go or repurpose them as rags for cleaning.

Ditto for blankets and quilts—exceptions being handmade heirlooms and hand-me-downs. If the heat were to fail, how many blankets would you really need? If it were really dire, wouldn't you go to a friend's or neighbor's house or to a hotel? It's okay to let some of these go. They won't go to waste—veterinarian clinics, human and animal shelters, and some secondhand stores will all accept donations of used linens.

I suggest that smaller and frequently used table linens—napkins, place mats, table runners—live in a sideboard or somewhere closer to the dining table. Infrequently used fancy tablecloths with coordinating napkins could be stored in the same closet where the leaves to the dining table are stored, preferably in a coat closet nearby. If you fold tablecloths lengthwise and hang them on a wooden suit hanger at either end of the rod inside the closet, and the napkins in a tub or basket above, you'll always know where to find them.

NOTABLE NOTE

Many of us may have lovely vintage or antique linens—crocheted tablecloths and place mats, delicate linen napkins and table runners, etc. Like fine silver, they "tarnish" with age and disuse as we wait for that "someday" when there will be an occasion worthy of such finery. That is a shame.

Get them out and start using them. If inevitably they will end up yellowed and frayed, why not enjoy their journey there? What a missed opportunity if we allow them to decay from neglect rather than from vigorous and enthusiastic use.

If relocating table linens to the kitchen or dining room is not possible, then these linens should also be sorted according to suite—create small piles of matching tablecloths and napkins, and store them with the other linens. If you're more bohemian in your approach and like a mix-and-match kind of look for your table, at least put all the tablecloths together and all the napkins together. That way, when you're making the table, you have to look in only one place to find everything.

I also suggest always cleaning and ironing table linens after use and before putting them away. That way, you won't be trying to do this while also preparing dinner right before guests come over for your next gathering.

By now, you should also have a growing pile of everything from your linen closet that isn't linen or some kind of textile. Everything. If you store items such as surplus paper products or a sewing kit in the linen closet, that's fine—we'll find a place for those items in the closet when the process is finished.

Once you've sorted each linen into its family pile, it's time to address the strays. Either donate them or keep a few for rags. Only a few. I'd suggest that the rags live in the laundry room or someplace where the cleaning supplies are kept. It's important that the items now identified as rags are no longer mixed in with current and still useful linens. I use a permanent marker to label old napkins, T-shirts, and other repurposed items with an *R* in one corner so if they ever end up in the laundry with similar items, the rags are easily separated when it's time to put them away.

A good rule of thumb for bed linens is three sets per room or bed so that there is always a clean set of sheets on the bed, one in the laundry, and one in the closet. If space or resources dictate that you have room for more or less, that's fine as well.

The same holds true for towels—for each person, there should be one on the towel bar, one in the wash, and one on the shelf. Add in one set for each potential guest you could host at one time. For example, if you have a three-bedroom home (all occupied) and a pullout sofa in the family room that could possibly sleep two, that would equal 10 sets of sheets (three times three plus one for the sleeper sofa) and 11 sets of towels (three times three plus two for the guests).

If space is an issue and a closet can't be dedicated solely to linens, consider using a piece of furniture or built-in cabinets to store linens in the room where they'll be used. Likewise, extra pillows and blankets could easily live in the guest-room closet. Another option when space is at a premium is rolling up towels and sticking them in a decorative basket in the bathroom or under the sink.

Ideally, the only items that live in the linen closet are involved in making the bed and bathroom—sheets, pillowcases, shams, towels, blankets, quilts, bedspreads, duvets, and duvet covers. If you are so inclined, sprays and potpourri might find their way here as well. Some people line their shelves with scented, acid-free shelf paper. Others will scatter sachets throughout the stacked sheets. Alternatively, an open box of baking soda, activated charcoal, or calcium carbonate in the closet will help keep items smelling fresh.

NOTABLE NOTE

If you've ever struggled to neatly fold a fitted sheet, here are simple, step-by-step instructions to demystify this process once and for all. Note that this is done standing:

1. Start by holding the sheet by its two adjacent corners on one of the shorter edges. With the sheet inside out, place a hand in each of the two corners.
2. Bring your right hand to your left, and fold the corner on your right hand over the one in your left so the corner on top is right side out.
3. Reach down and pick up the corner that is adjacent to the one that was in your right hand (it's now hanging in front),

and fold it over the other two corners; this third corner will be inside out.

4. Bring the last corner up, and fold it over the others so it is right side out.
5. Lay the folded sheet on a flat surface and straighten it out.
6. Fold the two edges in until all the elastic is hidden.
7. Fold the sheet into a rectangle, then continue folding it until you get it the size you want.

You can also find a video of this process at unstuffbook.com/closets.

What doesn't belong in the linen closet is anything that generates dust—particularly vacuum cleaners. And no shoes or anything that spends time on the ground outside, such as sports equipment. You don't want to be shaking out towels or rewashing sheets you thought would be ready to use.

Once you've determined what's staying, fold everything neatly and as flatly as you can, then reload the shelves. If possible, keep each set of sheets or towels in their own stack. This way, you'll avoid having to drag everything out or toppling everything over each time you remove a set.

Store the items you use most frequently, such as towels and bed linens, on shelves at or near eye level. Table linens can be assigned to a less accessible shelf since they are used less frequently. And rotate usage—this keeps linens from sitting for too long and getting musty.

NOTABLE NOTE

The best way to fold towels is in half lengthwise, then in half again (matching the ends to each other), then in thirds; this way, they'll stack perfectly and fit most shelves. You can also find a video of this process at unstuffbook.com/closets.

If you have antique linens, store them out of the flow of traffic, and if possible, keep them in acid-free paper to avoid discoloration and decay. Bulky items, such as comforters, quilts, and pillows that are for guests or that are rotated seasonally, can be stored in vacuum-sealed storage bags. These compress all the air out of the items, taking up less space and keeping them moisture- and bug-free.

In my closet, I have each shelf labeled with the different sizes of linens: king (primary bedroom) and queen (guest room and blow-up mattress). This helps guests find the correct sheets easily before they pick the wrong set and unfold them. I use simple metal label holders to identify each shelf, but you could just as easily use a label maker, adhesive tabs, or decorative tacks—anything that suits your taste and is easily legible.

NOTABLE NOTE

I do really enjoy pressed sheets. But given a typical busy schedule, you can imagine that without help there's not a lot of time in a day to press and fold the linens. A tip I learned somewhere is to remove the sheets and pillowcases from the dryer while they are still slightly damp and drape them over a shower rod to dry or simply fold them—they'll dry in the closet. It's the next best thing to ironing them.

Some folks like to store each set of linens in one of the pillowcases. It's a simple way to keep each set together. I prefer seeing the individual pieces neatly stacked, but it's certainly another option. Seasonal sheets, like winter flannels, should live with other seasonal linens or stacked behind the everyday sheets.

Towels live on their own shelf, each set in a neat stack. Beach towels should be kept on a separate shelf with other seasonal items or behind your bath towels or in the back of the car with other beach supplies, which is where mine live.

I store extra blankets and guest pillows on the top shelf of my linen closet. They're not often used, but they still belong with their brothers and sisters. I find that they stack nicely up top and are in a logical place when someone goes searching for an extra pillow or comforter. I keep them in the clear, pliable zippered plastic bag that they came in from either the store or the cleaners. If you don't have any of these, similar bags (or clear plastic tubs) are easily purchased at any number of stores.

Cardboard boxes, paper bags, and some plastics can damage certain fabrics. Avoid them as storage containers. I also suggest avoiding cedar chests because they are often only semisuccessful at killing moths or deterring carpet beetles. Paradichlorobenzene moth crystals may prove more reliable at controlling pests; just remember they are not safe for animals or humans, so use with caution. Green alternatives include pheromone traps. They are usually free of pyrethrin, which means they're safe to use around children, pets, and food.

As I mentioned, this project doesn't necessarily call for any new purchases—so resist buying new gadgets or toys to help you get organized. Once you know what you'll be storing, you can put together an accurate shopping list and get what you need.

When all the linens are reloaded in the closet, assess the remaining space, if there is any. You can then fill that space with the other items removed—the sewing kit, surplus paper products, cosmetics, a first-aid kit (prominently located and easily reached), etc.

Once those are in place, if there is still room available, consider storing extra shopping bags, totes, and other bags or baskets here. If there's no room for these items, the entry or coat closet is an excellent alternative.

If you don't have a safe in your home, you may consider installing a kick-shelf underneath the bottom shelf of the closet. This is really more like a very thin, recessed drawer trimmed to match the base molding so as to remain undetectable. To gain access, you simply push the edge of it with your foot, and the shelf releases and rolls out on wheels or glides. It's an excellent place to hide important items or documents, provided you aren't worried about them burning in a house fire. Those kinds of items, if not in a fireproof safe, belong in a fireproof file box or off-site in a safe-deposit box at the bank.

Many folks consider the backs of doors to be valuable closet real estate. I typically disagree. While static fixtures such as towel bars could be used to store table linens or other oversized items, or a mirror or display board could be mounted to the inside as a pleasant accent when the door is open, things that slap and bounce around every time the door is opened (e.g., ironing boards, brooms and mops, even shoe holders filled with items) make opening the door noisy and a potential hazard. Wouldn't it be nicer, whenever possible, to just let a door be a door?

Guest-Room Closets

If your guest room is also your home office or your living or family room, the closet in that room is most likely doing double duty. Anything from board games to office supplies could be sharing quarters with guest linens, so keep it simple and place everything a guest would need in one clear container. That way, any time company comes, they can find exactly what they need, and you won't have to scramble around assembling everything for them at the last moment.

Underutilized closet space in guest rooms is another place where overflow and infrequently used items can find an out-of-the-way home. Bulky appliances, such as bread machines, chafing dishes, and heated serving trays, can all live neatly stacked away, ready for the few times each year they are needed.

Utility Closets

A utility closet is where everything you use to run and maintain your home lives. Things stored here include cleaning products, light bulbs, tools, surplus cables, paint and painting supplies, caulk, adhesives, brooms and mops, dustpans, rags, trash bags, and hardware. Flashlights, batteries, and emergency kits live here. If there's room in this closet, recycling and trash could also live here.

Take advantage of every square inch of this closet. Hang brooms, mops, and dustpans up and off the floor—business side up. Using Like with Like as a guideline, group cleaning supplies together and paint supplies together so that when repairing or replacing something, everything you need to complete the job is within reach.

What you don't want living here are random items that serve no purpose. It's fine to have one container of mismatched fasteners, but don't turn this space into a way station for things that should have been tossed or recycled when you were finished with them.

When you've completed assembling knockdown furniture and once you're certain that everything is attached and functioning, recycle any leftover hardware. Those unidentified extra pieces aren't going to come in handy someday—they're just leftovers.

Paint dries out and hardens, so keep small jars of each color for touch-ups, create a simple paint chart (a master list of rooms, colors, and finishes), and then toss the old paint. Color varies from batch to batch, so by the time you're ready to paint again, even if you're using the same color, you'll need enough fresh paint to completely cover the walls anyway.

Cleaning supplies lose their strength over time, so don't hang on to them indefinitely, and don't just shove them to the back of the closet for "later." Get rid of them now. Just be sure to properly dispose of any toxic cleaners.

Make sure that what is in the utility closet is current to your house and current for your life. This closet in particular demands a simple and accessible layout—you should be able to find whatever you're looking for within 30 seconds of opening the door.

Coat/Entry Closets and Mudrooms

These closets and areas are located near entryways to store outer-wear, foul-weather accessories, and athletic gear. Ideally, all coats and jackets will live here. Baskets on the top shelf can corral winter scarves, hats, and gloves, and another basket can be used for work and gardening gloves. A shoe rack and a floor mat catch snow and rain from snow boots and galoshes. Hooks hold pet leads and umbrellas.

In the case of mudrooms, ample cubbies and hooks for each member of the household provide plenty of places for book bags and knapsacks, lunch pails, and athletic gear. Any entryway benefits from a chair or bench where you can put on or take off shoes, boots, or inline skates.

High shelves in closets and out-of-the-way cabinets also offer great resting places for seldom-used overflow storage from other rooms. Coffee urns, punch bowls, seasonal serving dishes—all of these can be stored based on the frequency they are used.

For example, I keep the leaves of the dining-room table in my entry closet along with extra folding chairs and pressed table linens. When it's time to expand the table and set it for large gatherings, everything I need is in one location.

Consider if the mudroom or entryway is a good place to set up a charging station. Depending on family values and where electronics live in your ecosystem, they could be stored here if their primary use is for emergencies outside of the home. If personal electronics are used all over the house, find a central location where everyone can have an outlet or station to plug in their devices, particularly if you're trying to regulate or monitor children's screen time.

There is no limit to how these spaces can be organized and structured so everyone comes and goes each day with all their stuff.

DIRTY LAUNDRY

I really miss having a laundry chute. As a child growing up, I loved the convenience of dropping dirty laundry through a flap in the wall and having it land in the basement right by the washing machine. If your current home is also absent a laundry chute, where do you want to place a hamper or two? Where is there sufficient space for baskets for laundry, dry cleaning, and alterations/mending, and do you have room for three distinct baskets or just one catch-all basket?

Where are you most frequently without clothes? I'm guessing the bathroom, a dressing room/walk-in closet, or your bedroom, right? Ideally, your hamper is conveniently located in one of these areas and also out of sight.

My first choice would be in a closet. My second choice would be in the bathroom, and the third choice someplace not too visible in the bedroom. I have two rolling carts in my bedroom closet that do the job nicely. The key is to place the hamper or basket somewhere easy enough to get to and use so that you will actually use it. Too often, hampers, especially ones with lids, just become another surface piled with clothes and other things that now prevent the lid from even being opened. Let's avoid that in your home.

MAINTAINING THE SYSTEM

Like with the mail and keys, the way to keep your closets from reverting back to a jumbled mess is not to exert some Herculean effort in desperate frantic spurts but rather to maintain the system on a daily basis. What you've accomplished in completing this chapter should never have to be done in this same way again if you pay attention to the space daily.

You wouldn't avoid brushing your teeth for several weeks and then suddenly scrub them silly in the hopes of erasing weeks of neglect. The same is true for your home. If you have a crazy day where you find yourself trying on 13 outfits before running out the door, when you return home, hang up the 12 outfits you didn't end up wearing. Don't walk over them for another four days before restoring order. And drop the lucky 13th into the hamper when you take it off.

As discussed, if and when you reach stuff equilibrium in your wardrobe, going forward you're now replacing and *not* augmenting with new purchases. You should have enough clothes to wear for the variety of places and functions you're routinely called on to attend. There will, of course, always be an opportunity to pick up a new garment when you're attending a special or formal event or need a particular item you're currently missing. But if you're just replacing a pair of jeans, it's okay to actually replace them; that was the plan when you bought the new pair.

If resistance to letting the old ones go is based on some feeling of abundance or a fear of once again finding yourself with "nothing to wear," think that feeling all the way through. More of anything that doesn't serve you isn't more of anything you need—it's just clutter.

Surrounding yourself with that kind of "more" will not protect you from an imaginary crisis, whether that crisis is "nothing to wear" or suddenly finding yourself homeless and hungry. While that may seem like quite a leap, I've seen plenty of clients and students race from one irrational fear to another almost instantly. And once that happens, clinging to a pair of old jeans starts to sound like a reasonable way to prevent these imaginary disasters.

So let's inject some sanity back into the equation. Clothes are not groceries. You won't survive a blackout, hurricane, or blizzard by eating that extra pair of jeans. Looking for comfort from things and in places where comfort can't be secured sets you up for a frustrating merry-go-round of feelings that's like a junkie's worst nightmare. Desperate clinging is rapidly followed by forced deprivation, and round and round you spin between these two polar extremes—*I need more, I don't have enough, more is better, more feels safe, don't take that away from me, I need more, I don't have enough*—again and again and again.

And all over a pair of jeans. Imagine what's possible with a few cash-mere sweaters!

Buy another can of tuna or vegetarian chili, and give the jeans away. You'll prevent going hungry, and you'll finally break the cycle of addiction to "more." That's the surest way to keep your closets (and yourself) in tip-top shape—satisfied with and surrounded by every-thing you need and absolutely nothing you don't.

6

BASEMENTS · ATTICS · GARAGES · SELF-STORAGE
(INCLUDING SEASONAL DECORATIONS)

No person who can read is ever successful
at cleaning out an attic.
–ANN LANDERS

Only in America do we leave cars worth thousands of dollars
in the driveway and put our useless junk in the garage.
–AUTHOR UNKNOWN

WHAT WE'RE GOING TO COVER IN THIS CHAPTER

- What Auxiliary Spaces Are and Aren't
- General Suggestions
- Space Limitations, Structural Challenges, and Environmental Hazards
- The Particular Challenges Presented by the Garage
- Feelings and Stuff and Space, Oh My!
- Teamwork
- Scheduling the Time
- Creating Efficient Storage in Any Space
- Storage Systems and Shelving: An Overview
- Sorting and You
- Cleanliness Is Next to Garageliness (or Atticliness or Basementliness)
- The Kinds of Things You Store in Your Auxiliary Space(s)
- Containerizing the Categories
- The Importance of Labels—How, Why, and Where
- Organizing the Storage
- When Laundry Is Done in Auxiliary Spaces
- Managing Messy Projects Inside and Out
- Converting Auxiliary Spaces for Living
- Trash or Treasure? Delusions about *National Geographic*, eBay, and Early Retirement
- The Thrift-Store Bin Is Not a Grab Bag
- Maintaining the System
- Self-Storage: The Dos and Don'ts

DID YOU EVER think it possible that you would open the door to a closet in your home and see not a tangle of random items but some clear order? Did you ever imagine that you would quickly and easily be able to put your hands on exactly what you were looking for without disturbing everything around it?

Congratulations. You've already come a long way.

We're about to explore how to maximize bonus spaces at home while avoiding new messes and jumbles in the process, keeping in mind that just because you *could* store something somewhere, such as a garage, attic, basement, or self-storage unit, doesn't mean you *should*. Resist the urge to get drunk on space and think that random chaos and disorder are more manageable because these spaces are seldom seen or are outside of your home. Clutter is clutter whether it's constantly underfoot, encountered twice a day on your way to and from the car, or in a rented space across town.

Almost like closets on steroids, these auxiliary spaces offer tremendous potential—both for storage and for clutter. And given their dimensions, they often require jumbo-sized efforts in getting and keeping them organized. That means wielding One Home for Everything and Like with Like with precision and consistency, especially when confronting historic neglect and chaos.

We'll use the one-two punch of these two rules to clear out these spaces and, when appropriate, to reassemble them. For spaces you own, whether it's a crawl space or a four-car garage, you should be able to find anything within 30 seconds. And for any spaces you rent, except in rare instances, you should be able to clear them out, saving money, time, and energy as a result.

WHAT AUXILIARY SPACES ARE AND AREN'T

Basement (noun): The lowermost portion of a structure, partly or wholly below ground level; often used for storage

Attic (noun): A floor consisting of open space at the top of a house just below the roof; often used for storage

Garage (noun): An outbuilding (or part of a building) for housing automobiles; a building or indoor space in which to park or keep a motor vehicle

Self-storage (noun): Shorthand for "self-service storage" or "mini storage"; an industry that rents storage space/units (i.e., rooms, lockers, containers, and/or outdoor space) to tenants, including businesses and individuals, usually on a short-term basis (often month-to-month)

Three of these four spaces are basically dedicated to general storage with the fourth designated specifically for automobiles. It's not that other things can't also be stored there, but first and foremost, we want to be able to get a car (or two) in the garage.

From a storage point of view, if you're lucky enough to have any one of these spaces in your home, you're pretty fortunate. If you're lucky enough to have more than one of them, you could be swimming in so much stuff that you can barely breathe. And if you have so much stuff that you had to move it off-site to store it—well, we're going to put an end to that by the end of this chapter.

> **NOTABLE NOTE**
>
> Do you have the original cartons that electronics and other large items came in? My rule for these boxes is keep them for 30 days and then recycle them. If you haven't chosen to return the item within the first 30 days of its life with you, then you're

probably keeping it. Should you need to ship it in for service, the manufacturer will typically either ship its replacement to you in a box that you can then use to ship the original device back, or you can request that they ship you an empty carton.

To be clear, none of these spaces are museums to previous relationships or abandoned hobbies. They are not altars to future second homes and receding youth (yours or your offspring's) or archeological digs of deferred decisions and past design choices. They are not final resting places for lost and misfit things cluttering your life.

When tidy and organized, you can use them to store tools, building supplies, seasonal items, oversized items, and anything else that needs a home that doesn't seem to fit anywhere else in your house. But if these are so packed with stuff that you are considering renting (or already have rented) a self-storage unit, you'll be incurring additional monthly expenses just to house belongings you likely don't need or even want.

Do you have a sad, scary corner somewhere? Like a bad date that never ends, you continue to pile just one more thing into that corner, vowing that "someday" you'll tackle the ever-expanding mound of stuff. Well, apparently, today is that day.

GENERAL SUGGESTIONS

In any of these spaces, these tips and suggestions are useful:

- A working flashlight at or near the entrance to each space is a must. In case of power outages and burned-out bulbs, you need light to find your way in and out.
- Make sure you have adequate and proper lighting; you can't have too much artificial lighting in spaces that have limited access to natural light.
- Water infiltration in basements is a huge problem for many homeowners. An easy and significant tool in the

combat against wet basements is ensuring that roof gutters and downspouts direct water away from your foundation. Likewise, make sure that the grade of any soil around your house is sloped to channel rainwater away from the foundation.

- Review your homeowner's insurance policy to see what the limits of coverage are for sewer and drain backups or flooding. With limited coverage, think carefully before storing valuables (either monetary or sentimental) in your basement.

- Dryers should either be vented to the outside or ventless if your laundry center is located indoors.

- If you have an unfinished space, never store anything in direct contact with bare soil. This is an open invitation to termites and other pests as well as mold, mildew, and decay.

- Do not store anything within three feet of the furnace, boiler, water heater, or other major appliances. Objects too close present service obstacles and potential hazards.

- Do not store any flammable and/or heat-sensitive items near gas-powered appliances or anything that has a lit pilot light.

- Make sure you've installed a smoke detector and carbon-monoxide alarm in all auxiliary spaces. Likewise, a fire extinguisher should be easily accessible in case of fire. Because these are areas in which you're probably spending less time, they may be farther away from the main emergency notification devices or response equipment in your home.

- Do not run a frost-free freezer in your basement if you have moisture problems.

- Do store wine in your basement (think wine cellars)—just not in the same room with hot appliances, such as the dryer, boiler, or water heater.

SPACE LIMITATIONS, STRUCTURAL CHALLENGES, AND ENVIRONMENTAL HAZARDS

Some of these spaces come with built-in limitations. Working with rather than against those limitations will maximize your storage capabilities. Few things besides hand tools can handle fluctuations in temperature and humidity, for instance. Therefore, it's recommended to keep the temperature between 70 and 75 degrees Fahrenheit and the humidity around 50 percent.[2] That may not always be possible, but it's useful as a benchmark when deciding what to store where.

Attic ceilings are sometimes low, limiting mobility, and they may also feature exposed beams. The attic floor may be nothing more than exposed 2" x 4" or 2" x 6" joists intended only to hold up the ceiling of the spaces below. And there may or may not be insulation between any or all of these joists.

If that describes your attic, your first decision should be whether you'll invest the time and money to finish this space off to increase your storage or if you'll just balance what you can on the ceiling joists and look to other spaces for more serious storage.

Part of the basement may be the laundry center or a workshop that limits additional available floor space. Maybe the basement is just a small room with an attached crawl space where the mechanicals of the house (furnace, boiler, water heater) are located. And perhaps structural columns or walls create very real obstructions or barriers to accessible space. Unless you're prepared to do major reconstruction to eliminate or compensate for some of these limitations, your best alternative is creative thinking.

If you have structural challenges that aren't going away—for example, load-bearing partitions or exceptionally low ceilings—spend enough time in the space studying those challenges to discover

---

2   "The Best Temperatures for Home Storage," *Comfort Matters* (blog), Lennox, December 13, 2019, https://www.lennox.com/residential/lennox-life/everyday-living/the-best-temperatures-for-home-storage/.

the best long-term solutions. Short-term solutions may be fine for now, but in thinking them through, you want to make sure they have staying power. If spatial relations are not your thing or you find yourself particularly stuck, consult a contractor, structural engineer, or architect for a few hours—they may help you see a solution you've been missing.

Dampness in Basements

Below or above grade, dampness is always an issue when it comes to storage. Even if your space is sealed and finished and climate-controlled like the rest of the house, I still recommend waterproof storage anywhere dampness has been present or could still appear. I've seen more cardboard and other paper-based containers ruin treasures by being stored in fluctuating humidity than by direct contact with water. So just in case you had another cardboard box filled with your high-school yearbooks heading to the basement, I wanted to catch you first.

One solution is to run a dehumidifier in these spaces and empty its tank regularly. This won't work for a space with an absence of either a vapor barrier below the slab or sealed concrete, however. In that case, you may actually draw moisture in from the outside with a dehumidifier.

Also, mildew loves dark, damp places. Be careful with books, papers, photographs, artwork, or important documents where there is no direct sunlight. Packets of silica gel desiccant in the containers will absorb some moisture, but these are not a panacea.

Flood Zones (Sewer and Drain Backup)

Whether or not your basement is finished, the possibility of flooding still exists. Even if you've never experienced a flood, one could still happen, particularly if you have a source of water in the basement. Here are some ways to avoid damage from flooding:

- Store all valuable items on pallets, shelves, or tables above flood level (the calculated elevation of any expected flood based on site-specific conditions).
- Install a sump pump to fight floods. Make sure it has an alarm attached to it.
- Consider installing an additional battery-operated sump pump for backup during power failures or, alternatively, a generator that would power your sump pump (and other appliances) in case of power outages.
- Maintain critical equipment on a regular basis. Set up a maintenance schedule and post it visibly nearby.
- Keep the basement-floor drain clean and clear of debris.
- Do not risk turning your basement into a toxic soup by storing chemicals (gardening, cleaning, etc.) where rising floodwaters could reach them.

Heat, Cold, and Humidity in Attics and Garages

Unless your garage or attic has been converted into living space or is very well insulated, or you live in an extremely arid place, the temperature and humidity fluctuations that occur in these spaces prohibit storing valuable papers and other sensitive materials in them. The effects of moisture coupled with heat are never good for much beyond your complexion. Many things, particularly anything cellulose-based—made of wood or paper—could become a willing host for both mold and mildew under these conditions. In fact, the only paper I've found that can consistently and safely live here is surplus toilet paper or paper towels if still vacuum-sealed from the store.

Likewise, the attic or garage isn't the best place for luggage. You don't want to grab a suitcase at the last minute to find it teeming with mildew just as you're about to go on a trip.

It's best to consider these as outdoor spaces, albeit with roofs and walls. So while nothing may actually be rained or snowed on, the effects of precipitation and temperature changes may still impact everything stored here. Cold in the winter and swelteringly hot in the summer, these spaces should house only items that can withstand dramatic temperature swings.

And at the risk of sounding like a broken record, precious items should never be stored in any place where the climate is not strictly regulated. Countless photo albums, baby books, and notebooks have been tucked away in unregulated spaces only to be consumed by black, spotty mold and rendered completely unsalvageable. Save yourself a heap of grief and find another home for these irreplaceable items.

Go High: Ceiling Height and Storage

When creating a storage plan for your basement, attic, or garage, there's another option you probably aren't considering: ceilings. That's right, ceilings are a tremendous resource for storage space. Whether the space is finished or unfinished, a few well-placed hangers, hooks, or brackets will hold bicycles, ladders, lawn chairs, camping gear, and any other items used infrequently or seasonally. There are even nifty pulley systems designed specifically to raise and lower bikes up into the rafters. When hanging things overhead, always secure the fasteners (hooks, chains, etc.) away from structural elements such as ceiling joists.

If room allows, consider a lofted platform to provide additional space for everything from screens and storm windows to storm doors and spare lumber. The only limits on what you can store are the dimensions of the platform and its structural integrity. That said, rather than viewing any additional storage space as an invitation to shop and fill it to capacity, build it to suit the current volume of things you already own and use.

When going up, keep in mind the varying heights of people in your home. If everyone is five foot six or shorter, things dangling overhead may not present a collision challenge. If you or someone else is taller, be sure to hang things out of the regular paths of traffic and, if necessary, hang a brightly colored cloth off either end to alert folks of the item's presence.

Finally, never hang anything heavier than an empty clothes hanger from an exposed overhead plumbing pipe—too much weight will stress its joints and eventually cause damage. Install dedicated storage rails alongside the pipe instead.

THE PARTICULAR CHALLENGES PRESENTED BY THE GARAGE

Can you fit a car into your garage? If you have a multiple-car garage and multiple cars, is the number of spaces (or bays) in the garage actually available for the same number of vehicles? This is our starting point.

Imagine the garage as a giant cupboard. This cupboard should house

1. your cars;
2. any tools used to maintain the cars;
3. any tools used to maintain the physical structure of your home and your grounds;
4. seasonal "quality of life" items such as grills, inflatable swimming pools, and lawn chairs; and
5. anything else you can easily fit inside without crowding out any of the above.

Too often, the scale of a garage fools you into thinking that order is less important because there's so much room or that random piles of things are fine since you're in here so infrequently. But you still want to be able to find whatever it is you're looking for quickly and easily—even more so in such a large space.

If you cannot fit one or more cars into your garage, you need to know why. Do you have a pool table, ping-pong table, or home gym set up there, or is someone practicing hockey in the empty bays? Are you running a home-based business and you've set up your workspace there? Or is it a less noble reason, such as having an immovable pile of stuff that has accumulated over time with no discernable beginning or end?

If cars do fit and there's just a bunch of clutter lining the perimeter of the garage, you're ahead of the game. Your garage is fulfilling its basic function. If the garage is currently so overrun with things that it's impossible to put a car inside, we're going to dismantle those snarls of stuff and disperse the myriad parts into Like with Like zones within the garage (or somewhere else inside your home). If these items no longer serve you, we'll send them off to friends' and neighbors' and strangers' homes via gifts, garage sales, donations, and, when appropriate, placement at the curb (with a sign clearly stating Free!).

FEELINGS AND STUFF AND SPACE, OH MY!

Too often, these auxiliary spaces become repositories for the misplaced and forgotten until useless clutter overtakes whatever remaining free space there had been. And the stuff that ends up in self-storage is usually even less current or important. There are a few exceptions to this, and we'll cover that in a bit, but if these piles of things have become overwhelming and seemingly impossible to untangle, time and willingness (and maybe a few trash bags) are all that now stand between you and order. Together we can clean up any and all of this stuff.

But preventing this from happening again requires a shift in how you think and feel about space, possessions, and their accumulation. More on that soon. Right now, grab your phone or a camera and this book, and head to the auxiliary space that has you most troubled. I'll meet you there.

The Auxiliary Space's Effect on Your Self-Esteem

Excellent. Now snap a few pictures. Be sure to get some good wide-angle shots of the entire space. These will be your "before" shots.

When you're finished taking pictures, just look around and observe the space without starting to criticize or judge yourself. See what you're surrounded by. It might be kind of marvelous and horrifying at the same time, the sheer volume of it.

Everything lying around in a jumble is pretty much useless since you can't easily access it or use it, so ask yourself if its practical absence from your life has negatively impacted you. Is there anything in these heaps that you have already replaced when you needed it—because you couldn't remember that you already owned it or simply couldn't find it? Are there duplicates and triplicates of things piled up here for similar reasons? How about things someone has outgrown or discarded?

Take it all in. Pay attention to any conversations that may be starting up in your head. Perhaps you're hearing a voice describe you as lazy or stupid or wasteful. If you're getting overwhelmed and want to head back to the safety of a nice clean room, take a deep breath instead. You're fine. It's just stuff.

And it really doesn't matter who's speaking as long as you recognize that it isn't *you*. You would never speak that way to a friend in need; instead, you'd roll up your sleeves, put your arm around their shoulders, pop a big grin, and say, "Is this what's making you crazy? It's no big deal. Let's dig in!"

So sidestepping any name-calling, fear, or shame at where you find yourself right now, let's focus instead on how all this stuff got here in the first place.

Departed Relatives and Friends, Part I: The Quick and the Living

It's quite possible that what you have in your auxiliary space belongs or belonged to someone else not currently in residence with you. If that is the case, these are your choices in dealing with these things:

1. Continue to store the items, but organize them in the snuggest way possible to minimize inconvenience for yourself.
2. Contact the owner and request that they collect the items by such-and-such date or you will move them to some off-site storage where they can collect them within a longer deadline.
3. Contact the owner and inform them that you are disposing of the items by such-and-such date if you do not hear otherwise.
4. Don't contact the owner at all and simply dispose of the items.

I'm not crazy about number four, but it is an option. Certainly if the items belong to someone you're not on good terms with, it can be uncomfortable to suddenly get in touch with them, particularly to discuss possessions. Even so, it's a courtesy that you may wish to have extended to you were the shoe on the other foot. Consider that before calling your local charity to come collect everything or announcing a free-for-all at your curb. You've waited this long to get rid of these things—if doing the respectful and courteous thing would be contacting the owner and giving them a clear timeline for the removal, another few weeks for a lifetime's worth of clear conscience seems a small price to pay.

Let's look at an example. Clients of mine, Patti and Nina, were already frustrated by their own lack of functional space, but it got worse when Patti began to work remotely. Suddenly, she was spending most of the week working from home where that lack of space was made worse by a piano and some furniture that her father had loaned them some time ago. The piano occupied prime real estate in a small room off the dining room where Patti wanted to set up her new home office. The furniture was stacked in the garage, so it was less in the way but still taking up too much space.

At first, Patti couldn't conceive of even raising the subject with her dad. This is how our conversation went:

Patti: I just know he'll think me selfish and ungrateful.

Andrew Mellen: Why is that?

Patti: Because that's how I feel. I mean, I borrowed these things years ago; we had no furniture in the living room, and the piano was a great addition to our home.

AM: Okay. But do you really believe those things about yourself? Are you selfish and ungrateful?

Patti: No, of course not. And more importantly, we really need the space. We've had this stuff here forever. No one plays the piano, and we bought replacements for his furniture as we could afford to. Besides, I've got to get off the floor and out of the family room. I'm on the phone and computer all day, and if Nina comes in with the dogs, it becomes way too crazy and disruptive.

AM: Okay. Is money an issue for him?

Patti: No. He can afford to pay to move and store it. I just feel bad asking.

AM: Can you let go of those feelings about asking?

Patti: I can try.

AM: Great. Here's what I suggest. When you make the call, thank him for the use of everything. But rather than asking if it's okay with him for these things to be returned, ask him when and how you should arrange for this stuff to leave. Offer to contact a mover for him (ideally, with him reimbursing you) if that would be easier for him. Give him specific dead-lines for things to leave.

Again, be friendly and gracious about it. Just because you're finally asserting yourself doesn't mean you have to become defensive or confrontational. It's not his fault that you've had this stuff here as long as you have; you are as responsible as he is for the duration. There's also nothing to feel guilty about; it's simply a fact that you now need these things to be removed.

The phone call went off without a hitch. Her father easily arranged for a family friend to come by and collect the furniture, and by week's end, a desk and a printer had replaced the piano and furniture.

You, too, can encourage the still living and fully functioning to once again become the stewards of their own possessions, whether it's your best friend or a grown child who's happily settled into their own home. If storing these things is no longer convenient or prevents you from properly storing your own things or fully utilizing your home, then I encourage you to make a phone call and kindly and firmly suggest that they make arrangements to reclaim their belongings.

Departed Relatives and Friends, Part II: The Late, the Great, and the Broken Plate

If the items you're storing belonged to a deceased relative or friend, they typically fall into one of two categories—either they are deeply sentimental things you treasure or they are things that ended up with you by default. In either case, you have the following choices:

1. You can go through everything and find whatever you'd like to keep for yourself and then offer the balance to other family members who also were close to the deceased.

2. If there are no other family members, after you've selected things, you can give the rest away to charity or attempt to sell anything with significant value.

3. Without reviewing the items, you can offer them directly to another family member or friend or to someone who is setting up house and needs things.
4. Without reviewing the items, you can donate everything directly to charity.

Certainly for anything you feel no attachment to, its absence should cause you no pain or inconvenience. If, on the other hand, these things are charged with emotional tugs and memories, it's important to allow enough time to adequately go through them, whether it's one box or an entire houseful of items. It also may be useful to have either an impartial and disciplined friend or a professional on hand to guide or accompany you through the process.

For a client and friend of mine, my purchase of a house in New York came at the perfect time. While we were still renovating the mostly empty house, Valerie brought stored items there from four different facilities to go through it all at one time in one place. An unfortunate series of losses came rapidly on top of one another for Valerie—first her grandparents died, then her remaining parent, and then she sold a home outside of Providence where she had lived and raised her children. Unable to deal with the sequential losses and overwhelmed with moving, self-storage seemed her best solution at the time.

But the storage costs were more than $1,200 a month, and because the things had mostly belonged to others, she didn't even have a working knowledge of what she was storing. So we made arrangements with each moving company to deliver the contents of her storage units to my new house, and then with my help, she was able to examine everything and make critical decisions about what to keep and what to let go of.

Timing also allowed her three children to come to New York and go through the items with her so they could each select anything they wanted. Valerie and I then arranged for those items to be shipped to their homes. Everything left over after she and her kids went through the stuff was given to friends and donated to local charities.

I realize not every situation works out this conveniently and smoothly. Still, the idea is there—get help if you need it, don't keep things in storage indefinitely, and do not allow the burden of other people's belongings to prevent you from ultimately moving forward.

In all cases, nothing is to be kept that doesn't mean something to you. It may be uncomfortable to hear, but you are not responsible for archiving the family's history unless you choose to. There's nothing requiring you to live with the accumulated possessions of deceased relatives—it does not make you ungrateful or selfish to let those things go. You inherited these things because someone thought you might have use of them or because you were the only surviving person left. Either way, nothing freely given is ever meant to be a burden. That is a certainty.

If you're feeling resistance right now, if a conversation is starting in your head that I just don't understand your unique position or the responsibilities you shoulder, or if that conversation holds you apart and isolates you in its insistence that you must do something you do not want to do or keep something that you don't want to keep, then know that I *do* understand. The fear, guilt, and other feelings that rise up are powerful when these kinds of notions are challenged. Remember, this process is about nothing less than liberation. Of course you will feel the shackles tighten most just before they are unlocked and fall away.

If you have any sense of your own independence or happiness, call that forward now. Draw strength from any experience you've had when you asserted yourself successfully, when you clearly defined the end of someone else and the beginning of you. That's where this work takes place. Feelings can be overwhelming and frightening and confusing, but feelings cannot kill you. Breathe deeply and deliberately.

And my favorite part of all this is that as soon as you actually take the action, as soon as you move a muscle, your feelings will change. Try it right now, and you will experience that for yourself.

Madison Avenue, the Internet, and Your Wallet

If the items overwhelming your auxiliary spaces are things you bought yourself, you've got to acknowledge your own role in how they got here, how they'll leave, and how you'll prevent something similar from happening again.

First, let's look at what happens out in the world or online. Studies show that we're exposed to 6,000 to 10,000 ads every day.[3] We are invited to purchase something, anything—mouthwash, snack foods, a new car, clothing, soda pop—with the promise of a better life (although that promise often remains surprisingly vague).

Better how? Smarter, more stylish, more loved, better smelling, always happy? Yes, but only after our purchase, of course. Until then, I suppose we're just dull, stupid, stinky, lonely, unhappy people. Thank you, Madison Avenue, Amazon, and every other online seller, for rescuing us from our wretched state.

None of this is an excuse for irresponsible behavior, certainly, but it does explain the pervasive grip so many of us feel caught in, consciously or otherwise. With a constant feed demanding we consume, consume, consume, how do we break free from this often self-destructive habit? Because after our purchase, we may be no smarter, stylish, loved, or happy than before, but we certainly have more stuff.

I'd like to say, "Just stop shopping," but that's too easy and probably unlikely. Most of us need to shop for some stuff—unless we're living off the grid. So how about this: Stop shopping indiscriminately. Pay attention and move a little slower. Separate your happiness from consumption. Don't confuse the temporary rush of a new purchase with deep, soulful contentment—they are not the same, regardless of how many times you see that contradicted on TV and in print.

In a moment of boredom, distractedness, or desperation, you may buy something thinking, *I'm better safe than sorry.* But looking around now, you may actually be a little more sorry than safe.

---

3 Sam Carr, "How Many Ads Do We See a Day in 2024?," *Lunio Blog*, Lunio, February 15, 2021, https://lunio.ai/blog/strategy/how-many-ads-do-we-see-a-day/.

A Practical Exercise

Pick three items you can easily see from where you are that you purchased but have never used or have used only once. Think about how they got here. Try to remember if you went shopping specifically for the item or if you just put it in your cart when you were looking for something else. Record that information below, in your notebook, or in your companion workbook.

Item: _____
Were you shopping for this when you bought it? Y / N

Item: _____
Were you shopping for this when you bought it? Y / N

Item: _____
Were you shopping for this when you bought it? Y / N

Great. Now I'm going to suggest that you fish them out of wherever they're currently resting and put them in the donation pile as soon as you can. Regardless of whether you were actually shopping for any of these items when you bought them, you don't use them now, so there's no sense in keeping them.

The value of this exercise is that it reveals how prone you are to impulse buying and how likely those purchases are to end up forgotten and taking up space. You don't need to feel bad about what you discover—what's done is done. The corrective action is leveraging any discomfort you're feeling now the next time you are tempted to add something unplanned to your cart. In fact, flag this page so you can revisit this exercise as often as necessary until you never forget the likely outcome of impulse purchases.

Nasty Talk—and Not the Good Kind

Since both Hamlet and the Buddha seem to agree that "there is nothing either good or bad, but thinking makes it so," let's turn our attention to those conversations we sometimes have with ourselves. Like everything else when it comes to getting and staying organized, the right mindset is key.

For myself, when I feel I'm wrong or I've made some error in judgment, it's very challenging to have some compassion for my mistake. I can easily jump right on that bandwagon of calling myself names and putting myself down for being all too human. It's difficult to see an opportunity for growth in those mistakes instead of feeling as though my whole world is falling in on itself. It's easy to think that, rather than having made a mistake, I actually *am* the mistake, and that how I feel in that moment is the way I'm going to feel forever. This can happen regardless of scale—whether I've disappointed a friend or just left the mail at home on my way to the post office. Again.

It's different when we see someone else beating up on themselves for being human, isn't it? It's so much easier to feel empathy for them and to see that what *feels* like a big deal to them really isn't in the big scheme of things.

It's useful to remember this when we start shaming ourselves for mistakes, and ideally, we remember before our hearts start racing and panic shows up. If a simple mistake can be either good or bad depending on our point of view, the sooner we can shift that point of view, the sooner we can get back on track and forgive ourselves. And I've found that a belly laugh or singing out loud or a phone call to a good friend has a great ability to facilitate that shift quickly and easily.

New Tools, New Choices

Now that you better understand how certain thoughts and emotions are connected to storage, space, belongings, and the pileup of stuff, you can start considering how to avoid becoming overwhelmed with it all in the future. These three perspectives will help keep new stuff from showing up at home unexpectedly:

1. Shift your thinking from viewing shopping as pleasure, diversion, or escape to viewing it as a practical necessity.
2. Shift your thinking from seeing mistakes as failures to seeing them as opportunities for learning something new.
3. Stay present when running errands to avoid daydreaming or getting lost in your feelings.

You don't want to spend valuable time clearing out clutter only to find new things mindlessly filling up all that available space down the road. Not to mention those debilitating conversations with yourself—let's be done with those, too.

With these concepts helping to slow, if not eliminate, the inflow of new things that end up unwanted, you can now get down to the business of unstuffing these spaces. Another deep breath or two, a look around, and you should be seeing through the clutter to what you now know are actually opportunities for change, albeit piled high in some very interesting configurations!

TEAMWORK

When approaching historically cluttered spaces, it's best to have help. And if you have a family, this is an excellent project for everyone to work on together. Chances are these spaces are filled with the result of more than a few people dropping and running, so you should not feel compelled to take this on by yourself. That's a surefire way to develop a resentment and strap on your martyr suit. And we know how that pinches and binds—never very flattering.

If you have the fortitude to survive the inevitable groans from these family members and their dramatic whining that they'd rather have a hot poker stuck in their eyes than sort through their stuff on such a lovely/rainy/busy/lazy day, you should be able to gently and firmly convince them that if they don't want to return home and find their precious treasures on the curb, joining you for a fun day in one (or more) of these spaces is in their best interest. Once they dig in, provided you have ample beverages and snacks, they will come to see the benefits of participating, not only on the micro level of reclaiming valuable space for proper storage but also on the macro level of laying claim to new ways of thinking about stuff and how you all share your home.

Working together to reclaim these spaces strengthens self-esteem—there is power in the we-made-it-together-we'll-correct-it-together spirit of team building and committing to common goals. It also presents ample opportunities to model healthy behavior. No amount of talking can compete with actually doing something—think of how frustrating it is to hear some version of "Do as I say, not as I do." So picking up a piece of trash and putting it in the garbage speaks volumes, particularly when done not as a burden but as a step toward liberation. As a family, you are now engaged in building the life you desire, one moldy shoe or broken hockey stick at a time.

Perhaps more important is putting into place the very thing that will prevent this from ever occurring again. And that is a fundamental shift in how you all view space and stuff. As you sort through everything, it's imperative to discuss two things:

1. The scale of appropriate consumption and what it should look like going forward to bring things in and out of the house
2. How easily this space was turned into a chaotic mess and how effortlessly it could return to this condition again if anyone in the family backslides on number one

This is not a threat or blame conversation but a call to action for future prevention. Communal living demands rigorous participation and vigilance. Otherwise, you risk this project becoming a Band-Aid for a wound requiring surgery. Anyone can clean out a space—you and your kin may even have done this before. But making that core adjustment as a family, as a working unit, of how you manage your space and objects is what is necessary. Seeing stuff in a different way has to become a part of your daily lives to ensure that in a year's time you won't be back here again with a different set of objects but the same exact problem.

And, of course, if you live alone or it's clear that everything in these spaces belongs to or got there by you alone, it's going to be just you and me.

SCHEDULING THE TIME

Whether working alone or with others, the work we're about to embark on—installing or modifying storage systems and sorting the contents of these spaces—will likely take two weekends or four days, at least two days of which should be consecutive. Those days are the sorting and reloading days.

If you are working with others, you'll likely shave a day off the process since building and installing the storage systems will go faster with more hands. If you live alone, consider enlisting a friend or two to help you. Depending on your level of friendship, everyone can determine exactly how involved they'd like to be. Particularly if the scale of your project is extensive, consider a time swap where you help them with a major project on their list in exchange for their assistance here.

To protect against future resentments, consider this a contract—you don't need to memorialize it on paper, but you should put your friend's work session on the calendar right away—before you even start your own work session. That way, you avoid future scheduling conflicts and any hard feelings, and everyone remains enthusiastic while working.

Use the guidance from the following sections to develop a plan of attack so you can direct the project from start to finish. Make a list of the tasks to be done, and divide those up among your helpers to keep everyone on track without you needing to appear bossy or controlling.

CREATING EFFICIENT STORAGE IN ANY SPACE

While there are seemingly infinite flavors of storage components, the basic structures are pretty simple and finite. You're either storing things *on* something (shelves, either wall-mounted or free-standing; hooks; and hangers) or *in* something (cabinets, hanging baskets, or bins). Your budget and aesthetics will determine what these things look like—the materials and finishes. Your space and skill will determine whether your belongings end up on things or inside them.

You may already have some of these elements in place. If what currently exists seems adequate and stable and well located, that's great. You just need to eliminate everything superfluous and reload. If some parts are there but a cohesive design is lacking, build around what's already installed.

On the other hand, if all you've got are wobbly shelves and a few recycled kitchen cabinets threatening to fall off the wall, now would be the time to replace them with a new system. Always seek the balance between practical and efficient, keeping utility and conservation in mind.

Garage Space Bonanza

Most garages have two feet of depth on each wall before breaking the plane of the bays. In the average garage, those three 24-foot-long walls equal 72 linear feet of potential storage from floor to ceiling—impressive. And that's without a single thing taking up any floor space at all.

Speaking of which, the less stored on the ground, the better. Concrete is porous and constantly wicking moisture up through it. Tools can rust and paper bags disintegrate when left on unfinished floors over time. It's also safer and more convenient to minimize the need to bend over as one matures.

STORAGE SYSTEMS AND SHELVING: AN OVERVIEW

As mentioned, shelves and storage systems come in a variety of materials, styles, and price points. Your budget, an understanding of what you're storing (both volume and kind of object), and the flexibility to modify the design as your needs change will be the guiding factors in determining which types of storage you'll choose. Different shelving types will obviously be better for storing certain kinds of items.

While prefabricated systems offer tremendous diversity among their individual components, they are also the most expensive. If you're comfortable with several styles or designs living alongside one another and are not afraid of potentially clashing looks, you can choose the best that each of these has to offer and custom design your own system. That way, you get exactly what you need and still keep your eye on the bottom line.

Stand-alone shelving units, whether plastic, wood, or steel, provide flexible storage while keeping things up and off the floor. Some shelving units can be fitted with casters or wheels, allowing even more flexibility in placement and access. Either roll them out of your way to gain access to more remote areas, or roll them closer for immediate access to their contents.

Guidelines for Sizing and Positioning of Shelves and Other Storage Systems

Use the following guidelines to help you design and configure your storage systems:

1. Choose shelf heights that allow enough space between the shelves and items of assorted heights. The lowest shelf should be between 18 inches and 24 inches from the ground. The distance between the lowest shelf and the next shelf above it should also be between 18 inches and 24 inches. After that,

as you continue up, the minimum distance between finished surfaces is typically between 12 inches and 16 inches.

2. Make sure to leave enough space between the ceiling and the top shelf for any tall (and infrequently used) items you plan to store there. Think camping equipment and tall coolers.

3. Make sure that all shelves, brackets, and hooks have clearance and will not interfere with interior doors, service doors, garage doors, and garage-door tracks.

4. When hanging things directly from the walls, be sure to anchor hooks, nails, and screws into studs for secure support.

5. Make sure that in all foot-traffic areas—near laundry machines, car doors, and doorways—you keep brackets and braces above head level so you won't bump into them.

6. In the garage, do not cover every inch of wall space with shelving. Allow several areas, especially near the garage door, for hanging storage for gardening tools (rakes, hoses, and wheelbarrows) and winter tools (snow shovels and buckets of ice melt).

7. In the garage, allow additional space for SUV or pickup truck doors to open fully, ensuring that any shelving doesn't restrict them.

8. Ensure a free-and-easy path from indoors to your trash and recycling areas and from these bins to the curb. You don't want to run a gauntlet each time you bring something to the bins or on your weekly trip taking the bins to the street.

9. Consider stackable recycling bins and the addition of a handcart. That allows you to wheel the entire tower of bins—metal, glass, and plastic—right to the curb.

10. Ensure an unobstructed path for any motorized service vehicles. You don't want to move cars (or bikes or the grill) every time you want to get the riding mower or snowplow out. Design a space that makes using these machines easy and accessible.

You can also find this guide in your companion workbook or download it from unstuffbook.com/auxspaces.

Shelving, Storage Systems, and Hanger Options

The following are most commonly used in garages, but many of these can also be used in basements and attics, too. Some modifications may be required for shorter walls or lower ceilings, but in all cases using the full height of your walls will greatly increase your storage capacity.

These are listed roughly in descending order of cost by component, although costs may vary. A small amount of research up front will save both time and money, and you'll end up with exactly what you want at a price that's reasonable for you. Remember when calculating costs to consider the measurements of the area(s) to be covered, the cost for the materials themselves, and any labor costs if you're not going to do the installation yourself. Given the proliferation of freelance labor sites and apps, not being "handy" is no longer a barrier to installing any of these systems.

CUSTOMIZED WALL SYSTEMS

Each whole-room conversion system offers similar features and installs directly onto your walls. These systems provide a series of panels or tracks that various cabinets, shelves, and hooks lock into. They are the most flexible should you want to modify your design down the road.

SLOTTED WALL PANELS

These are solid panels with rows of horizontal slots. Brackets and clips fit into the slots and suspend baskets, bins, cabinets, hooks, and shelves. Everything about these systems is uniform and proprietary, so once you commit to a certain manufacturer, you'll have to use only their components to complete your system. One potential advantage with this type of system is that you can also use this to finish off unfinished walls. Simply cover the wall with panels from floor to ceiling.

WALL TRACKS

These are metal rails that attach horizontally across studs. Some offer a decorative cover that disguises the rail. They come in standard lengths and can be installed at any height. Again, with proprietary brackets or clips you can attach a wide variety of baskets, bins, cabinets, hooks, and other holders.

With some systems (typically seen in residential closets), they also offer vertical standards that attach to the top rail. You can then attach brackets and support horizontal shelving across the brackets. This gives you the flexibility to break up shelving with other components from the rail's manufacturer.

WALL STORAGE CABINETS

Like kitchen cabinets, these come in a variety of materials, including wood, metal, and plastic, and are available in many different sizes, styles, and finishes. Some are freestanding (on legs or wheels), and some are wall-mounted. While these can be relocated once they're installed, you should consider these semipermanent. Just like laying out a kitchen's cabinetry, you'll want to be fairly certain of your design before you purchase and install these.

UTILITY STORAGE CABINETS

These are made from multiple materials in multiple finishes and are freestanding but cumbersome to move once placed. You'll certainly have to empty them before you can relocate them. In addition, unlike shelving units, you'll need to allow clearance for door swings on these cabinets when figuring out placement.

FREESTANDING SHELVING UNITS

These come in a variety of materials and combinations of materials from steel to wood to plastic. They come in standard dimensions, and because each unit is independent, they offer great flexibility as they can be moved from place to place. Units with wheels allow for even easier relocation.

METAL STANDARDS AND BRACKETS

These offer a low-cost, flexible alternative to both wall panels and wall tracks. Standards come in several lengths and attach vertically onto the studs, either over Sheetrock or directly (in unfinished spaces). Interlocking brackets come in various depths and allow for incremental adjustment up and down. The only limits to height are the length of the standards themselves.

For tall spaces, you can install standards on top of one another from floor to ceiling. Steel or wood or wire-mesh shelves can be used as long as they fit and are stable on top of the brackets. The thicker and more rigid the shelving material is, the less likely that it will buckle or warp under weight or humid conditions. One advantage to wire mesh is its breathability. Fabrics and other materials that need air circulation will benefit from mesh shelves.

WIRE GRIDS

These grid panels are made of metal, are sometimes coated, are available in various sizes, and can be used to cover entire walls. They come with clips and spacers to secure them to studs. Baskets, bins, hooks, racks, and shelves can all be attached to the grids to customize storage.

PEGBOARD (PERFORATED HARDBOARD)

This is the original grid panel. This ready-made surface is dotted with holes that accept a wide variety of clips, hooks, racks, and shelves. There are great accessories that let you store even heavy or bulky items without fear of things falling off or ripping free. Pegboard is fastened directly to exposed studs or with spacers over drywall. The spacers hold the panels far enough away from the wall to allow hooks to be inserted or removed.

There are different thicknesses of pegboard, so be sure to buy the correct corresponding hardware. If you have ever seen Julia Child's kitchen, she cleverly installed pegboard on her walls, then outlined all her pots and pans with a marker so anyone could return things back to the right spot.

TOOL HANGERS AND HOOKS

Many hardware companies now sell individual and highly specialized hooks and tool hangers. These are designed for everything from rakes and shovels and wheelbarrows to ladders and bicycles and hockey equipment. These attach to studs and are perfect for all those narrow or corner spaces. They get things up off the ground and keep them easily seen and reached.

Before you install any of these systems, measure carefully and consider access to them from both the front and the sides. You don't want to have a great-looking system that you can't easily get to.

Why You Don't Want to Do This Out of Order

Since these spaces are being "built to suit," if you cannot easily access every wall you plan to use for storage *prior* to sorting, I suggest studying your options and doing some research but waiting to install a system until after everything's been cleared away and sorted. When designing your layout and installing storage components, you need to be able to get to every part of the space so your layout will have integrity and accessibility from inception to execution. A half-baked cake may taste sweet, but it's a mess to deal with.

Likewise, do not start to load any storage before everything has been sorted and categorized. It may be tempting to cut a corner here and there, thinking, *Well, I can certainly put X right here. I know where that wants to live,* but you'll discover that as you sort, the volume of items in each category and the preferred location for these categories will continue to shift until everything has been touched and decided on. Until you have a completely empty space without any obstacles or space commitments, you can't actually see where the most efficient place to put each thing will be.

Having to move things twice is not the end of the world, but a lot of loading and unloading is a waste of time during an already large project. Patience and being methodical will pay huge dividends as you work through this process. Trust me.

SORTING AND YOU
Things You Will Need for This Work

Once you've assembled and installed whatever storage systems you're going to be using or are clear that it's preferable to wait until after the space is cleared, it's now time to start sorting. So get these supplies and bring them to the work area:

- Smartphone or camera
- Trash cans and bags
- Broom
- Dustpan
- Mop
- Wet-dry industrial vacuum
- Tubs/containers/baskets/tarps (to isolate, corral, and contain like things)
- Old carryout or food storage containers (clear plastic with sealing lids for smaller storage items)
- A sizable magnet (for picking up nails, screws, or random pieces of metal)

Find a spot for your trash cans, a spot that you can easily get to with the trash bags you'll soon be filling. And make sure there's enough room around them for the extra bags you'll end up with when the cans reach capacity. It'd be better not to have to move the trash twice before setting it at the curb. If you can arrange this process to fall close enough to trash-collection day, take it all to the curb immediately.

Clever Attempts to Delay or Avoid Sorting

Having already taken your "before" pictures, at this point you may feel tempted to sidestep examining your possessions and instead rush to get some containers—hoping that just corralling it all will be enough. This is another variation of "out of sight, out of mind." By tossing everything into containers, you may be thinking you'll do the actual sorting later or "someday" when you win the time lottery and have an influx of unstructured time with no plans. At least everything's up off the floor and into bins, so that's progress, right?

Wrong. Randomly stuffing things into bins and boxes brings you no closer to knowing where everything is or eliminating the things that you don't need, want, or care about. This hasty "fix" just delays the inevitable.

> **NOTABLE NOTE**
>
> When you eventually do shop for proper storage containers, do not be seduced into thinking that you need a new lamp, frying pan, or power tool since you're "already out shopping." You're in the middle of a project, and you're on an errand, not an excursion.

Alternatively, you may be thinking that stocking up on all different sizes of tubs and bins will help you in your sorting process and is the best way to proceed. This, too, is a mistake. No amount of shopping will cure this mess. Until you know the exact volume and content of the items to be stored, you can't possibly buy the right types or sizes of containers. And the last things you need are odd-sized and surplus containers creating more clutter and wasting money!

Sorting in Two Easy Steps

Armed with the sorting categories and Stay-or-Go questions listed below, you're ready to begin sorting. This is where the rubber meets the road. Once you've sorted through everything, you'll evaluate whether there's more to store than room in which to store it. For now, let's focus on examining each individual item that makes up each category.

STEP 1: ELIMINATE TRASH

The first thing to do is find everything that can clearly be identified as trash and discard it.

Trash (noun): an unwanted or undesired material or substance; broken, discarded, or worthless things; also referred to as rubbish, waste, garbage, or junk, depending on the type of material and the regional terminology

So now find the items that are unequivocally unwanted, broken, or worthless, and throw them out. That includes anything missing key components that can't or won't be replaced; anything actually broken, including toys; and anything that no longer works, even when plugged in or after the batteries are swapped for fresh ones.

Electronics and other things that contain heavy or toxic metals, chemicals, or batteries should be isolated into a recycling pile—a quick search online will show you places that offer recycling programs where you can drop off these kinds of things either for a small fee or for free. Likewise, paint cans and other toxic liquids should be isolated for proper disposal.

See the Resources section in the companion workbook or visit unstuffbook.com/resources to download information about how and where to dispose of electronics, paint, and other hazardous items.

STEP 2: LIKE WITH LIKE

With the trash gone, that leaves you with everything else to be sorted into families of like objects. If there are still random items in a tangle, pry everything loose from its neighbors. Cords and cables have a way of strangling anything they come in contact with. No need to get frustrated or angry; just take it slow and work on one thing at a time. Of course, any additional trash you come across should immediately get tossed.

If you're in the garage, move out of the way any motorized vehicles that are staying, whether they're cars, ATVs, riding mowers, motorcycles, or scooters. Likewise, move any single large items such as grills, bicycles, ladders, and wheelbarrows. These also need to be out of the way to create enough sorting and organizing space. Once you've established categories for sorting, some of these items can be brought back in and placed with other items that share the same category.

Whichever space you're in, create areas into which like items can be sorted. Spread out tarps or bins to define areas, or take old cardboard or damaged sheets of foam core and a large marker and create signs, staking out specific areas around the space. This way, camping gear doesn't spill over into seasonal gardening supplies.

When spreading things out and sorting, keep things to one level as much as possible so you can easily recognize category contents and minimize handling times. Books and other flat and uniform items can be stacked while clothes and other soft goods may end up in piles—just remember that ultimately you'll have to dismantle these piles as you make further decisions.

Below are some global categories we've used elsewhere in this book. You can use them for some high-level, Like-with-Like sorting:

- Keep
- Return to Others (soon!)
- Donate (soon!)
  - » Thrift store
  - » Specific people or organizations

- » Online classified sites (The Freecycle Network, craigslist)
- » Out at the curb with a sign
- Sell (only things that have significant value and easy-to-identify markets)
- Recycle (as in "green" recycling)
- Trash
- Sentimentaland
- The Fence

For those items that you're keeping that will be containerized and stored, below are some categories to get you started. Review this list and then your belongings so you can identify any additional categories that you'll need for the proper labeling and storage of your stuff:

- **Artwork:** intact or damaged, two- and three-dimensional
- **Automobile:** all things to do with your cars (motor oil, windshield wiper fluid, tires, etc.)
- **Books:** in or out of boxes, current or historical or school-books, etc.; ultimately, only books that you're keeping
- **Camping gear:** tents, sleeping bags, portable grill, folding chairs, coolers
- **Cleaning supplies:** opened cleaning products, buckets, mops, brooms, dustpans
- **Clothing, children's**
- **Clothing, "fat"**
- **Clothing, seasonal:** separated by season as well as by owner/wearer
- **Clothing, "skinny"**
- **Cold-weather tools:** snow shovels, scrapers, ice-melt products
- **Collections:** from Pokémon to Barbie to Hummels to stamps
- **Electronics, computer:** surplus computer parts, printers, monitors
- **Electronics, other:** iPods and other personal listening devices, stereo components, TVs, adding machines, calculators

- **Fasteners:** nuts, bolts, screws, nails (store near tools)
- **Financial documents:** supporting documentation for tax returns, bank and credit card statements, receipts
- **Furniture:** current and no longer used, intact and broken, missing parts, torn
- **Games and toys:** board games, jigsaw puzzles, children's toys
- **Gardening, lawn, and landscaping:** summer yard tools such as hoses, rakes, shovels, leaf blowers, chain saws
- **Hobby supplies:** scrapbooking; knitting and crocheting; model cars, planes, or trains
- **Holiday decorations:** separated by individual holiday
- **Inherited things:** in or out of any containers they arrived in
- **Laundry:** as in dirty laundry, if you do laundry in this space
- **Media:** LPs, cassette tapes, 8-track tapes, 78s, 45s, VHS tapes, DVDs, CDs, floppy disks
- **Newspapers:** either current or old (for example, documenting the day Kennedy was assassinated, your child's birth, the first moon landing)
- **Nonmotorized recreational vehicles:** bicycles, tricycles, unicycles, inline skates, skateboards, pogo sticks, stilts
- **Office supplies**
- **Original cartons for equipment:** just in case we have to return them!
- **Paint and painting supplies:** including drop cloths, rollers, brushes
- **Pantry items:** foods, dry goods, paper products
- **Periodicals:** current or old magazines, catalogs
- **Photographs:** in boxes, in albums, or loose
- **Seasonal lifestyle:** grills, lawn chairs, cushions
- **Seasonal pastime supplies:** pool equipment and toys, croquet equipment
- **Sports equipment:** all seasons, from Frisbees to ice skates, further separated by sport

- **Surplus china and dishes:** including crystal, stemware
- **Surplus goods:** bulk cleaning supplies (unopened), light bulbs, batteries
- **Surplus kitchen equipment:** appliances, pots and pans, dishes, silverware
- **Surplus planting supplies:** for houseplants rather than gardening, includes planters and vases
- **Tools, all-season:** ladders, saws, drills, hammers

You can also find this list in the companion workbook or download it at unstuffbook.com/auxspaces.

NOTABLE NOTE

Temporary or supporting financial documents that you don't want to store in a filing cabinet should be stored in clearly labeled water-resistant plastic containers. Many of these can be discarded after three to seven years, but check with your attorney, accountant, or tax professional before doing so.

Permanent financial documents (tax returns) and financial instruments (stock certificates) should be stored with other documents that cannot be replaced and might be necessary in an emergency (insurance policies, health care proxies, wills, deeds, vehicle titles). These should be copied and/or scanned and the originals stored in a fireproof, waterproof safe or filing cabinet on the main level of the house.

The problem with storing them off-site in a safe-deposit box at a bank is that banks aren't open and available 24/7/365, so if you need one of these docs in an emergency, you'd have to wait for the next business day to retrieve them. If you do store things in a safe-deposit box at a bank, make sure there are multiple keys to each box with clearly noted and identified locations.

Stay-or-Go Questions

Once everything has been sorted using Like with Like, it's time to handle each object or set of objects and ask the following 12 questions. You'll also find these in your companion workbook.

1. Do I really need this?
   No. Great, then let it go. Place the item in the trash or donation pile depending on its usefulness to others.
   Yes. Explain to yourself why keeping this is a need and not a want.
   Go on to the next question.

2. Do I need all of these?
   Yes. If so, record the number of items and establish this number as your limit.
   No. Decide how many you truly need, and once you pick a number, stick to it. Don't amend the number when you come across another item; swap the newest object you'd like to keep for one of the objects you've previously sorted.
   Go on to the next question.

3. Am I keeping it because of sentimental attachment?
   Yes. Okay, what is the story behind the item and is it still valid and meaningful?
   No. Keep it and put it in a pile with other like items.
   Go on to the next question.

4. Would a photo of it suffice?
   Yes. Take a photo or two, then place the item in the trash or donation pile depending on its usefulness to others.
   No. Explain to yourself why a photo is insufficient—avoid defensive posturing or deflection and be specific.
   Go on to the next question.

5. Do I already have a better one?

   Yes. Place the item in the trash or donation pile depending on its usefulness to others.

   No. Great, then decide if you need to replace it or if the existing one is still usable.

   Go on to the next question.

6. Is this better than the one I have?

   Yes. Install this one as your new version, then place the previous one in the trash or donation pile depending on its usefulness to others.

   No. Release this version and don't look back.

   Go on to the next question.

7. Am I keeping it for "someday"?

   Yes. Acknowledge that "someday" doesn't exist and that with many items, having more of them isn't the best way, or even the only way, to avoid an emergency. Then, place the item in the trash or donation pile depending on its usefulness to others.

   No. Explain to yourself when this item will be useful and be specific.

   Go on to the next question.

8. Will I actually do the work required to restore or repair this?

   Yes. Make a plan for when you will restore/repair it and commit to that plan.

   No. Accept this fact without regret or shame, then place the item in the trash or donation pile depending on its usefulness to others.

   Go on to the next question.

9. Am I keeping it only because it was expensive and it's "still good"?

   Yes. Acknowledge the story, then place the item in the trash or donation pile depending on its usefulness to others.

No. Explain the reason why you want to keep this if it's not about the money, then decide if that's a valid reason. If it is, marry the item into its Like-with-Like siblings or let it go.

Go on to the next question.

10. Will my life change for the worse if I let this go (in actuality, not just in your imagination)?

Yes. Keep it and put it in a pile with other like items.

No. Celebrate your clarity and then place it in the going-out pile.

Go on to the next question.

11. Am I keeping it because it's part of a set?

Yes. Examine this story and see if it's valid or just a knee-jerk reaction or other habit. If there's no good reason for keeping it, let it go.

No. Place the item in the trash or donation pile depending on its usefulness to others.

Go on to the next question.

12. Do I use the whole set?

Yes. Keep the whole set and put all the parts together with other like items.

No. Release the parts you don't use.

Go on to the next question.

Depending on your answers, you should now have a good sense of whether each item should stay or go. When in doubt, toss it out or let it go.

Other than breaks for snacks or the bathroom, this should be a continuous activity, and you should not stop until everything has either been separated into a smaller pile of one category or in a pile to be released. If it's getting dark or you're exhausted, you can stop before you've made decisions about everything. Of course, if you've taken things outdoors, you'll want to either cover everything up or bring any big-ticket items indoors for safekeeping overnight.

More Pesky Conversations about Thoughts and Feelings

Sorting and purging may bring up questions or thoughts or feelings. This is natural and not to be feared or judged as a sign of anything other than your humanness. The mind is a thought machine and the heart a feeling machine. Generating thoughts and feelings are what they do.

If these kinds of thoughts or feelings have stopped you in the past or prevented you from even beginning, you're not alone. And while they may be demanding and intrusive and annoying, they are nothing more than a product of your fertile imagination and vulnerable constitution—not always a great combination when sorting through random things but certainly not deadly.

I recently spent three weeks in Chicago with a client, Iris, who had decided that she wanted to put her house on the market and move on. This was the house she had raised her two children in, and after 20 years, it was jam-packed from the attic to the basement with everything from fine art to toy drums.

As we sorted through the basement, we came across lots of her kids' old clothes and toys. She never broke down and cried, but she told me the story of each thing we touched. Iris would hold each item and tenderly relate how her son had worn this little baseball cap or her daughter had performed in her ballet recital in these slippers.

We kept three tubs and some trash bags nearby—one tub for each child, one tub for her, and trash bags for the local thrift store. As we sorted through box after box and pile after pile, some things were set aside for each child and a few for her—I could always tell which thing she wouldn't be able to part with by the way her smile lit up as she first handled it. She'd start to laugh, and I'd know this tiny jumpsuit was going straight into *her* tub. Anything that didn't make the cut was bagged and earmarked for charity.

We continued this process through storerooms packed with books, sporting equipment, and old bolts of fabric. Other than a few more sentimental objects, everything else was gathered up to be taken away.

There were times each day when Iris was clearly overcome with feelings as she sifted through years of accumulated belongings, each one representing a particular event or time in her life. When I sensed she had reached a threshold of emotion or exhaustion, or she just seemed to lose focus, I'd check in with her. Was she okay? Was she tired? Did she want to take a break, get a snack or a cup of tea? Did she want a hug? Most of the time she'd laugh and say she was fine, let's keep going, but there were times when we did pause, head downstairs, and put the water on for tea or grab a snack.

If you're working alone, you'll have to do that for yourself. Check in with yourself and pace yourself. I've laid out a rigorous plan of action in these pages, but you should consider the human component in this process as well. You don't want to get too hungry or tired when doing this work.

Likewise, if strong emotions come up, shift gears; if you're overwhelmed going through your kids' childhood clothing, an old dissertation that's not quite finished, or love letters from any number of exes, start shredding or go sort towels or do something equally unemotional. Get a snack. Take a walk around the block.

No one's keeping track of the time. The goal is to complete the task or tasks described from beginning to end. If that takes three hours or three days, that's fine. As long as you keep coming back to it, you can walk away for some fresh air as often as you need to. Just be mindful not to allow strong feelings, exhaustion, or hunger to derail you and prevent you from finishing altogether.

When we got to the attic, Iris and I found an old bedroom set that had belonged to her daughter. We cleaned it off and brought it down to the main floor to set up in one of the bedrooms. Unfortunately, most of what else was up there had been overrun by mice or moths.

Surrendering to the situation, we filled bag after bag with trash and hauled it down to the curb. I think it was that much easier for Iris to empty the attic without looking back, having already sorted through the basement and selected her precious totems of two childhoods' worth of memories.

We can take away several lessons from Iris's experience. A few selective items can distill and capture the feelings behind whole swaths of time. And more practically, if you have the sense that time and unwelcome pests have destroyed the contents of some area of your home, sort through another area first and cull your treasures there. It will make the inevitable losses more tolerable as you assess the damage and finally let things go.

Our Feelings about Trash

Undoubtedly, as you sort, you will discover additional things that can't be considered anything other than trash. Put them directly into a trash bag. There's no need to fret or talk yourself out of tossing something that is worthless or beyond repair. For those items that are still worth something, if not to you but to someone else, they can be gathered in another area (labeled Donate) and taken to your local resale shop or a shelter, or to some other place that accepts donations of still-functional things.

It can be sad to throw things away for a variety of reasons—most of them emotional and spurred on by stories we tell ourselves about either the monetary or the sentimental value of an item, or sometimes the monetary *and* the sentimental value. At some point, most of us will tell ourselves a story about a thing and that the frugal and prudent choice would be to repair or restore it to full functionality "someday" or even "someday soon."

The truth is that if you have not attempted to fix something in the last 12 months, it is almost certain that you never will. You may argue with me in your head, but I have been a party to this conversation countless times with clients, and in every case, not a single item needing repair was ever successfully repaired without my intervention.

And, of course, beyond money and feelings, there are also the environmental consequences of throwing things away. Most of us are mindful of the growing mountains of trash just outside our cities or floating on barges on our waterways, and we want to keep as much as possible in circulation and away from these (mostly) dead ends. There are programs that convert some trash back into energy, and every day there are more options for recycling things that just last month were considered exclusively trash. I urge us all to pursue every avenue for the proper dismantling and recycling of any and every thing we discard.

There will be times, however, when something is still destined for the landfill. And in those cases, no one wants your trash any more than you do. If something is missing crucial parts or is destroyed beyond use, be responsible and dispose of it properly. Do not pass along garbage to a local nonprofit, assuming they'll do the sorting for you. You may believe that the remaining shoe of a pair might still find some use in the world, but unless it is an athletic shoe that can be recycled, you are mistaken. Throw it away.

NOTABLE NOTE

When considering the toxic nature of something you're about to discard, a good rule of thumb is if you wouldn't put it in your mouth, then it most likely has a correct way to be dismantled and recycled, and it should not just be tossed into the trash to leach into water tables or food supplies.

I realize this places a particular burden on some people who have limited mobility or live in more remote locations— even so, this just brings mindfulness further into focus. Before bringing home something potentially toxic and thereby tacitly agreeing to be responsible for its eventual disposal, consider your alternatives. Is there a "green" or nontoxic yet equally effective version of the item you could buy? There may not be. In those cases, I encourage you to assume full responsibility for seeing your product/item through the complete arc of its life cycle—from arrival at your door to its departure for eventual dismantling and comprehensive recycling. See the Resources section in the companion workbook or online at unstuffbook.com/resources for more guidance and instruction on this.

The surest way to keep things out of a landfill is to use less and be more mindful about what you invite into your life. If you don't want to be responsible for something at the end of its life cycle, perhaps you should leave it where you found it in the first place. If we really do live in a supply-and-demand society, the sooner we stop demanding, the sooner they'll stop supplying.

CLEANLINESS IS NEXT TO GARAGELINESS (OR ATTICLINESS OR BASEMENTLINESS)

Once you've sorted and purged everything from one of these spaces, before you load anything back in, sweep or vacuum and mop the floor. If you are in the garage and there are any oil spills or other fluid stains on the floor, try to get them up now. A quick search online should turn up solutions for any stain situation you might have on your hands. Wipe down every surface, paying special attention to cobwebs and other dust collectors. If you have cabinets or shelves that remain as part of your storage system, wipe them down as well.

THE KINDS OF THINGS YOU STORE IN YOUR AUXILIARY SPACE(S)

Look around at the various Like-with-Like zones, then get out your companion workbook or notebook. Find the page in your workbook titled "The Kinds of Things I Store in My Garage (or Basement or Attic)" or start a new page in your notebook and label it with this title. Then, begin to record the categories you've identified and sorted things into.

Remember to think in terms of groupings and categories rather than specifics—not My Navy Heavy Wool Slack Suit but rather "Clothing, seasonal." For fine-tuning, refer back to the list on pages 208–210 or at unstuffbook.com/auxspaces for guidance—you'll find suggested categories there to get you started.

Do this exercise for each auxiliary space. Then take all the lists and look for duplicates. Have you historically stored the same kind of thing in more than one place? If so, was the bulk of a particular category in one space with just a few stragglers in another space, or were items fairly evenly divided among spaces?

This will help you marry together items from the same category so that when you finish, all of any one category will be found in only one location. One Home for Everything and Like with Like come to your aid once again.

Also review the lists for any spatial limitations, looking for ways to maximize how you use each space by fitting the largest, bulkiest items where you have the most room and where it is easiest to move things in and out. If you only have one or two of these kinds of spaces, this shouldn't take too long.

This exercise, like every exercise in this book, is designed to help you focus your efforts, clarify the kinds of things you're storing, and figure out where and how best to continue storing them for their protection and your easy access.

Depending on the size of your spaces, consider adjusting the scale of your belongings to match the available space. For example, if you often shop in bulk but it's also important to have generous open space around you when you're doing laundry, consider how much bulk shopping you should actually do. Rather than cramming 48 rolls of toilet paper and 500 paper plates into your laundry-folding area, perhaps you can cut back to 24 rolls and 250 plates so you don't feel unnecessarily crowded.

As you make and review your lists, just remember—there is no absolute right or wrong way to organize your home. The guidelines are simple:

1. Do you have adequate room for everything you own?
2. If there is adequate room, is everything easy to locate and use?
3. If there is not adequate room, you either need more room or less stuff.

And, of course, in the case of number three I always vote for less stuff.

CONTAINERIZING THE CATEGORIES

Once everything has been sorted, it's time to put things away in containers. Measure or carefully guesstimate the volume of each category so you know which size and how many containers you need. Anything that is part of a set or is not a stand-alone item should be containerized with its siblings—exceptions being lawn furniture (too bulky), bulk supplies (these just need to all live together in one area), and collections of small things, such as fasteners. It's enough to have each kind of fastener together in their own container; we don't need a container of containers of fasteners. And as always, keep Like with Like—put the fasteners near the tools and other hardware, for instance.

If your camping gear comprises a tent, two sleeping bags, a mess kit, a portable stove, two propane canisters, a tarp, and some stakes, find containers that are large enough to house all these items in the fewest number of containers that will still fit someplace in your garage, basement, or attic. That said, when loading larger containers, make sure they don't become so heavy that moving them becomes awkward or requires more than one person.

Now would be the time to go shopping for containers, if needed, since you have an accurate measurement of each category's size requirements. I'm not a big fan of plastic in everyday living, but I am a huge fan of clear plastic tubs and bins for storage.

You may choose lovely decorator containers for all your storage needs *if* these containers are specifically labeled, and you update those labels anytime something is added or removed. Otherwise, you need to be okay with wasting time hunting through several look-alike containers searching for some item because you don't remember *which* lovely container you stored that item in.

> ### NOTABLE NOTE
>
> Do not buy containers, bins, or tubs to containerize your items before sorting. Wait until you are certain about the volume and quantity of things you're storing—you don't want to guess and end up with a bunch of containers in odd sizes and shapes that you can't use. And remember—it's not a bargain if it's not what you need or want, so resist buying containers just because they are on sale. Thinking that you'll make something fit doesn't make it true.

If repeatedly opening and closing a container to determine its contents seems like too much trouble (and it does to me), the alternative is a container you can easily see through. This way, regardless of how often you change the contents, there's never any confusion about what it contains. Under no circumstances should you hold on to decorative containers if they don't serve you, regardless of their cost— sell them or give them away.

When you have the right sizes and amount of tubs on hand, begin filling them. Continue to put everything into a container until only singular items remain. Because not everything is equally sturdy or has the same storage needs, it's important to further break things down into smaller categories so nothing is damaged while being stored.

For categories like books or seasonal clothing, uniform stackable tubs are fine to house everything. It's unlikely any book would crush or damage another book when they are stacked on top of and against one another inside a container. But the same is not true if you combine fragile items like a punch bowl or your grandmother's china with model airplanes. Just because they could all fit into one tub doesn't mean they should.

By now, you may recognize that many of these suggestions involve evaluating how honest you are with yourself. If your default unconscious response is immediately *Oh, that's no problem; I'll always remember which container has the X in it* but in reality you don't know which drawer in the kitchen holds your ice cream scoop, admitting that fact to yourself doesn't make you a bad or stupid person. Let that judgment go. It just means that even though you want to remember, the truth is you are unlikely to remember.

The opportunity here is working with that knowledge to make your life easier and simpler. And if having a clear tub is less pretty but infinitely easier for finding what you're looking for, which is the better solution for you—an opaque decorative container or a clear plastic one? Make the best choice for the real you, and you won't regret it.

Christmas Decorations (as an Example)

I'm going to show you how to take a single category, Christmas decorations, and break it up into all its different subcategories, so you can use this as a roadmap for other large categories that have several subcategories.

LIGHTS, INDOOR AND OUTDOOR

Here's the first subcategory (Lights) of a subcategory (Christmas Decorations) of a category (Seasonal Decor).

Start by bringing all the lights together but separated by indoor and outdoor. Also gather up all the extension cords, power strips, and spare parts/light bulbs for the Christmas lights. It makes sense to keep these wires, cables, and spare parts living here with the lights rather than putting them with other electrical parts. They have more in common with Christmas than they do with electricity.

Ideally, each string or strand of lights is individually wound around a paper towel roll, the core of an old roll of gift wrap, or a very fat and short dowel. Lights should have their own container *unless* you have only one or two strings of lights, in which case you could store them in a smaller container within a larger decoration category and container. Three or more strands are worthy of their own container.

TREE ORNAMENTS

Put all the tree ornaments in as many tubs as required. Only the tree ornaments. These are fragile, and you don't want these shifting and bumping into heavy items as you move the tubs around. If you have the original boxes they came in, you can store them in their boxes inside the tubs. If not, repurpose used tissue paper from gift boxes/bags to either wrap the ornaments individually or to create layers, like a lasagna of ornaments and paper.

Do not overpack these or crush them, and use as many tubs as needed for the number of ornaments you have. Included in one tub should be any packages of ornament hooks/hangers. If the hooks/hangers are loose and no packaging exists, use a ziplock bag to corral them.

ARTIFICIAL TREE, WREATHS, GARLANDS, SWAGS, AND OTHER EVERGREEN TRIM/DECOR

The tree, wreaths, and any other artificial evergreen decorations should all live together. While sturdier than glass ornaments, these are also vulnerable to crushing and other damage.

Take the tree apart into its smaller pieces. Lay the pieces in tubs, allowing their own weight to determine volume. Never apply weight or pressure, attempting to fit one more piece in a tub. If you have cardboard available, you could also place a section of cardboard between layers of greens, repeating the lasagna technique mentioned earlier.

Even if space is at a premium, do not overstuff the tubs, or you'll damage the contents when you close the lid.

Natural wreaths and similar decor will need to be discarded, ideally composted or chipped into mulch.

FLOCKING, STOCKINGS, OTHER SOFT FABRIC GOODS, AND HOLIDAY-CARD HOLDERS

These should all be kept together, laid flat, and layered. Included in this tub should be stocking holders and any holiday-card holders.

NATIVITY SCENES, SMALL FIGURES, SNOW GLOBES, AND TABLETOP DECORATIONS

Wrap each fragile item in tissue paper or Bubble Wrap, and lay them all neatly into the tubs. Everything else can be either wrapped or gently loaded into the tubs.

LARGE FIGURES, INDOOR AND OUTDOOR (INCLUDING LAWN ORNAMENTS)

All large figures should be stored in an open tub or in some sort of corral if possible (think repurposed playpen). If any are too large to containerize, store them together and near their siblings—a top shelf or shelves is often a great location for these oversized items.

An alternative if you have a garage is to make or use a loft area to store these big items. If the garage is not climate-controlled, make sure to wrap the indoor items in some sort of protective material; the outdoor figures should be just fine unwrapped.

CHRISTMAS COLLECTIBLES

Like the Nativity figures, any fragile items should be individually wrapped. Plush items or items that will not break, chip, or damage one another may be laid into the tubs carefully.

CANDLES, THINGS THAT BURN

If you never burn these candles, they may be stored with other table-top decorations. If you do burn them, keep them all together. Do *not* store matches in the tub with anything flammable. Also consider the climate and temperature when storing candles and other items that may melt, drip, or combust when exposed to prolonged heat.

NOTABLE NOTE

This chapter mentions storing things that burn as an example of a category of Christmas items. Here's where discernment and critical thinking come into play. While Sterno is something that burns and that you might use during the holidays, it is not a seasonal item, and so it should be stored with other fuels and chafing dishes someplace where it could be found year-round. You might use it for any number of other events during the year.

When things belong to two categories or could be stored in two different places, we sometimes get stuck making a decision and either put things in the wrong place or don't make a decision at all. Since everything needs to have only one home, it's important that we really think through where that home is. Often, the broader choice is the better choice, as with the Sterno.

TRAINS AND OTHER ANIMATED DECOR

For trains, group all tracks, track-related fasteners, power adapters, etc. together. Keep the cars separate, and wrap delicate, fragile, or antique cars individually. All signs, signals, lights, buildings, and other decor for the tracks and scenes should be stored separately as well. Things with moving or removable parts should be dismantled and all specialized parts stored together in a ziplock bag. Do not mix similar-looking pieces without labeling them if there is any chance that you won't be able to tell them apart in a year.

THE IMPORTANCE OF LABELS—
HOW, WHY, AND WHERE

Once everything is in a container, create an inventory of all containers and label them. Labels don't need to be fancy; they do need to be legible. Write in large block letters—cursive and lowercase letters are hard to read from a distance.

I prefer labels to writing directly on the container because you may want to put something different in the container in the future. That way, you'll avoid a series of crossed-out names every time you change contents.

NOTABLE NOTE

When storing things, find the balance between hyperspecific and vague—Books is probably specific enough for most of us. Unless you have a sizable library, you don't need to break them down into Novels and Other Fiction, History, Poetry, Art, and so on. On the other hand, you don't want to label them something as general as Printed Materials and wind up combining books with magazines, pamphlets, and owner's manuals.

How to Label Something Properly

- Label all boxes/containers/tubs so you can tell at a glance what's in them.
- When you label your containers, label them with large and clear letters that you can see and read from a distance of at least five feet.
- If printing labels or inventories from a computer, print an additional one and drop it inside the container or tape it to

the underside of the lid. This is helpful in case the labels fall off the outside.

- There's no need to label the top of a container if you are stacking them—you'll never see it.
- Label both sides and either the front or the back of a container so you don't have to face it in a certain direction when you put the container back in its place.
- Be mindful of label materials and where things are being stored. In hot climates, masking tape often dries and cracks off or the glue melts. When removed, some duct tapes leave a gummy mess behind.
- Be specific with your labels. Don't just label something Christmas Decorations, especially if you have multiple boxes of Christmas decorations. Instead, label them Christmas: Lights, Indoor or Christmas: Artificial Tree or Christmas: Wreaths. That way, you'll only have to open one container.
- If you are using any drawer-cabinet systems, a clever hack for a label for the individual drawers is gluing an example of each drawer's contents to the face of the drawer for an easy-to-see guide.

ORGANIZING THE STORAGE

With everything successfully containerized and labeled, it's time to organize the containers on shelves or pallets and put them away until you need them next. Two things will determine where you store everything: frequency of use and volume of stuff. Use Like with Like to identify where to store which items. Try to keep similar items on one shelf or on adjacent shelves.

Begin to load each cabinet and shelf with your sorted and containerized things. It may be that your best guess of a category's volume does not match up with the actual capacity of a shelf or cabinet. When this happens, don't be discouraged. You have two choices—either reduce the volume of things in that category or find a different location that can accommodate the entire category.

If you feel strongly that everything you have is necessary, I won't argue with you. If you feel that maybe you padded out your category with a few questionable items, now is the time to come clean and let them go.

Keep in mind how much things weigh, and always load heavier and bulkier items lower; lighter things can go up high. For hazardous materials such as chemicals, pesticides, and sharp tools, use storage cabinets with doors that can be closed and possibly even locked, well out of the reach of children and pets.

Once everything is up off the ground and on a pallet or shelf, in a cabinet, or hanging from a hook, take some pictures. These are your "afters." This is the way your space now looks, and with a minimum of consistent effort, this is the way your space will continue to look.

Frequency of Use: Storing Holiday Items, Seasonal Items, and Bulk Items

Bulk staple items that you're often accessing to replenish supplies should be the most accessible. Seasonal items that are rotated out for use more than once a year should be the next priority. For things used only once a year, such as holiday decorations, you'll want easy enough access, but these things don't need to be at your fingertips.

Sentimental or nostalgic items or memorabilia (wedding gowns, yearbooks, etc.) should go in one section, usually the least accessible as these items aren't taken out very often, if at all.

WHEN LAUNDRY IS DONE IN AUXILIARY SPACES

If your laundry center is in one of these spaces, make sure that you have ample room for sorting and folding clothes, hanging up damp clothes to dry, and using the ironing board. You should also have a shelf or cabinet overhead or nearby for laundry soap, spot removers, and other products.

A turntable is useful to store liquids; it will condense the space required, and if it has a lip, it'll also collect any spills. If space is tight where you do the wash, you could also hang damp clothes to dry in a nearby shower and set up the ironing board in a nearby room or hallway.

When evaluating your space, look for ways to improve efficiency and minimize the footprint, and think about how you like to do laundry by asking yourself the following questions:

- Can I finish the laundry in the same room or area that I wash it?
- Is there room for a table or countertop to fold laundry on?
- What about an ironing board? Do I or does someone in my family press clothes?
- What about damp clothes that either shouldn't be dried at all or should be pulled out while still damp to avoid shrinkage or wrinkling?
- How often do I do laundry?
- Do I usually or only go to this space to do the wash?

All of these are factors to consider when laying out your space, including where you'll place shelving and other storage.

MANAGING MESSY PROJECTS INSIDE AND OUT

Consider whether there are activities happening indoors that generate dirt, dust, or other particulate matter that could possibly get into things being stored. How about proper ventilation for hobbies, crafts, or repairs that involve toxic substances?

Certainly, you'll want to locate any sort of shop as far away from the laundry or stored food as possible. That's one more argument for airtight containers with resealable lids. Beyond that, keeping any sort of woodworking, grinding, drilling, or chemical use isolated is your best bet for keeping your storage area clean and dust-free.

If you do have a workshop indoors *and* also have a climate-controlled or all-season garage, consider relocating your shop to the garage. That's a sure way to prevent generating dust indoors.

When the garage doubles as a work area or any mixed-use space, pay attention so that projects and their supplies don't migrate into common areas.

And just because there is better air circulation in this somewhat outdoor space, you'll still want to prevent sawdust and other particulate matter from finding its way into items stored nearby. Regular sweeping, vacuuming, and air filtering will keep debris from ending up anywhere other than the trash.

As you've been sorting and purging, you may have come across some things needing repair or a project that has been unfinished for more than a year. If so, take a realistic assessment of what you actually have the time and interest to complete.

If you are someone who is often building or fixing things, that's great. If, on the other hand, you've had a chair on your workbench for two years waiting to be reupholstered, consider taking it to an upholsterer or passing it along to someone who has a better history of completing these kinds of projects. You don't need to feel bad about it. Just be clear about where your interests and free time intersect with one another. Just because you could do something doesn't mean you need to or should. Your time, your choice.

CONVERTING AUXILIARY SPACES FOR LIVING

If you've been planning to or are in the process of converting an attic, basement, or garage into living space, consider carefully what you're going to do with the things currently stored there.

As I outlined earlier, I am adamantly opposed to using self-storage facilities unless you are wealthy or only parking things there temporarily. If you have things in the auxiliary space that could be relocated somewhere else in your home, take them there now and marry them with their siblings.

If you have no intention of ever using some of these items again and if you're not saving them for family members (or if you are saving them for family members, but they don't want them), it's time to let them go. If you want to sell them, figure out where, how, and who's going to do that.

Once you've successfully downsized in preparation for your auxiliary space conversion, make sure that you design sufficient storage into your new space for everything that you'll want to put back into it once the renovation is complete. Work smartly and cleverly to maximize storage wherever you can.

A bank of closets or even a storage room in your new layout will pay off handsomely, not only for your usage but also in resale value when you eventually put your house on the market. As they say, you can never be too thin, too rich, or have too much storage.

TRASH OR TREASURE? DELUSIONS ABOUT *NATIONAL GEOGRAPHIC,* EBAY, AND EARLY RETIREMENT

Have you been threatening to have a yard sale as soon as the weather clears up or warms up or cools off? Or are you thinking you'll go online and auction off all your treasures?

With few exceptions, if you think that you're sitting on a gold mine, you probably aren't. No doubt with good used merchandise, you could possibly make some money selling your leftovers. It's unlikely, however, that you'll become wealthy.

People don't go to garage sales looking to spend top dollar; they go looking for a bargain. Even with online or private auctions or any number of auction apps, you always need to consider what your time is worth because you can't get it back.

And while there are people who collect anything—Beanie Babies, celebrity trash, and lawn gnomes—it again seems unlikely that the copies of *National Geographic* you're stockpiling in the basement are going to put anyone through college, even a community college.

So while garage/yard/tag sales can be a great way to meet your neighbors and a few strangers, they are also a lot of work. If you're really serious about having the sale, commit to a date or a series of dates and put them on the calendar. Once that's done, go online to find the best advice on organizing a garage sale. This information changes seasonally, so I won't detail it here. Suffice it to say, I hope you don't find the same pile of stuff still lying around six months from now.

If you can't get it together to have a yard or garage sale, how likely is it that you'll get it together to sell things online? If a garage sale seems labor intensive and unappealing, online auctions and sales can be 10 times worse. Between taking photographs, uploading them, describing each item accurately, answering all the random emails from potential buyers, packing things, and running to UPS or the post office, you could burn through hours of your time for relatively little money.

Fortunately, there are plenty of services that will do the selling for you, but it won't come cheap. They'll keep a percentage of the selling price (typically 50 percent), plus *you'll* pay commissions to the listing app. Still, while you'll net less than half of what you think anything is worth, you'll be ahead of where you would be with everything still lying around your basement. Don't be penny-wise and pound-foolish about this one.

THE THRIFT-STORE BIN IS NOT
A GRAB BAG

Regardless of whether you're setting things aside to sell them or not, you should establish a box or tub that becomes the donation bin. This container should be easy to get to and clearly marked for everyone in the house to find. Anytime you come across something you're finished with, whether it's an article of clothing that doesn't fit, a piece of outdated technology (as long as the item still works properly), or a book you don't feel compelled to keep, these things should find their way into the donation bin.

As the title suggests, this bin is *not* an ongoing grab bag of surprises and treats. With the exception of small children who may mistakenly deposit something here you would not want donated to charity, once something is in the tub, it should stay there until it is dropped off at the appropriate charity.

If you live with other people, they alone decide when they are finished with something and what they want to do with it. Don't go rooting around inside the box and then become bitter when you discover that someone decided to donate an item rather than offer it to you. Instead, celebrate their generosity and thoughtfulness, and let it go. Of course, if you find that they've mistakenly tossed *your* belongings into the box, by all means, rescue them.

MAINTAINING THE SYSTEM

The best and most reliable way to maintain auxiliary spaces once you've organized them is twofold. First, now that everything clearly has a home, make sure whenever you take something out of its home, you return it to its home when you're finished.

Second, create an organizing schedule. If everyone uses and returns things to where they came from, you should never have to take on a project this size again. But no one and no system is perfect.

So put a quarterly or biannual decluttering-and-organizing day on your calendar—because if it doesn't actually make it onto your calendar, it's unlikely to happen. And if you live with other people, make sure it ends up on their calendars as well.

If you schedule the day to coincide with a change in the season, you can combine swapping out seasonal items with cleaning the spaces as well. That way, it will seem less unpleasant, and you'll have the added bonus of getting two necessary chores out of the way at the same time.

SELF-STORAGE: THE DOS AND DON'TS

As you've worked through this chapter, a thought may have crossed your mind a time or two: *I wouldn't have to sort or purge any of this stuff if I just threw it all in a self-storage unit.* If you're tempted to do this, please don't. Self-storage is a short-term solution at best. Like an unused gym membership, it's a monthly drain that's easily forgotten until the charge hits and you think, *I really have to take care of this* this month.

Storing old bedding, marginal appliances, old magazines (old *National Geographics*, anyone?), lawn furniture, etc. for nearly a hundred dollars each month makes no sense. Do the math. The average length of rental for self-storage is 14 months.[4] At an average cost of about $90 per month, it would cost you $1,260 over those 14 months. If your goods aren't worth that much going in, they certainly won't be worth that much coming out.

If money is not a concern, the psychic burden of lingering stuff may be enough to motivate you to make different choices. And if money *is* a concern, the math speaks for itself. Either way, self-storage should be used strategically. In the U.S. alone, this industry brings in almost $40 billion a year. That's a lot of deferred decisions.

---

4   Colton Gardner, "Self Storage Industry Statistics (2022)," *Neighbor Blog*, Neighbor, February 1, 2024, https://www.neighbor.com/storage-blog/self-storage-industry-statistics/.

I have some high-net-worth and ultrahigh-net-worth private clients who have a lot of stuff and may or may not use their surplus things again. They can afford to park things away without feeling the impact of monthly storage bills. For some of them, we catalog and isolate fine art and antiques in premium storage facilities and keep the rest of the furniture and belongings in indoor, climate-controlled, long-term storage facilities.

These folks are the exceptions. For most of us, self-storage should only be used in one of the following 10 instances. I've listed them out with their suggested maximum duration:

1. You're moving and need to store things temporarily. Six months or less.

2. You're renovating a home and need to store things off-site while the work is being done. Up to two years depending on the scale of the renovation.

3. You want to get a jumpstart on some serious decluttering and need to create enough space to work. Six months or less.

4. You're blending or consolidating households and need time to sort through all the duplicates. Three months or less.

5. You're staging a home for sale and need to temporarily hide things that don't necessarily show your home to its best advantage. Three months or less. (If your home hasn't sold by then, you have a pricing or realtor issue).

6. You're between school years, either at boarding school or university. Four months or less.

7. You're downsizing and need to move quickly. Six months or less.

8. You've got a transient or nomadic job or life (e.g., working overseas or in the military). Until you set up a new permanent residence.

9. You're in real estate, either as an agent or a staging expert, and you store your stock of furniture and decor here. As long as you are actively working.

10. You are a contractor, furniture dealer, retail shop owner, or other professional, and you store your business inventory here. As long as you are actively working.

A Storage Story

Here is a cautionary tale about self-storage units. For some readers, it might seem extreme but for others, surprisingly familiar. Either way, there is at least one major takeaway from this story: What typically drives procrastination around self-storage units is either ambivalence about the contents or fear of a potentially difficult conversation. Sometimes, it's both.

This story begins in Portland, Oregon, at a weekend decluttering workshop I was leading. During an interactive round-robin with the participants, one woman—let's call her Robin—shared that she had a storage unit in New Orleans where she hasn't lived in over 10 years.

She explained that the unit was filled with her adult daughter's things from when the daughter was a child and young adult. She had raised her daughter in New Orleans, but by now, no family remained there. It's also important to note that her daughter is currently living in Amsterdam, is married, has children of her own, and has not been living in the U.S. for over 15 years.

The bottom line is that the things in storage have not been seen or used in many years.

As Robin was sharing the story, she became overwhelmed with grief and shame several times—to the point of breaking down in tears and crying so intensely that she was incapable of forming words. When she caught her breath, we did a simple math exercise—not to humiliate her but to gain clarity on exactly how much money she had already spent on this space and storing its contents. My hope was that, once the total amount she had spent became real and not some vague number easily forgotten except on the day her credit card was billed, the realization would prompt her into speedy action.

Here's the math: at $500 a month for 10 years and seven months, she had already spent $63,500–no small sum.

To stop this monthly drain, I suggested Robin take the following steps as quickly as possible:

1. Contact her daughter and have a frank conversation with her. Find out if the daughter cared about the things that were in storage, and based on that, take one of the following actions:
   a. If the daughter didn't care about the belongings, Robin should fly to New Orleans ASAP and arrange for some help to clear out the space and donate all of the contents.
   b. If the daughter did care about the contents, Robin should either go to New Orleans herself and FaceTime with the daughter as they went through the storage space remotely or offer to fly the daughter to New Orleans and meet her there so they could go through the space together over a long weekend and dispatch everything—meaning, select which things, if any, would get packed and shipped to Amsterdam and which could be let go.

By the end of the workshop, Robin had experienced a major mindset shift and was no longer despondent—she was eager and enthusiastic. She declared that she was looking forward to going home and contacting her daughter.

One month later, I got an email from Robin reporting that she had met her daughter in New Orleans three weeks after the workshop. After four long, surprisingly pleasant and not overly intense days, they had set aside some things that Robin paid to ship to Amsterdam, and the rest of the things had been donated to some local charities.

She shared that a tremendous weight and financial burden had been released along with all the accompanying stress and that it had also been a beautiful and powerfully intimate weekend with her daughter that had brought them closer than they had felt in many years.

The moral of this story is that regardless of how long you may have been avoiding something, once you decide to act, you can make tremendous progress in very little time and that your biggest fears may actually offer you your biggest opportunities.

Packing Your Stuff for Storage

If after all this, you still want to use self-storage, here are some suggestions to maximize this investment.

PACK YOUR BELONGINGS SMARTLY

Consider storing items inside clear bins instead of cardboard boxes. While cardboard boxes in climate-controlled spaces are okay to use and less expensive, plastic bins make it much easier to keep track of what's inside your storage unit. Unlike opaque cardboard boxes, clear plastic bins allow you to see what's inside a container without having to dig through it. This doesn't mean you don't also want to label each container.

Uniform-sized containers make stacking things much easier, so stick with bins of the same size whenever possible. Likewise, if you have a bunch of smaller, random-sized items, consider packing them in one larger container to help with stacking.

As you're packing, especially items that were in the kitchen, be sure to wipe away any food particles that could attract pests. Likewise, wipe away any moisture from anything that might have come from the bathroom, laundry room, basement, or other damp locations. Remove batteries from all electronics before you pack them. And always leave appliance doors slightly open once you've placed them in the space.

It might sound obvious, but put heavier items on the bottom of your containers, with your smaller and lighter things on top. This will help keep your belongings safe from any damage and allow for better stability when stacking.

Remember to make sure you can properly lift and move your containers once they're packed—particularly when working alone. You can't afford to injure yourself while trying to wrestle with a container that's too heavy or too large for you.

If you're using a portable moving container, like a PODS unit, things may shift in transit. So make sure fragile items are well wrapped and cushioned inside each container.

LABEL EVERYTHING

If you're using self-storage and unless it's to buy you some time to declutter, chances are you won't need the items you're packing up for at least a couple of months. And if you're using clear plastic tubs, you might think you don't need to label every box and container. But even if you have an amazing memory, you're probably going to forget what's in each container once everything is sealed up.

Labeling the containers also makes unpacking much easier, and it's also useful if you ever need to come in and grab something. The easiest way to label containers is to do so as you pack. Take pictures of the contents as well. This will help if there's an insurance claim down the line. Being able to show things well packed and protected and in perfect condition will go a long way in settling any disputes.

Label each container with the following details:

- The room the items belong in
- The contents of the container
- Whether it contains any delicate or fragile items that may dictate where the container goes

It's a good idea to ensure your labels are clear to read and understand, and that, when you're stacking items, they can be easily seen. So put labels on at least two sides of the container and also on the top (unless the container will go in a stack), and place one inside the container as well. Make sure at least one label on the container is facing outward so you can clearly see it when you're in the storage unit. You can use printed labels or a permanent marker to handwrite on labels.

DO NOT STORE VALUABLES

With the exception of fine art and antiques in premium storage spaces, do not store anything super valuable in these kinds of places. As a general rule, if you can't afford to lose it, you probably shouldn't be putting it in your storage unit. A majority of the time your belongings will be just fine and there's nothing to worry about, but self-storage always comes with a risk that items will get damaged or lost.

To be safe, find an alternative way to house fine art, antiques, jewelry, family heirlooms, and other valuable items, somewhere that is highly secure, elevated, and protected from theft as well as climate catastrophes.

Packing the Storage Unit

KEEP A WALKWAY

Even if you don't plan to take items in and out of self-storage regularly, leaving walkways so you can access items throughout your storage unit can save you a ton of trouble down the road.

Open aisles allow for easy maneuvering and take the hassle out of finding what you need when you need it. Stack your containers and belongings in a way that allows you to reach any corner of the space without having to move a lot of containers or heavy furniture out of the way first.

USE WOODEN PALLETS

Using wooden pallets to raise your items off the concrete floor helps keep air flowing throughout the storage unit. This is a great way to avoid moisture buildup that happens when items are sitting directly on the floor.

USE SHELVING AND RACKS

Storing shelves, a dresser, or other similar items? Put those items to work to help maximize the space in your storage unit. Even garbage and recycling bins can be used to store items. Don't let hollow space go to waste.

If you don't have any furniture that can get things up and off the floor, consider getting some sturdy shelves or storage racks to organize your unit. They can help you store any awkward items that don't quite fit in a container and help you make the most of your space, including the height of your unit.

ZONE THE SPACE

Keep your most frequently used items close to the door. Seasonal clothing (heavy coats, boots, hats, flip-flops, swimsuits), holiday items, and/or important documents should be stored near the front in well-labeled containers or bins so they're easily accessible.

Then, as you load things into the unit, arrange them according to category. Those categories should be based on their previous (and likely future) location within your home or office. Be sure to group similar items together.

After installing any shelving or racks, place large, heavy belongings toward the back of the storage unit. The heaviest and most bulky items should be placed against the walls and down low whenever possible.

Make use of small spaces by stuffing any gaps with smaller items. Ensure your belongings are packed in tightly to prevent damage and maximize the available space.

Remember that smaller and/or lighter containers should always be on the top of any stacks or shelves, although fragile items shouldn't be stacked too high. They should be well-protected on shelves.

USE THE FULL HEIGHT OF THE SPACE

When packing and organizing your storage unit, remember to go vertical with your belongings. Though a storage unit as small as a 5' × 5' has only 25 square feet of storage space, it has 200 cubic feet to work with.

Containers should be stacked high and furniture should be stored upright. Just make sure that no small containers are stored at the very top of the unit if it has no ceiling/roof and no secure fencing. Otherwise, you might end up with a shifty neighbor removing smaller items from over the top of the wall.

If the storage unit is particularly high, you may want to consider keeping a foldable ladder or step stool inside the unit with your belongings.

CREATE AN INVENTORY

When putting a lot of items in storage, it's difficult, if not impossible, to remember all of them. While large furniture pieces are easy to remember, smaller items such as mementos, artwork, photos, electronics, and clothes are often forgotten until you start unpacking.

To account for everything going into storage, create and maintain a list of all items inside the unit. A spreadsheet is the best tool for this, but if you'd prefer, you can certainly handwrite your list. Taking photos of stored items is also a great way to catalog what's in your storage unit. Be sure to save all photos and inventory descriptions in one place.

Once the space is loaded, draw a simple map for yourself of where each category of things is located inside your unit. This will save you (and anyone else who wasn't with you when you loaded the space) a lot of time when you want to put your hands on something fast.

USE PROTECTION

Don't leave items unprotected. You'll help prevent damage by properly packing and wrapping them. Furniture should be covered with blankets or moving pads (not plastic, which can trap moisture, resulting in mildew and mold), and anything small should be boxed up. Fragile items should be carefully wrapped in packing paper or Bubble Wrap and stored in a way that they can't move around.

Once everything is in place, you can also drape all of it with some drop cloths or dust sheets. Given the materials these buildings are constructed out of and how many things are moved in and out each day, it's not a bad idea to cover your stuff before you lock up.

INSURE YOUR UNIT AND BELONGINGS

Most large-scale storage unit companies require that their customers maintain adequate tenant insurance against loss or damage. This is to make sure everything inside your unit is safe and accounted for at all times. Having adequate storage-unit insurance will protect you in the unlikely event your belongings are compromised.

There are a few different ways you can attain coverage: use an applicable renter's insurance policy, add the storage unit to your homeowner's insurance, or purchase third-party insurance through the storage facility.

Start by checking to see if your renter's or homeowner's insurance will cover personal property in storage. If it doesn't, you may be able to add it on or purchase a separate storage insurance plan through your insurance company.

If you can't get coverage from your existing insurance company, you can often get coverage from the storage company. However, given how some insurance companies operate, this would be my last choice and probably should be yours as well. It would suck if there was a need for a claim, and you then had to fight with the insurance company to get them to pay.

So if you need to get coverage from the storage facility, be sure to do your research upfront and confirm the third-party vendor is reputable, reliable, and has a strong history of making good on claims.

KNOW WHAT YOU CAN AND CAN'T
PUT INTO STORAGE

It would seem obvious, but don't store anything perishable. You should not pack anything in your unit that could spoil. In addition to the smell, rotting food and plants could attract bugs, rodents, and other pests—none of which you want in your unit or in your things.

Make sure you know what you can and can't store, such as flammable, hazardous, or corrosive materials, or live animals. Be sure to check the guidelines of the storage facility *before* you move in.

ASK FOR HELP

Moving things in and out of storage is still a move, and it can be difficult to tackle it on your own. Get help from friends, family members, professional organizers, or freelance workers, especially if you're loading heavy items or stacking things up high. An extra set of hands will always make the process run smoother and faster and reduce any risk of injury when lifting furniture or other heavy things.

Check to see what, if any, additional amenities, such as free moving trucks, dollies, or packing materials, may be available from your storage facility. You never know unless you ask. Some facilities offer moving-in bonuses such as free or discounted rates, too.

PROTECT YOUR KEYS AND ACCESS CODES

Be mindful of who you share your key or access code with. Always use your best judgment, and never allow someone into your unit unless you already know and trust them around your belongings. It sounds convenient to send a freelance helper to your storage unit, but people with bad intentions are everywhere, including on websites advertising day labor. Carefully vet anyone before hiring them, and unless it's a person you know and trust, you shouldn't be letting anyone in.

GET THE BEST LOCK YOU CAN AFFORD

Just like good fences make good neighbors, a strong lock is critical to securing your unit. If you're buying the lock directly from the storage facility, spend a little more to get the sturdiest lock you can afford—one that can't be easily tampered with. Even storage facilities with cameras and on-site staff can't monitor everything, so to prevent someone from gaining access to your stuff, put a strong, secure lock on your unit. It'll be one less thing to worry about.

UNDERSTAND INDOOR VERSUS OUTDOOR STORAGE

Unless you're storing heavy machinery or other things typically used outside like a car, tractor, or tools, *or* you're in a very dry and temperate location and only using storage for a short time, meaning three weeks or less, you're going to want climate-controlled indoor storage. The only benefit of an outdoor storage unit, besides the price, is the convenience of being able to drive right up to it.

NOTABLE NOTE

If you have storage off-site right now and you are ready to address it, schedule a trip there with a friend or two to start sorting through the contents. Bring some containers and trash bags, and decide what's going back to your house, what's going home with your friends, and what's going to a local thrift store or charity. If you need to do this in stages, consider each trip a chance to whittle away at the contents, moving yourself into smaller and smaller units with each subsequent trip until that last visit when the unit is empty.

7

CAR

If all the cars in the United States were placed end to end, it would probably be Labor Day weekend.
–DOUG LARSON

Take care of your car in the garage, and the car will take care of you on the road.
–AMIT KALANTRI

WHAT WE'RE GOING TO COVER IN THIS CHAPTER

- What a Car Is and Isn't
- What Belongs in a Car and What Doesn't
- One Home for Everything and Like with Like (on Wheels!)
- Organizing the Car
- Maintaining Order on Four Wheels
- Dead or Mortally Wounded Cars and Their Final Destination (Which Isn't Your Lawn)
- Procrastinated Repairs, or Driving on Borrowed Time
- License and Registration, Please
- Traveling and Road Trips
- Checklist before a Trip

IN THE LAST CHAPTER, we talked about the car's home, the garage. Now we're turning our attention to the car itself.

Whether you own, lease, rent, or rideshare, there are many reasons you spend so much time in cars. You commute for work, for play, to visit family and friends, and to take vacations. If you do not live in a small town or large city where walking, biking, and public transportation are viable options, chances are you are spending time—considerable time—in a private vehicle.

For those who drive to work in the United States, the nationwide average commuting time is now about 55 minutes each day. That means that the average American now spends more than 330 hours a year commuting to work.[5] Think about it—that's nearly 14 days a year spent just getting to and from work. I'm already exhausted typing it, let alone living it.

Wherever you live, if getting to and from work means driving a car, you're in that car for a while. Add into the mix that even the biggest vehicle (a Hummer, 87 cubic feet) is still smaller than most people's homes (3,200 cubic feet). So managing this limited space is even more challenging in some ways than tackling clutter in the home.

In such a small space, it would certainly make driving easier, safer, and more pleasant to only have the things you need—and anytime you're a passenger, to get in and out of the car without leaving anything behind.

---

5   Jack Flynn, "15+ Average Commute Time Statistics (2023): How Long Is the Average American Commute?," Zippia, February 13, 2023, https://www.zippia.com/advice/average-commute-time-statistics/.

WHAT A CAR IS AND ISN'T

Automobile (noun): A self-propelled passenger vehicle that usually has four wheels and an internal combustion engine; used for land transport

So that's what your car is.

Your car is not a rolling filing cabinet, portable closet, phone booth, library, hobby center, "date magnet," snack shop, head shop, vanity, or cosmetics counter in a department store—it's a vehicle used for land transport. Driving is a privilege and comes with rights and responsibilities. We'll get deeper into what should *not* be happening in your car a little further on.

If you consider your car to be an extension of yourself, meaning its purpose beyond transportation is to signify to others something about your personality, status, or rank, does that carry over to the car's contents?

- Do you consider your car to be an extension of your handbag, knapsack, or briefcase? Or your office?
- Are there schoolbooks or library books on the floor or seats?
- Do you carry work documents on the seats and/or in the trunk—not just when you're on your way to a particular meeting, but always, just in case?
- Do you have cosmetics stuffed into the glove compartment or between the seat cushions?
- Have you ever not offered a ride to someone because of the clutter in your car?
- Have you ever parked farther away from your destination than necessary to avoid having people see you exiting your car?

If you do not have blackout windows, any person passing your car on the street or in a parking lot can see into your car and assess its current state. Your secret, therefore, is not so secret. The solution is not to race out and get blackout film applied to your windows. The solution is to clean out your car once and for all and to organize its contents in a systematic way so you can find exactly what you are looking for in 30 seconds or less.

When it comes to doing this, it's helpful to think in terms of zones with specific areas of focus and function. We'll get into what these zones are in a little bit. For now, let's look at what should and should not live in your car.

WHAT BELONGS IN A CAR AND WHAT DOESN'T

There are plenty of things that are helpful to have in a car and many things that are not so useful. Visit unstuffbook.com/car or refer to the companion workbook for a checklist of things you may want in your car, things you may currently have in your car, and things you should probably remove from your car.

NOTABLE NOTE

Your insurance card and your vehicle registration should be kept on your person, not in your glove compartment. Find a place in your wallet to keep them.

Many insurance companies and car professionals agree— these are not things you'd want a thief to have if your car were ever stolen. Do not let optimism or laziness lull you into thinking you are exceptional in this regard—a vehicle is stolen approximately every 32 seconds in the United States.[6]

You must carry these two pieces of paper at all times when driving your car. You may make additional copies to give to other people who often use your car as well. Failure to produce these documents if you are ever pulled over by the police likely means a fine and a hassle, especially if you're involved in an accident.

6   National Insurance Crime Bureau, "New Report Shows Full-Size Trucks Have Highest Theft Rate," news release July 27, 2023, https://www.nicb.org/news/news-releases/new-report-shows-full-size-trucks-have-highest-theft-rate/.

Work Product in the Car

Whether you're a digital nomad, real estate agent, or other traveling worker, there are plenty of reasons why you'd have printed materials like brochures, samples, displays, and even lawn signs in your car. Any materials you do keep in your car should be containerized and organized so you can easily find what you're looking for when you need it. One thing you shouldn't still have in your car is a box of stuff you emptied from your desk at your last job.

A Few Words about Trash

If you have purchased food from a convenience store or fast-food restaurant, that food probably came in a bag of some kind. A simple way to deal with food trash in the car is to put any food wrappers, napkins, etc. back into the bag they came in when you are finished eating. This is also a good time to collect any other trash lying around the car.

The next time you exit the car, take the bag with you and deposit it in the first trash receptacle you see. No more trash in the car.

Please, for the sake of others, never throw trash out of a car window onto the side of the road. Never spit gum out onto the sidewalk, and the same goes for cigarette butts. We all share the world outside our homes, and it's common courtesy to put any unfinished food, gum, wrappers, popsicle sticks, cigarette butts, empty packages, and bottles or cans in the nearest receptacle rather than leaving a trail of trash behind you. If you're littering, you're unconscious and need to wake up. Please do so—you'll benefit and so will the rest of us.

ONE HOME FOR EVERYTHING AND LIKE WITH LIKE (ON WHEELS!)

Because cars have limited space, these two principles are essential to getting and keeping your car organized. Look for and gather together like items, and assign each of these groupings a home. Use frequency of use and ease of access to guide you in selecting each home.

ORGANIZING THE CAR

If you are doing this alone, an area near your home (driveway, parking lot, or at the curb) is the best place to do this. If you have someone with you who can watch your stuff, a car wash is another excellent place to empty your car and get it organized. That way, you can run it through the wash while the other person keeps an eye on your belongings. A mild, sunny day that is not too windy is your best choice for this activity—you don't want the weather to interrupt your process once you begin.

Step 1: Empty the Car of Its Contents

Things you'll need for this task:
- Bins/tubs (8)
- Bucket of soapy water or other cleanser
- Cleaning rags, sponges, or cloths
- Smartphone
- Clear 9" x 12" envelopes or pocket folders
- Ziplock bags
- Tarp
- Trash bag (or several)
- Vacuum cleaner

By now, this should be familiar, if not easy. Make sure you have all the items listed on hand before you start this process. If you don't have them assembled, put down the book and go get them—we don't want to interrupt the flow because of a missing component.

Great. Now open the tarp and spread it out. Open a trash bag and set it aside.

Before you remove anything, take a few photos to document the current state of your car. Open and photograph the trunk as well, especially if there's chaos in there.

Now begin removing everything that isn't actually a part of the car and lay it all out on the tarp to examine. Avoid placing things in piles or clumps or stacks for now. When we begin sorting and arranging, you'll group items Like with Like.

For now, throw away any trash as you remove it from the car—trash is one thing we don't need to sort through. If you need a refresher on what exactly trash is, see the definition below:

> An unwanted or undesired material or substance; broken, discarded, or worthless things; also referred to as rubbish, waste, garbage, or junk, depending on the type of material and regional terminology

Any items you find that originated in your home (coffee mugs, water bottles, reusable food storage containers) should be set inside a bin or tub to return to your home.

Be sure to empty out

- any roof compartments,
- ashtrays,
- behind the visors,
- cubbies,
- cup holders,
- door pockets,
- glove compartment,
- rear cargo areas,
- rear-of-seat pockets,
- trunk, and
- under the seats.

Now would be an excellent time to clean and vacuum the interior and possibly wash the exterior of your car. Start with cleaning all the interior surfaces. Vacuum between all the seats and their backs, between cushions, and under every seat. Remove, shake out, and vacuum all floor mats. Fold down any foldable seats to get deeper into seldom-reached areas. Wipe down the dashboard and inside any cubbies and compartments; wipe down all the doors and clean the windows. When that is done, we'll begin the sorting.

Step 2: Sort

These are the categories you're going to sort everything into:
- Emergency Needs
- Maintenance
- Travel and Comfort Aids
  - » Winter
  - » Kids
- Work Product
- Going Away—Keep
- Going Away—Donate

Refer to the lists in your companion workbook or that you downloaded at unstuffbook.com/car for examples of which items belong in each category. Remember to apply Like with Like so that all adapters end up together, all tools together, all service and repair receipts together, etc.

The Going Away category has two parts: Keep is for anything that still has a purpose but doesn't belong in your car. And Donate is for things that still have a purpose but no longer belong in your life. Items in Keep will end up someplace in your home or your garage, and Donate things will be given away to become a part of someone else's life.

Just like with trash before, anything that can easily be culled from the former contents of your car at this time should be. If you see that you have four flashlights, test them all, find the ones that work, choose the best one for the car, and set the other three aside. For anything that you need to think about, it's fine right now to just group Like with Like and wait for the next section to begin whittling down the number of things. It will become apparent soon enough that you have things you can let go of when you see them all grouped together.

Step 3: Purge

As you did for your kitchen, think about how you use your car:

- Do you work from it—are you a digital nomad, salesperson, regional rep, or real estate agent?
- Do you shuttle kids all day in it?
- Do you volunteer for Meals on Wheels or use it for other kinds of deliveries?
- What are you regularly reaching for and not able to put your hands on—mobile phone, pen and paper, sunglasses, etc.?

Touch everything. Physical contact is important as it shifts your relationship from hypothetical to actual. This is not a step to avoid. If you make yourself touch each item as you're going through the piles, you will be clearer as you determine what is necessary to have with you in your car versus what you think may be fun or useful to "someday" have in your car.

Things that are obsolete or outdated can leave. If you have work product in the car, realistically assess if you have enough for the next few weeks or the next few years. How many chargers do you need? How often do you hand out brochures? How many lawn signs do you need right now? If you're not even working today, perhaps those lawn signs can live in the garage until you *actually* need them?

Recognize the faulty logic in thinking that the more things that surround you, the better prepared you are for anything, should a situation suddenly come up. Unless you literally live in your car, you can't be in need of that much stuff for a day's outing. When taking a serious road trip, you would, of course, be packing things specifically for that trip. For day trips around town, you don't need a wilderness survival kit at your fingertips.

Pay attention to multiples of the same item—a bottle of water is a welcome addition. Random half-empty bottles, not so much. Likewise, you don't need multiple bungee cords, screwdrivers, etc.—if they aren't unique in size or shape, consider how many are necessary. And if you struggle with how to answer that question, I'll give you the answer: one. These items are already spares—you don't need spares of spares.

Anything that could still work but doesn't, such as flashlights missing batteries, can be set aside to either cure what needs curing or just let go of.

When purging, if you find yourself getting stuck or having conversations with yourself about how useful something might be "someday," then what you're struggling with does not belong in your car. This kind of debate is easily solved by using the junior version of the question "If your house was on fire, what would you grab?" In this case, if your car was on fire, what would you grab?

Ask yourself, *When was the last time I used this?* If the answer is either more than six months ago or never, it doesn't go back into the car. The welcome exceptions to this are, of course, emergency supplies and the first-aid kit. I hope you'll never need either, but you should always have both.

Whenever you have to spend time either debating or convincing yourself of something's ultimate usefulness, pay attention. Whether it's another abs exerciser or a third pair of sunglasses, if you have to really search for the answer, you already have your answer. It may not be the answer you want to hear, but it's there, and it's speaking as loudly and as clearly as it can. And what it's saying is, "Let me go."

Once you've set aside everything that doesn't need to be in your car, do not revisit those items. Don't second-guess yourself. Let them be, and turn your attention to organizing the remaining items so you'll be able to find them whenever you need or want them.

Step 4: Organize Everything That Remains

Now that we have our piles of Like with Like items, it's time to corral them. Enter the bins, tubs, or crates. If you find all the containers you've brought are too large, load things into them anyway. This will give you the best understanding of what size containers to replace them with. Then you can either find those containers inside your home or purchase the right-size containers for what you'll be carrying around in your car.

NOTABLE NOTE

Just as you keep only seasonal clothes in a closet, you don't need your winter kit of supplies for cold weather rattling around in your trunk all summer. Once this kit is assembled, containerize it, then store it someplace convenient so at the first hint of inclement weather, you can put it back in the car.

Here are the essential items you want in your winter kit:
- Snow brush
- Ice scraper
- Collapsible utility shovel
- Pet-friendly granulated de-icer and/or traction mat
- Spray windshield de-icer
- Two-gallon ziplock bag of kitty litter
- Low-temperature washer fluid
- Warm hat/cap
- Insulated gloves
- Warm socks
- Nonslip boots
- Lightweight down/down-alternative or heated blanket
- Body and hand warmers

Unfortunately, this works the opposite way as well. If you've overoptimistically brought a series of shoe boxes to this party and everything requires a laundry basket, you simply have too much stuff. Return to Step 3 and take another pass through your things.

Step 5: Reload the Car Using Zones

Now that everything is organized and containerized, you can start putting things back in the car. This is easy to do if you think of your car as having zones. Here is a list of the items you should put in each zone so they are accessible when you need them:

- Trunk
    - » Emergency needs
        - Road flares
        - Jumper cables
        - Portable car battery starter
        - Portable power bank and cables (in addition to any typically plugged into your console)
        - Flashlight
        - Tactical knife
    - » Maintenance items
    - » Bungee cords
    - » Camping gear (if you camp frequently)
    - » Cooler or other insulated container for groceries requiring refrigeration
    - » Tote bags and/or reusable shopping bags
    - » Old cloth towel (or two)
    - » Roll of paper towels
    - » Resealable ziplock bags (gallon, quart, and sandwich sizes)
    - » Sporting gear (if you are in a league or play weekly)
    - » Winter kit (for the duration of the cold-weather season where you live)
    - » Work product (if you frequently work out of your car)

- Under front passenger seat
  - First-aid kit
  - Emergency hammer
  - Window breaker
- Glove compartment
  - Owner's manual
  - Envelope with coupons (only for places you drive to)
  - Envelope with warranties, receipts, cheat sheet, etc.
- Driver's side visor
  - Garage door openers (if your car doesn't have a ceiling compartment for these)
- On the windshield
  - Toll-road transponder (behind rearview mirror)
- Seat-back pockets (or better yet, over-the-seat pocket organizers)
  - DVDs (if you have players in the car)
  - Kids' stuff (somewhere the child can get to quickly and without assistance)
- Door pockets
  - Napkins and tissues
  - Wet naps/baby wipes
  - Trash bags
  - Umbrella
- Center console
  - Phone chargers
  - Cradle for mobile phone
  - Bottle of water (or two)
  - Pen or pencil
  - Permanent marker
  - Pad of paper
  - Parking permits (as needed)
  - Seatbelt cutter

MAINTAINING ORDER ON FOUR WHEELS

Now that the car is clean and organized, how will you keep it that way? The best principle for this is: bring something in, take something out.

That is, if you bring something with you into the car, unless it needs to live in the car, take it with you when you leave. Keep a trash bag or small container handy, and use it rather than tossing trash on the floor or on the seat next to you.

All people who use or ride in the car are also to be responsible for removing what they bring into the car. If they fail to do so, let them know that items left behind for more than 48 hours will be considered abandoned and could be discarded.

These kinds of rules take a bit of time to establish, so once the rule is put in place, allow two weeks for learning and complying. After two weeks, no one can act surprised when they find you've kept your word.

Make it a habit to empty the car immediately when returning home from a sporting event or other activity involving gear, and it will soon become second nature. Don't allow items to pile up. Make a daily or weekly sweep through the car, searching for items out of their bins or needing to be returned to the house.

Empty the trash bag frequently. An easy time to do this is when stopping for gas or going shopping. Almost any store or mall you'll drive to also has trash receptacles outside—use them. Likewise, get into the habit of removing the trash when exiting the car at the end of the day and tossing it in the trash can at home. It's that much nicer to get into the car the next morning not faced with yesterday's or last week's garbage.

Plan a regular washing schedule. If your kids like to get wet and play with hoses, make it a family affair. You could add the incentive of paying them what you'd pay for a drive-through car wash if they need extra motivation. If the idea of washing the car yourself is unappealing, take the car to the local car wash—just make sure you've organized your things first. If the workers at yours are anything like the workers at mine, they're seldom interested in moving anything out of their way to vacuum beneath or around any obstacles.

DEAD OR MORTALLY WOUNDED CARS AND THEIR FINAL DESTINATION (WHICH ISN'T YOUR LAWN)

There are always local charities ready and willing to take dead or dying cars off people's hands. There are also junkyards and auto-parts places that may be willing to buy or haul your car away for parts.

In either case, if a car is no longer roadworthy or is beyond repair, don't clutter your yard or your neighborhood with dead vehicles. Pick up the phone and have it removed.

PROCRASTINATED REPAIRS, OR DRIVING ON BORROWED TIME

Besides keeping your car clean and neat, you'll also want to keep it running smoothly and efficiently and, therefore, safely. The car is a machine, and as such, it needs to be cared for and maintained in the ways that all machines need care and maintenance.

In your calendar, enter the date of the most recent services performed on your car. While many service providers now place a little plastic tag in the upper-left corner of the windshield as a reminder for your next oil change, other services can easily be overlooked until it's too late.

And take it from me, the time to respond to warning lights is when they first go on, not weeks later. When I was seventeen, I was driving a Plymouth Duster I got from my mom. It was a little top-heavy, as Dusters were, but it was a neat and clean car in excellent working condition.

The oil light went on one afternoon on my way home from school, but I didn't do anything about it. I saw that light every time I started the car and drove somewhere. I was young, and I figured I had plenty of time to eventually get around to it.

Fast-forward to an early evening several months later. I'm driving my friend Ann Ritchie and myself down to Cobo Hall to see Rod Stewart in concert. We are very excited. WRIF is playing back-to-back-to-back Rod Stewart songs, even old Faces songs, and we're having a great time anticipating the show.

About seven miles from the exit of the expressway, there's a sudden loud bang and the car shuts down. I manage to pull us over to the side of the road, out of the way of traffic, and open the hood. Lots of black smoke. Bewildering. What could possibly be the problem?

The state police pull up soon, and after explaining what had happened and where we are heading, in a stroke of luck, they decide to drive us down to Cobo Hall so we can make the show. And it was amazing. Rod Stewart was in rare form and good voice—for Rod Stewart. We had a great time. Of course, my father had to come down there at 11 p.m. to collect us. That was less of a good time.

The next day, the car was towed to a mechanic friend of my dad's who examined it and determined that a piston rod had been blown through the engine block of the car. Cause: insufficient oil. The car was totaled.

The cost of replacing the engine was more than I could afford or my dad was interested in spending. As the saying goes, "for want of a nail" or in my case, for want of a quart of oil. A painful and costly lesson learned.

NOTABLE NOTE

Anytime you have repairs done that come with a guarantee, make sure to keep the receipt and any printed warranty papers you receive. Store these in a clear envelope inside your glove compartment.

You may also take a picture, scan, or add a copy of these receipts and warranties to your home filing system, and if you are prone to misplacing things, a few digital and hard copy backups are a good idea. The key is to have a copy with you if your car ever breaks down while on the road—this ensures that any work covered by the warranty will be completed with few questions or fuss. While dealing with the inconvenience of an interrupted trip, you don't also want to deal with less-than-helpful staff trying to verify your claim for warranted coverage.

LICENSE AND REGISTRATION, PLEASE

As mentioned earlier, always have the registration and insurance card with you when driving your car. It's a good idea to add reminders to your calendar for the renewal dates for your vehicle's inspection and registration. I set these reminders for four to six weeks prior to the actual expiration date, which gives me ample time to take the car in if an inspection is needed and still get the new materials back in the mail.

In some states, registration and inspection run concurrently according to month—however, a vehicle's registration is often renewed for multiples of years whereas the inspection is due each year. Check with your local DMV or secretary of state's office to avoid a ticket for lapsed inspection because you assumed that everything renewed at the same time.

TRAVELING AND ROAD TRIPS

I always pack the night before any trips and stack everything by the door, so I know I'll never walk out of the house without everything I planned to take with me. I even stack my empty refillable water bottle on my bag so I remember to fill it up before I walk out of the door.

It's a good idea to check traffic and weather reports before you leave and download any maps or directions while you're on Wi-Fi so you'll have them on your phone. If you're going on an extended trip, review your emergency kit and make sure everything is fully stocked and up to date.

Make any important phone calls *before* you get in your car to avoid unnecessary distractions while driving, particularly if there's any chance you could be upset by the call. You don't want to get overly emotional while trying to pay attention to the road.

CHECKLIST BEFORE A TRIP

Go to unstuffbook.com/car or refer to your companion workbook for a handy checklist you can use a week before your trip to make sure everything for your car is in good working order. That will give you enough time for any necessary repairs. You don't want procrastinating on any repairs to delay your departure.

You can also find there a cheat sheet for all the basic information you need for your car, including VIN, tire size, oil weight and type, and most recent service appointments.

8

SENTIMENTAL OBJECTS • GIFTS • COLLECTIONS

Souvenirs are perishable; fortunately, memories are not.
–SUSAN SPANO

Sentimentality—that's what we call the sentiment we don't share.
–GRAHAM GREENE

Most of those who make collections . . . are like men eating
cherries or oysters: they choose out the best at first,
and end by eating all.
–NICOLAS CHAMFORT

WHAT WE'RE GOING TO COVER IN THIS CHAPTER

- Mementos, Sentimental Objects, Gifts, and Collections: What They Are and Aren't
- One Home for Everything and Like with Like
- Sentimentaland
- If You Visit It, You Will Bring Me Home: Travel Mementos, Part I
- Departed Relatives and Friends, Part III: From Houston to Heaven
- Good Gifts, Bad Gifts
- I Am My Own Museum
- Collections—Cool or Crazy?
- Will You Hate Me If I Get Rid of . . . ?
- This Might Be Worth a Fortune—*Antiques Roadshow* or Thrift Store?
- Dry Storage Versus Wet Storage (Reminder)
- Approaching Sorting and How to Sort
- Actually Sorting
- Containerizing the Objects
- The Importance of Labels—How, Why, and Where
- Organizing the Storage
- Maintaining the System

IN THIS CHAPTER we turn our attention to conceptual clutter as opposed to location-specific clutter. The subjects of this chapter—mementos, sentimental objects, gifts, and collections (and by extension, decor)—are the kinds of things you may find all over your home. When on display, they are a matter of taste. When lying in piles, unsorted, underfoot, or in the way, they are clutter. Learn to tell the difference, to honor one and safely store or discard the other.

Things You Will Need for This Work

- Trash bags
- Timer or stopwatch
- Eight tarps or blankets for sorting items into categories
- Dust cloths
- Acid-free paper
- Noninvasive adhesives (tapes, glues, etc.)
- Tubs, containers, or baskets to corral and contain like things
- Label maker or labels and a fine-point marker

MEMENTOS, SENTIMENTAL OBJECTS, GIFTS, AND COLLECTIONS: WHAT THEY ARE AND AREN'T

Mementos and Sentimental Objects

Memento (noun): An object or item that serves to remind one of a person, past event, etc.; keepsake; souvenir

Sentimental (adjective): Having or showing tender, gentle, or delicate feelings as in aesthetic expression; having or showing such feelings in an excessive, superficial, or maudlin way

A memento could be just about anything from a Roman Catholic relic to an old soda-pop cap and everything in between. And sentimentalism can range from heartwarming to harmful. In fact, later in this chapter, you'll read a cautionary tale of what sentiment can morph into when indulged in the worst ways.

Because of this, I encourage clients to retain sentimental objects and mementos in a focused and disciplined way—almost as if distilling the memory or experience and charging the item with clear intention. In cooking, we work to reduce the sauce with steady heat, but in this case, we reduce using steady focus so that the objects selected to hold the memory are saturated with the experience rather than it being thinly spread out over many random objects. The idea is to discriminate in the best sense of the word.

When sorting through sentimental objects and mementos, find a quiet place where you won't be disturbed as you examine them. Set aside a comfortable length of time, between 15 minutes and two hours. If you struggle to stay focused for 15 minutes uninterrupted, set the timer for less time. If you need to get up and walk around or fidget as you're working to stay engaged, do whatever it takes.

This is deep work, and you want to be able to go wherever you need to go to get clarity and make smart choices. As a rule, barring

ADHD or other neurodivergences, 15 minutes is a good starting point. But brain science tells us that after two hours, we tend to lose focus,[7] so it's best not to work past that threshold.

Beyond that, as long as you're using the timer to keep time rather than any part of your brain, work for as long as you can make thorough and thoughtful decisions. The key is to remain sharp, undistracted, and productive for the entire allotted time.

So pick an amount of time, set your timer, and work for that duration. When the timer goes off, even if you find yourself on a roll, finish the last piece, clump, pile, or area you're working through and take a break. If you want to then reset the timer and dig back in, great. And if not, you're finished until the next time. It's always better to be pleasantly surprised and looking forward to sorting than cranky and exhausted and watching the clock.

When working with sentimental objects, you don't want to stray into reminiscing. It's dangerous territory and a slippery slope. A certain amount of reverie is acceptable and expected, but the time to linger is on the other side of the sorting process.

As you're sitting still and reviewing these items, really imagine yourself going through this same tub in another 20 years. What do you think you'll want to be handling at that time? Old chewing gum (really, food in any form) is inappropriate as a souvenir. Ditto for dirty clothing; while the smell of someone on a worn garment may seem evocative today, in 20 years their sweet aroma will turn sour—not to mention how body oils and perspiration accelerate the discoloration and deterioration of most fabrics.

It's a mistake to idealize any object, elevating it above the actual memory. Too often, we charge the object with so much responsibility for holding complex and extended memories that the object's significance becomes distorted. As a result, our ability to actually remember events and people can fade without the object present.

---

7 "Brain Focus and Concentration Problems," LifeSeasons, https://lifeseasons.com/glossary/brain-focus-and-concentration-problems/.

And of course, any object can get lost or broken at any time, and it would be a drag for the memory or memories to disappear along with the object.

Also, I strongly suggest that any item that evokes maudlin feelings or hurtful memories be discarded. Promptly. There's no need to sustain that form of grief.

Gifts

Gift (noun): Something given voluntarily without payment in return as to show favor toward someone, honor an occasion, or make a gesture of assistance

I do not believe in obligatory gift-giving—it contradicts the very definition of a gift. I'm not a grinch, but I strongly believe that nothing freely given is ever meant to be a burden. If you receive anything that feels imposing or awkward or comes with strings attached, I suggest that you respectfully decline the offer whenever possible.

If that's not possible for any number of reasons, which we'll discuss later on in the chapter, release the "gift" as soon as possible. You may regift it to someone who has no relationship with the original giver or donate it. Either way, cut the strings and set it free from any negative associations.

Collections and Decor

Collection (noun): Something that is collected; a group of objects or an amount of material accumulated in one location, especially for some purpose or as a result of some process: a stamp collection; a collection of books on Lewis and Clark

Decor (noun): Decoration consisting of the layout and furnishings of a livable interior

They say that beauty is in the eye of the beholder. Nowhere is this more evident than in one's taste in decor. I am not a big fan of collections of objects as decor. They seldom reflect a strong curatorial vision and, as a rule, typically devolve into clutter. There are exceptions to all rules, this one included, and the best examples of standing exceptions include most museums and libraries where collections are both actively curated and consistently revolving. We'll explore both of these concepts as they relate to collections later in the chapter.

ONE HOME FOR EVERYTHING AND LIKE WITH LIKE

These two legs of The Organizational Triangle are your foundation for getting organized, *particularly* with sentimental objects and mementos. I cannot stress this enough. These principles should be rigorously and consistently employed, not saved for special occasions. One Home for Everything and Like with Like ensure that when you need to find something, anything, you have to look in only one place, and there it will be together with all of its siblings.

SENTIMENTALAND

In previous chapters, we created the virtual place called Sentimentaland, which exists in our imaginations as well as in a number of tubs and bins. Here again is the definition:

> Sentimentaland is a mythical land defined by clear plastic tubs containing objects of dubious monetary value but that are ultimately priceless to you.

As we've worked through other areas, we've uncovered various things that ultimately belonged in Sentimentaland. Now, with our focus directed specifically on mementos and sentimental objects, Sentimentaland is about to become far more populated.

It's possible that you'll need more than one container for Senti-mentaland before you're done with your entire home and this chapter. That's okay. The containers just all need to live together, and we need to ensure that their contents are consistent. Never mix general things still needing a home with meaningful touchstones of life's important moments. Like with Like!

The ultimate location of these Sentimentaland containers is open to negotiation. You may store them in a closet, the basement or attic, under the stairs—anywhere you have room, provided that it's some-place climate-controlled. Sentimentaland, like everything in Goldi-locks's world, wants to avoid extremes of too hot or too cold; we want the temperature to be just right.

While Sentimentaland is a country without borders, it does have a few laws. There are only two of them, so they shouldn't be too chal-lenging to obey.

Sentimentaland Laws

LIKE WITH LIKE

It's everywhere! Here it means, for example, that all baby clothes and other childhood artifacts reside together. If you still retain your own baby clothes in addition to the clothes of your children, they should be further subdivided by child or generation.

What I typically suggest is that each child be given their own con-tainer so that childhood art, report cards, crib blankets, stuffed animals, and the like can all remain together, and that each child's stuff is not com-mingled, requiring later sorting. Think of these as time capsules carefully and lovingly curated by you for yourself, your children, or both.

WHEN EVERYTHING IS PRECIOUS, NOTHING IS PRECIOUS

In curating these items, you'll select what will ultimately be kept. This process is highly personal and subjective, and it should reflect what you value as both memories and history. No doubt you'll remember which outfits most amused you and tormented your child. Likewise, you'll hopefully be able to identify the artwork that heralded nascent genius versus the scribbling that expressed core rage at being cut off from another juice box.

You get to decide what is significant and what is not significant. Relax, though. It won't be that difficult. When sorting through things, you'll be amazed at how what's important will assert itself. If, years later, you can still giggle at a memory simply by handling a tiny shirt or pair of shorts, you'll have your answer. You really only have to stay present and pay attention. Like most things, showing up is the most important piece of the work.

Remembering that *you cannot keep everything* will help you make strong and confident choices. It's helpful to leverage the following concept if that ever feels constrictive or limiting: When everything is precious, nothing is precious. Museums are the only places where everything is precious, and no one wants to live there. Most of us get sleepy after only a few hours in one, and the only furniture you can sit on is typically a bench without a backrest. It's just this simple—special things lose their specialness when there are too many of them.

Also recognize that this is mostly an exercise for you—your kids either have already rescued the things that are most important to them or will be pleasantly surprised by whatever you've kept from their childhood since they were busy living it. Iris's story in Chapter 6 illustrates a few examples of this process.

NOTABLE NOTE

I've talked a lot about childhood and childhood artifacts because, for parents, this is often the most difficult category of objects to sift through and select from. The Sentimentaland laws in this chapter apply to all objects—yours as well as your children's. Old baseball cards, concert tickets and playbills, T-shirts, sports equipment, Christmas decorations, school textbooks and class notes, journals and diaries, games and toys . . . the list is seemingly infinite. Every grouping of sentimental objects can benefit from careful editing.

One of the benefits of creating these tubs is to corral and preserve these items. If they remain in a jumbled heap, you will be less likely to find something if and when you want it, and the contents are less likely to be properly maintained or protected.

IF YOU VISIT IT, YOU WILL BRING ME HOME: TRAVEL MEMENTOS, PART I

Trips away from home exploring the world can be some of the most memorable events in our lives. And reflecting on them when we are back home is a great way to relive those adventures. Sometimes, we use physical objects to trigger those memories, but scientists suggest that smell is actually the most influential sense for evoking stored memories. Keep this in mind when choosing which mementos you will collect, making sure that they are specific and evocative enough to be worth bringing home.

One simple guideline I find helpful is to document the event, not the approach or preparation. Simply put, the sandwich was special, not the wrapper that it came in. Free maps and brochures from tourist centers are printed every day, so they probably aren't worth keeping.

Instead, consider what was unique about *your* trip. Find that, and *that's* the souvenir to hold on to, not a random empty envelope from some hotel. If the hotel is a place you'd like to stay again, add it to your notes or contacts, then recycle the envelope.

Use this decision-making process as a guide for future travel and adventures as well. Avoid mass-produced junk, and instead, seek out local curiosities so each memento is something specific and meaningful for you. Did you stumble upon a funky dive somewhere and decide it was the perfect place to propose marriage? That's the site of something special—keep the matchbook or coaster from there. A disposable paper cup or T-shirt from Walt Disney World is something anyone could have brought home—and probably has.

NOTABLE NOTE

I'm all for photos from trips and travels, but I also find that many people spend so much time documenting everything that the first time they actually experience having been away is when they get home and look back at their photos! By then, the experience is over, and all they're left with are the artifacts from it.

Put your phone or camera down and explore, experience, and drink up the adventure while having the adventure—you'll have more interesting stories to share when you get home than can be conveyed in even a stellar slideshow put on for friends and family.

DEPARTED RELATIVES AND FRIENDS, PART III: FROM HOUSTON TO HEAVEN

Now to inherited things—including broken clocks, chipped dishes, and the like. For whatever reason, however it happened, these things are now in your possession. Things you love, things you use—these are not the issue. Things you love that don't work or are broken, things you love but don't use, and things you don't love and don't use—all of these *are* the issue.

Let's start with the last one first.

Things You Don't Love and Don't Use

Simply put, let them go.

The fact that a family member once owned an object is never a good enough reason to keep it. You are not the family archivist—if your family is that significant in historical terms, find a historian or archivist who can advise you about what belongs in a museum or archive.

If you are not from a storied or notable family, find the family member who actually wants the role of preserving history, and if no one does, *pay attention to that*. You don't have to take it on by default.

You're not a bad child, parent, or sibling for not wanting to keep and store things that you don't like or can't use. They are only objects, even if Grandma traveled from the old country with it strapped to her back. She chose to do so for her own reasons, not to saddle you with it 100 years later. If it has some actual value, consider selling it online or through an auction house. If not, donate it, and the charitable organization can liquidate it.

Things You Love But Don't Use

Waiting for "someday"? As mentioned in Chapter 6, if these items are charged with emotional tugs and memories, it's important to allow enough time to go through them, whether it's one box or an entire household. Consider enlisting an impartial and disciplined friend or professional for support and guidance.

Ask yourself, *Why am I keeping things that I don't or won't use?*

Are you afraid of damaging them, thereby diminishing their value? As an example, let's look at antique sterling silverware. You always run the risk of someone cleaning them improperly or accidentally dropping a piece down the drain and turning on the garbage disposal. Things happen.

If the monetary value of the silver is the most important thing to you, then perhaps you should consider selling the set and using the money to buy something you wouldn't be afraid to use. Or pass it along as a gift or trade it with another family member who has something you *do* cherish and would use.

Given that financial and secondary markets are unpredictable—including fine art, antiques, and precious metals—it seems imprudent to hold onto the silverware, hoping that it will hold its value or even appreciate while sitting in a closet somewhere. There are smarter ways to handle things of value.

Or perhaps you're not using something because you're afraid doing so will speed its decay. The truth is, it will. If you use antique linens, for example, they will eventually fall apart—but probably not tomorrow. Fabric, in particular, is remarkably strong and resilient unless it's dry-rotted, in which case it's already ruined, you just don't know it yet.

Gandhi told his followers to imagine that *anything* broken, even if it was brand-new, was at the end of its usefulness, as this was its natural life cycle. He felt that by doing this, the preciousness of any item was dispelled. And if you were in touch with the inevitable end from the very beginning, when that end finally occurred, it wouldn't be a surprise.

It's a good point.

Lovely things are lovely. And doing one's best to keep them that way is appropriate. But denying yourself the use of lovely things to preserve them for future, perhaps unknown generations seems sad and pointless, despite what the Patek Philippe ads say to the contrary ("You never actually own a Patek Philippe. You merely look after it for the next generation.").

So if you find yourself the steward of beautiful heirlooms, use them. Celebrate the fact that the people who came before you acquired something so durable and enduring. And in passing these things down to you, they must have wanted you to use them, too, creating another generation's memories in the process.

Things You Love That Don't Work or Are Broken

Meet Laurie. And her father's broken clock. From as far back as she could remember, Laurie's dad had a small mantel clock on his desk. It took pride of place at the center of the rear edge of his desk. So whenever she would visit him in his study, the clock was there—solid, reliable, warm, and steady. Just like her dad.

It's now many years later. Laurie's father has passed away. And the clock no longer keeps time. The hands are loose and don't move, and the internal workings are frozen. She even took the clock to several watchmakers hoping to get it restored, but each horologist confirmed that the clock was beyond repair. Laurie was disappointed and emotionally stuck.

Laurie is an in-demand educator and trainer with high EQ. She is also extremely practical, so she typically doesn't keep broken or unusable things around. Her things are either working, being repaired, or discarded.

But this was her father's clock. Getting rid of it would be like getting rid of her dad. At least, that's how she felt. So, in an eerie and unsettling way, the broken clock sat on the credenza behind *her* desk now.

Andrew Mellen: So, Laurie, tell me about the clock.

Laurie: It was my dad's.

[She tells me about learning to tell time on the clock, the pipe that used to sit in a stand next to the clock, and the great conversations she would have with her father in his study underscored by the gentle rhythmic ticking of the clock.]

AM: Wow. Lots of memories.

Laurie: Yeah. That clock was always there, keeping time.

AM: Yep. It sounds even more like your dad was always there, keeping time. Steady and reliable, and now he's not around, either. Does that sound accurate?

Laurie: But it's the last thing I have of his. I can't let it go. I mean, there's a part of me that totally wants to let it go, but it feels like too much of a betrayal.

AM: I know it feels that way, but I want you to know that letting the clock go isn't the same thing as letting your dad go. Your dad is not the clock, and of course the clock is not your father. You had great times with your dad, in and out of that study. Those memories are not, will not be, diminished by the absence of this clock. I'd like you to consider a few things.

One, it's possible that in holding on to the clock—which if it had not been your dad's would have left a long time ago—you're actually idealizing the clock, charging it with the responsibility of holding all your memories of your dad. And you could be scared that if you let it go, then all the memories will leave with it, too.

Maybe you can first release the clock from carrying all that weight, and that will open up other ways for you to remember and celebrate your dad. How else can you evoke a memory of him? Maybe through a favorite book or meal or song?

And two, when you shift the focus off the broken clock, take some time to reconnect with the person you're missing. What do miss about him, when do you miss him, what are the conversations you may still be having with him? This will let you move back into your powerful imagination and memory to spend time with your dad there—all the great times you had with him.

None of those memories or images can be diminished or altered by whether the clock is here or not. In fact, you could take it a step further and choose not to reduce them all down to a broken clock, which, both literally and metaphorically, doesn't even work. We both know the clock is definitely not your dad—he's so much more. Why not let him be more than a broken clock?

Laurie: It just bums me out that it doesn't work, that I can't get it working.

AM: I know.

Laurie: And I would have let it go if it hadn't been his.

AM: I know.

Laurie: Ugh. [pausing] He's not the clock, is he?

AM: Nope, that's for sure. He is not the clock.

Laurie: He's not the clock. I love him, and he's not the clock. He is not the clock. [pausing] Okay. Let's let it go, I'm ready, I'm done. I'm done with the clock. The clock that doesn't work. My dad is not a broken clock.

AM: Excellent. Good work, my friend. Really good. Congratulations.

If you, like Laurie, find yourself caught between guilt and releasing a treasured object, consider taking a picture of the object in question as a step in the letting-go process. As you journey toward releasing the actual object, the photo can be a way to soften the transition for you. You can look at the photo as a touchstone and active reminder of your process.

And once you do decide to let the photographed object go, you can choose to keep the photo—that way, you can still see the object, but it takes up a fraction of the space occupied by the original item.

If you decide to try this out, make sure the photos are in focus and well lit. And if you like art projects or scrapbooking, the photos might even find their way into a new piece of artwork.

Things You Love and Use

Bravo! The only issues that might arise around these items are where they live and whether they are living with their sisters and brothers. For these items, it just comes down to One Home for Everything and Like with Like.

GOOD GIFTS, BAD GIFTS

Nothing freely given is ever meant to be a burden. Gifts are an expression of someone's appreciation, recognition of a significant event or that event's anniversary, or a token of affection. They are not offered, and should not be offered, as a punishment or a pointed reminder of what you should or should not be doing. A framed photo of someone suffering from mouth cancer given to someone who smokes is not a gift—it's an assault.

When these kinds of gifts are from a relative, a colleague, or someone you see regularly, social custom requires you to accept the gift graciously, but you are under no obligation to retain the "gift" a moment longer than absolutely necessary. Get rid of it as soon as possible.

Any object that causes you pain, grief, regret, embarrassment, disappointment, or any other form of debilitating sorrow has no place in your life. There is a clear distinction between torment and the bittersweet sadness we feel when remembering certain past tender moments. *That* sadness is colored by the absence of a particular time or a loved one; it's not the sorrow I'm describing here. One feels aggressive and abusive and the other is a natural result of intense feelings of loss or separation.

Short of veiled criticism or judgment arriving in the form of a gift, let's assume that most gifts are offered in the spirit of kindness and thoughtfulness and with desire to enhance the quality of your life, not to burden you with an unnecessary object. If any gift doesn't seem either aesthetically pleasing or practical—say, a brightly colored sweater but you wear only earth tones—you may pass it along. There is nothing wrong with regifting; just avoid everyone's embarrassment by making sure that the regifting takes place well beyond the extended network of the original gift giver. If there's any opportunity that the giver will cross paths with the regifted item, you're too close to home.

These principles should inform our gift-giving as well. No strings attached, or it isn't a gift. And always consider the recipient.

I have a friend; we'll call her Louise. Steve, Louise's boyfriend of many years, read a book that he loved. It was about relationships and communication between couples. Steve talked to Louise enthusiastically about this book several times while he was reading it. He even mentioned giving Louise a copy of the book as a gift.

Louise is a particularly self-possessed woman, though. She had, of her own accord, glanced through the book while Steve was reading it and found the tone of the book and the message rubbing her the wrong way. She shared as much with Steve.

Steve was understandably hurt and disappointed. The book's content had been powerful for him, and he felt that some of the information in the book would be useful for them as a couple since they had some recurring challenges and conflicts within their relationship. Still, Louise was adamant that she was not interested and that he should not give her a copy of the book under any circumstance.

I hope I have successfully conveyed how direct and clear Louise was in her communication.

Valentine's Day arrives.

You guessed it. In spite of her direct plea to Steve, he presented her with the book, neatly gift-wrapped along with some gourmet chocolates.

Louise was livid. A huge fight ensued, so huge they almost broke up—that's how upset Louise was.

Steve seemed genuinely confused. He could not grasp that in his willful desire for her to read the book, he had explicitly ignored her wishes. For him, it was a loving expression of something significant that he wanted to share. He could not wrap his mind around the concept that *her* desires should have been the guiding principle for any gift he gave her.

And, of course, for Louise, that was what was so disturbing—not the book as a gift, but that in his insistence, he completely dismissed her, disrespected her, and rendered her invisible. Not an effective way of expressing affection on a special occasion.

The lesson is clear: The gift is for the intended, not for you. It ceases to be a gift when you give someone something they don't want or won't use simply because you think they should want it or should use it.

Endless opportunities exist for expanding our thinking around gift-giving. There are many ways to express or demonstrate your affection for someone. In some ways, the easiest choice is to buy something, but that may not be the best choice. When considering the quality of the intended's life, in supporting their choices, what else might make a noticeable impact that doesn't involve buying anything? Perhaps a home-cooked meal or some day care for their kids? Maybe a scholarship to attend a workshop or class? A week's worth of carpooling or running errands?

Really imagine what you have to offer besides cash or a cash equivalent—no doubt money is sometimes the perfect gift, but there are so many other great ways to show someone you care.

I AM MY OWN MUSEUM

No, you're not. Pull back the drapes and let in some light and air. You can't live for posterity and for the moment at the same time. And shrines to your youth, deceased movie stars, or the hot clerk at the local drugstore are equally disturbing. Hold things gently in your hands, and if that isn't possible, it may be better to simply set them down or let them go.

Remember the principle that when everything is precious, nothing is precious. Learn to distinguish between trash and treasure. A dime-store hairbrush is not the same as your last published article. No one wants your discarded toothbrush or used Q-tips except maybe a stalker or an unstable ex-lover. Find value in who you are and what you do—whether that's giving your child a bath or just listening to a friend without judgment.

If you're an artist or other creative, an archivist somewhere may actually be interested in your notes and research and working process. But completed projects, particularly published work or work that is out in the world, should be able to stand on its own merit. Of course, film-makers can sift through outtakes and unreleased footage for bonuses and extras, writers through old notes for an anthology of works and the creative process, and photographers through old prints and negatives for a new view of an older image. But in all of these cases and others, almost everything has a finite time limit or expiration date.

At some point, as an artist, it's helpful to acknowledge that an opportunity has passed and you'd be better off turning your attention to current and future projects rather than hauling around or digging through old files hoping to find a hidden gem.

If your work process and product are important enough to be retained, there will be entities interested in preserving them that will probably do a much better job of inventorying and cataloging them than you. And for those entities, it won't be helpful if your materials are jumbled together in your studio with old junk mail and other less specific stuff.

COLLECTIONS—COOL OR CRAZY?

Do you have a matchbook collection? A large jar full of coins you're using as a doorstop? Coasters from around the world? Sand from every beach you've ever visited? A glass menagerie of woodland creatures?

Do you use the matchbooks or just collect them? And do you now just pick up a book of matches anywhere, from a corner bodega to a restaurant you recently visited? What qualifies inclusion in the coaster collection—a particularly memorable brew or just the last place you grabbed a beer? Will you eventually cash in the jar of coins and use them for a rainy day? Have you carefully labeled the sand, noting the beach's name and country of origin? Attached a photo of you in your swimsuit?

Do you see where I'm headed? My point is, what makes a collection special? It is the care with which the collection is curated. Rather than going for sheer volume, there ought to be a reason for each piece to be included. Each piece should be able to stand on its own. It should be an excellent example of whatever it is in its own right—that's what makes a collection a collection.

Consider carefully when beginning a collection of anything—typically, there are one or two pieces that give birth to the collection in the first place. Don't let those be the strongest examples and your favorites, or there's no reason to have more. You can just have one or two things you really love because padding your collection with a bunch of filler so you can call it a collection doesn't actually make it a collection. So ask yourself, *Do I really need or want to collect anything*? Perhaps it's better to just keep the few items that you cherish and let the rest go.

In addition to people who have embarked on collecting things themselves, I've also encountered many people surrounded by objects from well-meaning folks who think that because they like rabbits or elephants or turtles, they must want to collect them. My clients, Carol and Becca, can illustrate this point.

On a trip once, and not a safari, Becca bought a single giraffe figurine as a gift for Carol. They displayed it on a glass curio shelf in the main hallway of their home where everyone could see it. Suddenly, as if floodgates had opened, every time a friend or colleague was stumped for an appropriate gift idea, the light bulb went on and bingo!—another giraffe found its way to their home.

Likewise, mermaids. When I arrived at Carol and Becca's home for the first time, their bathroom was lousy with mermaids—not an uncommon image for a wet room, particularly in the home of playful and creative women who appreciate other women. Cards depicting mermaids were taped to the walls, the nightlights featured frolicking mermaids, and the tub and shower area was literally swimming in them.

It all started because they had one framed picture of a mermaid hanging in the bathroom. This one picture became an unspoken invitation for anyone and everyone to bring Carol and Becca mermaids in every form—from Disney figurines and stickers to apparel and even toothbrushes. What was once a note of whimsy became a stifling theme, and one not of their own design. They were either too embarrassed or too polite to say, "No, thank you," so instead, they resigned themselves to decorating their bathroom with every piece of mermaid memorabilia they received.

Our work together gave them permission to dismantle the collection and "come out," as it were, about their desire to simplify and cease collecting.

So if you, too, have been the recipient of people's generous but misguided assumptions, you are empowered and encouraged to say, "Thanks, but no thanks," and start dismantling your collection as well.

WILL YOU HATE ME IF I GET RID OF... ?

I love my mom. This is not news. Years ago, she gave me her wedding china. It was all intact, full service for 12, and included a lot of serving pieces. She hadn't been married to my dad since the 1970s, so she didn't want it. And she had inherited *her* mother's china when my grandmother died, so she gave her china to me.

It was a lovely pattern and a lovely gesture. But upon inspection, the china was not my taste. I like simple and elegant lines and patterns and these were a bit too scalloped and floral for me. On the other hand, I didn't want to upset my mother or hurt her feelings. Clearly she was done with it, but I didn't want to assume that just because she didn't want it, it was okay for me not to want it, either. So I called her up.

I started the conversation by saying that I was thinking of getting some new dishes and that I wanted to know how she felt about that. I could hear her catch her breath and pause. I think she may have uttered, "Oh?" And then she changed the subject. When she starts talking about the Detroit Tigers or Pistons, I know she's uncomfortable—her default change-the-subject move is talking about sports.

I rushed in with, "Forget it, it's fine. You know I love the fact that it was yours, and I certainly appreciate the thought. It's fine. I won't do anything right now."

We talked for a few more minutes, and when the call ended, we both said, "I love you," and hung up. A few minutes later, the phone rang. It was my mom.

Mom: It's fine. Do whatever you want with the china. I'm done with it, and if you're done with it, let it go.

Andrew Mellen: Really? Are you sure?

Mom: Absolutely. You know that stuff just takes me a little bit of time to get over. And then I'm over it. So I'm over it. I'm fine with whatever you decide.

AM: That's great, Mom. Thanks.

Mom: Now, you're not getting rid of it completely, are you? You just want to get new dishes in addition to the china?

AM: I can do that. Is that what you want me to do?

Mom: It's good china, right?

AM: Sure. It's great. It's in great shape.

Mom: Well . . . I don't know. I guess not. This stuff is hard! This is what you do with your clients every day?

AM: Pretty much.

Mom: That's amazing. You're amazing.

AM: And that's my mom talking. But thank you.

Mom: Do you know anyone you think would like the china?

AM: Not off the top of my head, but I can give it some thought.

Mom: Or you could just give it to a local charity. There are a couple by you that you like, right?

AM: That's more what I was thinking. I spoke with an online company that buys china and cutlery, but they offer you a fraction of what they sell it for; you have to pack it up and ship it to them; if they don't want something, they ship it back. It just sounds like a nightmare. I'm more inclined to give it to some charity and let them sell it. It's in perfect condition, all the pieces are there, they should be able to get some good money for it.

Mom: That sounds better. Do that.

AM: Thanks, Mom. I will. I love you.

Mom: I love you, too. And you are pretty amazing.

The moral of this story is that you can and often should talk to family about these decisions; you don't necessarily need their permission when deciding to let a family gift go, but you also don't have to figure it out all on your own.

You may be surprised to learn you're on the same page about this choice. And if you're not, at least you can be upfront about your plans. That way, you avoid feeling shame or guilt over your decision, which may be amplified when that decision becomes a secret you're keeping from someone you care about.

If the other party doesn't like your choice or has a strong negative reaction, offer them the item(s) and invite them to do with it as they choose.

THIS MIGHT BE WORTH A FORTUNE— *ANTIQUES ROADSHOW* OR THRIFT STORE?

We discussed a version of this topic in Chapter 6 when we looked at garage sales, but let's revisit it here.

As I said before, resist the urge to hold on to stuff just because you think it *may* be worth some serious cash. If you think you have something valuable, take it to an appraiser or someone qualified yet impartial (meaning they don't stand to benefit from either a high or low appraisal) to determine if you're right.

We've all heard stories of a garage-sale Jackson Pollock or some other hidden, neglected treasure. If you have something similar in your possession, it would be good to know it. If instead you have a quirky and interesting thing that has no real monetary value, the local thrift store will be happy to take it from you.

Finding the best advisor for your possible treasure will require some footwork, so take the time to do it right once and the first time. Look online, ask friends and neighbors and colleagues for referrals, and check the appraiser's references. You don't want to turn a rare and beautiful thing over to a complete stranger until you're certain that they won't disappear with it and that they have demonstrated expertise with objects like yours.

In other words, don't assume that after a five-minute phone call, because you "had a good feeling" about the appraiser or know how to "read" people, you can tell whether or not they are reputable and reliable. Remember Bernie Madoff.

Once it's been properly appraised, if you decide to keep it, document it properly and get it insured.

DRY STORAGE VERSUS WET STORAGE (REMINDER)

As discussed in previous chapters, precious things should not be subjected to fluctuations in humidity or temperature. Mold, mildew, rot, and pests—you name it, and moisture will foster and welcome it.

Once you've gathered everything and completed the sorting process discussed in the next sections, make sure that wherever you ultimately store your mementos, they are safe and dry and protected from the elements.

APPROACHING SORTING AND HOW TO SORT

If you're apprehensive about sorting through things—in particular, sentimental objects and touchstones from your past—a calm and steady approach is best: Breathe deeply and settle down emotionally and mentally. You're not about to run a gauntlet of swinging, bloody spikes, so there's no need to be overly agitated or bring frenetic energy to the process.

The goal of sorting is knowing exactly what it is you're holding on to and why you're holding on to it. And the most direct way to achieve that goal is to sort through everything, make reasonable and heartfelt decisions, discard what you are finished with, and lovingly and respectfully store or display what remains.

So while this may not feel like a day at an amusement park at first, it is more like that than you realize. You'll be scared, you'll be thrilled, you'll be tuckered out, you'll laugh, and you may even surprise yourself and want to go back for more.

There are only three rules for sorting:

1. **Establish an amount of time for each sorting session.** We've already discussed that, barring ADHD or any other attention challenges, aim for no less than 15 minutes but not longer than two hours.

2. **Find a quiet place where you will not be disturbed.** If you're sorting in the space where everything is currently living, see if you can close off that space so other folks or pets are not randomly wandering through or constantly interrupting you. If having company (a pet, friend, or family member) will help you stay calm and focused, by all means have them with you. Just be sure they can be there while you maintain the equilibrium and the pace and not create or become a distraction.

3. **Be true to yourself.** No one is looking over your shoulder, and this is a private and personal task. So you have the final word on what you think is important and what you can let go of. You don't need to have imaginary conversations with anyone who is not in the room with you about whether you should let something go or not. And you absolutely do not need to answer to anyone else for your choices (unless the things still belong to someone living and that person isn't you!).

This is by no means a grave or overly serious task; it just requires concentration and deliberateness, which is why I'm being so explicit about how and where. You want to be comfortable and focused so that whatever comes up, you're in the best place possible to address it without those thoughts or feelings derailing your process.

If you haven't done so already, select a place in your home that can be dedicated to the process of sorting until the process is complete.

Even if the space is modest, it's best not to have to set up and tear down this whole operation every time you want to continue the work.

Once you've identified that space, collect all the mementos and sentimental objects you've accumulated and bring them to this place. If you've created Sentimentaland containers as you've worked through previous chapters, bring them here now.

Without tearing apart your home, be thorough in searching out every item of sentimental import and gather them all up until you've isolated them to this one area of your home. You can always address the random object you've overlooked and discovered later, but a comprehensive sorting saves time and minimizes emotional upheaval.

ACTUALLY SORTING

Great. You've found a quiet place to be. You're surrounded by things to sort. It's now time to gather the supplies listed on page 269. Once you've got your tools and supplies on hand, you're ready to begin.

Perhaps it's worth saying a little prayer or meditation at this time: "Let me be careful and conscious, respectful and thoughtful. Let me be deliberate and diligent and thorough. Let me be strong and patient and flexible and resilient. Let me be kind and generous and gracious and fearless. And let this be pleasant."

Now, define your workspace. You can do this by spreading out a tarp or blanket, setting up a table or even taping out the floor. This helps you to isolate smaller areas where like items can be grouped together and still be seen.

Remember not to stack things too high in piles when sorting; you want them to be mostly spread out on a single plane. This won't always be possible—space may be limited—and with books and other flat items, stacks are probably inevitable. In any case, all piles and stacks will eventually need to be dismantled as you make further decisions.

The following are the categories you should be thinking of when sorting sentimental objects:

- Keep
- Return to Others
- Donate
  - » Specific people or organizations
  - » Thrift store/Shelter
  - » Free online sites or at the curb with a sign
- Sell
- Trash
- The Fence

Keep: These are items that you really love today and feel confident you'll continue to love for many years to come. You'll either display these things or wrap them in acid-free paper or other protective coverings (as needed) and place them in containers for safekeeping.

Return to Others: These are things that belong to other people but are currently in your possession. It doesn't matter how long you've had them; they need to go home, and they should get there sooner rather than later. Do not procrastinate any longer; swallow whatever feelings you may have about the amount of time you've had them, and get them gone.

In the following rare cases, you may give the object to a thrift store *rather* than return it to its rightful owner:
- The owner is deceased and you are unable (not unwilling) to contact the next of kin.
- The return of the object would cause harm to the recipient or someone else.

Donate: These are things you are clearly done with for whatever reason that you're now willing to let go of. With personal mementos, it's uncertain how many of these kinds of things have a life beyond you— for example, things like old ticket stubs, playbills, or conference lanyards. If there's a secondary market for these items, great. If not, then they should be recycled or discarded.

For any items that could still be used by someone else, determine where to take them and then send or deliver them there. Do not allow these things to linger as you search for the "perfect" home for them.

Sell: These are things you are clearly done with that have some monetary value. You can take these things to a local consignment shop or sell them online. If you don't have the time or interest in selling them yourself, find someone or a service who will handle liquidating them for you.

Trash: These are the unfortunate things you've kept that have no value to anyone and are now to be discarded. Please recycle anything that can be recycled and lovingly toss the rest.

The Fence: As mentioned in Chapter 5, this is the category to use when you feel "on the fence" or unable to make a decision. However, use it only as a last resort. If every third item is ending up in this category, you are using it incorrectly.

Step 1: Like with Like

Set and start your timer. Then begin by simply putting similar things together. This means putting yearbooks with other yearbooks, journals with journals, baby clothes together, love letters together, etc.

Throughout this initial sorting into groups, toss out all the trash you come across—you don't need to leave that for later. Likewise, since you're handling things anyway, wipe everything down to remove any dust, mildew, or grime.

It's possible that all you'll accomplish in the first session is sorting into like categories. That's fine, and it's not a small achievement, so don't be discouraged. Make sure you set up your next date with yourself right away so you don't lose momentum and don't have to look at the sorted piles for too long.

Step 2: Stay or Go?

Once everything has been sorted into like categories and obvious trash has been discarded, it's time to make some more decisions. Sitting quietly and handling each item, carefully consider what has real meaning for you today. What seems lasting and enduring? What is mildly amusing? And what holds no meaning because the memory is no longer compelling, is unpleasant, or is possibly even forgotten?

It's okay if something you used to love doesn't move you any longer. It doesn't mean you're heartless or devoid of feeling. We all change. The things that used to delight and engage us may now bore us or at least not engage us. Don't judge yourself if you feel this way—just acknowledge it and move on.

Anything that doesn't seem essential should be released. If any of these items have adequate monetary value or they perform a function, such as an appliance or an electronic device or even a T-shirt or wine key, sell them or pass them along to a charity. If they are less functional, such as a menu or a wrapper or a plastic bag, they should be recycled or tossed in the trash.

Spend enough time with each object to make an informed decision but not so much time that you get lost in reminiscing or distracted by feelings, either fond sentimental feelings or any sort of shame, embarrassment, disappointment, or frustration. If or when you become aware that you're drifting and are no longer focused on the task at hand, stand up and move around. The surest way to shift feelings is to physically shift your body.

Go get a glass of water, leave the room and walk around outside—anything to physically break the mood. If you choose to call someone, make it someone who is supportive of you and this process—do not call anyone who might offer you any criticism, constructive or otherwise. Likewise, do not call someone who struggles to let things go themselves or who is related to the items being sorted if there's any chance you'll be drawn into further reminiscing.

Once you've gotten a pep talk or cleared your head and feel ready to resume, return to where you're working and dig back in.

This is really a rinse-and-repeat task. You'll keep sorting through these objects until each one has been touched and a decision has been made to keep it or let it go. As in other sorting projects, you may very occasionally set an object aside in The Fence—but only when you really can't make a decision, not in cases where you just don't *want* to make a decision. Keep in mind, too, whether the things you've come across are things you'd like to have in your home on display or neatly stored away in Sentimentaland.

When everything has been sorted, it's now time to containerize it.

CONTAINERIZING THE OBJECTS

If you have multiple people's mementos and objects, you should have a tub or series of tubs for each individual. If you have multiple containers for each person, consider segregating the contents by category as well (one tub for printed materials such as journals, yearbooks, and magazines; one tub for clothing; one tub for tchotchkes and other objects, etc.). All the containers should be see-through so the contents are easy to identify. Additionally, you may want to use different sizes and/or colored lids to signify each person's containers.

For example, you could use 10-gallon tubs with purple lids for you, eight-gallon tubs with blue lids for your child, and 12-gallon tubs with red lids for your partner. If this isn't practical, different-colored electrical or duct tape is an easy-to-read identifier. Of course, all the tubs will also be labeled as well.

At this time, if you haven't done so already, wrap anything that is fragile or requires additional protection to keep it safe from damage. Load heavier and bulkier items toward the bottom with lighter things resting toward the top. Do not overload the containers so that moving them is awkward or requires more than one person to manage them.

THE IMPORTANCE OF LABELS—
HOW, WHY, AND WHERE

In Chapter 6, I gave a detailed description and explanation of labeling. Please see page 227–228 to review that section. I'll just stress here that labeling the containers is a critical step in ensuring that you can easily find whatever you're looking for in these containers in the future.

ORGANIZING THE STORAGE

Once each category has been successfully containerized and labeled, it's time to store them until you next need or want the contents. Find an area of your home that is large enough to house the full collection of Sentimentaland containers. If this isn't possible, then divide up the containers by person, and find a home for each person's Sentimentaland.

Remember to store them somewhere climate-controlled and as accessible as these kinds of items need to be. If you frequently look through memorabilia, don't bury the containers behind old furniture and seldom-used paint. Common sense will inform how and where everything should be stored so it's out of the flow of traffic but still within easy reach.

MAINTAINING THE SYSTEM

Moving forward, whenever anything is destined for Sentimentaland, add the item to the appropriate container in a timely fashion. It's fine to set something aside for a few days until you can get back to Sentimentaland, but don't leave things lying around indefinitely. Find the container the item wants to be deposited into and place it inside. Obviously, if the item is fragile or requires additional packing, do that prior to putting it into Sentimentaland.

If you find that you have enough energy to identify something as Sentimentaland-worthy but seem to lack enough energy to then store it there, talk yourself through the procrastination. If it turns out you're more ambivalent than you thought, maybe you don't need to save this thing after all. And if you do want to keep it, reminding yourself of how easily it could be damaged if you don't store it properly should motivate you enough to pick up the object, travel to Sentimentaland, and put it away.

9

PHOTOS

All photos are accurate. None of them is the truth.

–RICHARD AVEDON

A photograph is like a recipe—memory, the finished dish.

–CARRIE LATET

A picture is worth a thousand words—but not if you can't find it.

–GOOD HOUSEKEEPING

WHAT WE'RE GOING TO COVER IN THIS CHAPTER

- What a Photograph Is and Isn't
- One Home for Everything and Like with Like
- Does This Photo Make My Butt Look Fat? Or Good Pics, Bad Pics
- If You Visit It, You Will Bring Me Home: Travel Mementos, Part II
- Who's That Strange Man Standing Next to Aunt Ida?
- Digital Versus Analog Images—Not an Either-Or Proposition
- Photo Albums—Fun or Frustrating?
- Digital Frames
- The Disease of I-Made-It-Ism
- Approaching Sorting and How to Sort
- Actually Sorting
- Organizing Digital Photos
- Maintaining the System

- ARE YOU OVERWHELMED by your photographs?
- Do you have envelopes of photos shoved into various drawers around the house?
- Do you have rolls of film lying around that have never been developed?
- Have you ever bought a new memory card rather than downloading images from your digital camera?
- Have you ever gone in search of a particular photo and given up in frustration?
- Do you think that "someday" you're going to create a photo album of your trip to Spain?
- Have you recently inherited old photos and don't even know who's in them?
- Do you contemplate stopping taking pictures because you're so overwhelmed by what you already have?
- Are you now overwhelmed with your answers to these questions?

Take a deep breath and count to 10.

This entire chapter is dedicated to photographs—sorting them and storing them, accessing them and utilizing/enjoying them. After all, if we don't enjoy our photographs, why bother keeping them at all?

The magic of photography offers us a static window into events we have lived or events we have missed (that may have been described to us or left for us to imagine). And photographs allow us to conjure those scenes each time we view them so we can relive and share past events in the present time.

Almost everyone has at least one challenge when it comes to photos. We love to take pictures, and then we are quickly overwhelmed with keeping them organized or storing them. And as with so many other advances in technology, digital photographs just complicate, rather than simplify, the situation. The fact that these photos live somewhere on our devices encourages an out-of-sight-out-of-mind attitude, particularly if we have lots of storage space and limited tech skills.

Together we'll tackle the challenges of sorting and organizing and storing photos, and by the time you're done with this chapter, your photos may not be in perfect order, but they will all be together, more manageable, and much easier to interact with.

Things You Will Need for This Work

- Trash bags
- Timer or stopwatch
- Spray can of compressed air
- Tubs, containers, or baskets to corral and contain like things
- Photo boxes and/or albums and/or scrapbooks and/or frames
- Lint-free cloths
- Acid-free paper
- Cotton negative sleeves
- Clean white cotton gloves
- Acid-free and noninvasive adhesives (tapes, glues, etc.)
- Label maker (but stick-on labels should not touch photos or negatives)
- Acid-free labels
- Acid-free markers
- Scissors or paper cutter
- Sorting surface (3' x 6' or larger and ideally not a surface that needs to be cleared off before the sorting is complete)

WHAT A PHOTOGRAPH IS AND ISN'T

Photograph (noun): A picture produced by photography

Photography (noun): The art or process of producing images of objects on photosensitive surfaces

> ### NOTABLE NOTE
>
> If you're intimidated or agitated when you think about protecting your photos because you've neglected them in the past, let that go. What's done is done. If you read something online that warns of the irreparable damage you are doing *right now* to your photographs, remember that whatever you've read is probably trying to sell you something to prevent damage or reverse years of neglect. Learn to avoid the hype and focus on current best practices, which are detailed in this chapter, and you'll be fine—it doesn't need to be any more demanding or scary than that.

People like to say that "the camera never lies" and that "one picture is worth a thousand words." While clever, how accurate are either of those statements? What is true is that many people rely on photographs to document their lives, sometimes depending on pictures more than their actual memories. While a good photograph can certainly transport us through time to a place or long-past event, there is value in doing at least some of that memory work ourselves.

Why? First, because a photo can get lost, damaged, or destroyed. Second, because our memories may contradict what we see in an image. Third, because even a burst of rapid shots can't fully capture the subtlety of a dynamic conversation or relationship as it is unfolding. So it's unlikely that a series of still images will ever be comprehensive enough to tell us the whole story.

Lastly, a picture itself may appear to be objective and without prejudice, but every moment captured is colored and shaped by many variables—the photographer, the subject, the location, and the circumstances, to name just a few.

I can show you a photograph of my father and me on a trip to Tahquamenon Falls in Michigan's Upper Peninsula, and you would see us embracing and smiling at the camera. The falls behind us are rushing with tannin in shades of deep copper and rust. The sunlight is fractured as it works its way through the thick canopy of green leaves overhead.

What the photo doesn't reveal is the horrible fight we had 15 minutes before we asked a passing tourist to snap our picture in front of the falls. We were so upset with each other that part of the argument was about whether we would cut the trip short and head home or not. But no one besides my dad or me would ever know that just by looking at the photograph. This doesn't diminish the beauty of the setting or the obvious affection my dad and I felt for each other at other moments in our lives—it's just a very real element of the memory that the image can't convey.

So photographs may be records, but even more, they are interpretations of events rather than completely accurate records themselves. The photos we take, the pictures we gather and hold on to are touchstones for real events and real encounters with real people; the photos are *not* the events or the encounters or the relationships themselves. They are powerful tools, certainly, they are expressions of creativity and artistry, of surprise and wonder and circumstance and timing, but they are not and should not be confused with intimacy and breath and scent and touch.

Cherish your photos as windows into places you have been or dream of going, and protect them as documents of people you have known or people you've never met that have made your life possible. But know that you will not and cannot replace the actual experiences with a two-dimensional image of light reflected and captured. Continuing to believe that would be a far greater tragedy than losing every photograph you've ever owned in a natural disaster because it would mean that you've surrendered your role in keeping those memories alive.

ONE HOME FOR EVERYTHING AND LIKE WITH LIKE

Applying One Home for Everything and Like with Like to photographs means digging out any developed rolls of film and their corresponding images that may still be shoved into various drawers, tucked into corners, or stacked up on shelves and bringing them all together to sort through and organize. It also means tracking down digital photos wherever they currently live or are being stored.

Once you've brought together printed photos with printed photos and digital photos with digital photos, you'll sort and organize them, then find one place in your home where they will live. If it's a photo, it's to be with its brothers and sisters in one place in your home or office.

The *only* exception to this is, of course, the hard drive of your computer. When we get to organizing your computer in Chapter 10, we'll address those photos as files on your computer; in this chapter we'll deal with getting them from the camera onto your hard drive, into folders, and properly labeled. The same techniques we'll use to organize your physical photos will be applied to digital pictures as well, so you won't be learning two different ways to manage your photos—one way fits all.

DOES THIS PHOTO MAKE MY BUTT LOOK FAT? OR GOOD PICS, BAD PICS

When we talk about sorting photos later in this chapter, we'll address the larger task of making sense of your accumulated photos. But from this moment on, whenever you take pictures, regardless of whether you're using film or a digital camera, make it a part of your process to review them within 24 hours and eliminate all of the following:

- Duplicates
- Bad exposures
- Blurry or out-of-focus shots
- Off-center shots
- Bloopers
- Photos you'd rather not remember
- Photos you're not proud to share
- Photos that don't evoke an immediate positive emotional response
- Photos with a foreign object obscuring part of the frame, be it a finger, a camera strap, or some other object

As we've discussed before, most likely you are not the subject of an anthropological study or documentary, so you don't need to keep any photos of you where the little tummy roll you've recently been sporting is pushing down the waistband of your slacks. Or the photo of you with food on your shirt or mascara running down your face. Or the one with your fly open.

Unless they amuse you, there's no reason to hold on to these kinds of images. Just like a bag of pistachio nuts—you accept that not all can be opened, that some are duds. Just because you pushed a button doesn't automatically make every picture a keeper. And the more you edit your collection of photos as you take them, the less clutter you'll have to deal with going forward.

IF YOU VISIT IT, YOU WILL BRING ME HOME: TRAVEL MEMENTOS, PART II

Taking vacation pictures can be fun, whether you're trekking the Himalayas or visiting family in Des Moines. But living behind your phone or camera as you descend into the Grand Canyon or teeter on a rope bridge over a gorge is both dangerous and foolish. Even taking excessive photos of your kids' various achievements means your children don't get an enthusiastic cheerleader while they're actually doing the thing. Plus, you're likely to miss the most important moments because you're so focused on capturing them on film.

When it comes to finding harmony between documenting your life and living your life, I'll always suggest erring on the side of living it. Sure, you want to remember what happened, but don't you really want to have been there experiencing it in the first place? And while some people will enjoy seeing photos of your adventures out in the world, they're mostly for you and anyone else who was there with you. What do you need to document so you remember where you were and what you did? That's a good place to start when deciding of what and when you'll take photographs from now on.

Certainly you'll take more photos than you intend to keep, knowing that not every photo will be worth keeping once you get home and review them. And I would never want you to be so scared of missing something important that you never take another picture again. So take some photos and also stay present to what's happening in the moment. That way, you'll have your memories to help you review your pictures as you look for the best of them to keep.

Just like with mementos and other sentimental objects, aim to capture exceptional, unusual, and unique moments in your pictures. There are masterful shots of the falls at Niagara that professionals have waited days, perhaps months, to capture. Buy a postcard—you won't do better. But the image of your companion leaning over the railing and getting drenched in their yellow slicker is a once-in-a-lifetime shot—don't miss that.

The moments that are never to be repeated without rehearsal are the images you'll cherish, and those are the ones that will instantly remind you of the smell of fresh-baked blueberry pie on a Maine summer day or a thick-and-syrupy coffee after dinner in Turkey or the thrill of your grandchild's first birthday cake. How many pictures do you need of your hotel accommodations, luxurious as they may have been, when compared to the moment a lion pounced on a gazelle on safari in Kenya? And while that first birthday cake may have been a triumph of baking and decorating, the bite that ends with frosting on the nose is far more evocative of the moment, right?

In capturing the shocking, the absurd, the ridiculous, the sublime, and the quietly mundane, you record the fullest history of your travels and your life. Those images become the emotional map you'll follow to remember each taste, each step, each sound, each smell. Be thoughtful and creative, and you cannot lose. Just remember to remove your lens cap and, of course, fully charge your phone or camera.

WHO'S THAT STRANGE MAN STANDING NEXT TO AUNT IDA?

Probably Uncle Albert, her first husband, who died tragically before your mother was born. But you might not know that if some other relative hasn't written on the back of the photo, identifying all the people in it.

Not long before my father died, we went through everything he owned that was important to him. He knew his time was shortening, and it was a beautiful and simple exchange between the two of us. He let me know what was important to him that I keep and was also very clear about what no longer meant anything to him.

His ease and matter-of-factness was refreshing and inspiring. Clearly, where he was going, these things weren't going with him, and he was as content to toss something in the trash that he was finished with as he was to place something meaningful in my hand and tell me its story, encouraging me to care for it as he had.

We also went through a bunch of old family photos. As we looked through them, he pointed out who was who. Some I knew, and others I had never and would never meet. There were also people he either couldn't remember or had no clue about. My dad was the youngest and the last surviving member of his generation—so if he didn't recognize someone, there was no other source to go to.

And while any old photograph holds some fascination for me—the clothes and cars, wondering about a stranger's life and what may have been going on when the picture was snapped—ultimately these people were now only memories for someone, just not for him or me. So there was no reason, good or bad, to hang on to those photos. Just like old coupons and calendars he was no longer interested in, he simply tossed these into the trash as well.

As we sorted, we came across various early photos of family members who are still living, and my dad gave me specific instructions on what to send to whom, which I did. And I found some great pictures of my grandparents and great-grandparents, cousins I'm fond of, and my dad and his siblings. These I kept for myself.

The point of sharing all of this with you is that when it comes to old family photos, sorting through them with someone old enough to know who everyone is is a time-sensitive endeavor, and that just because a photograph comes into your possession, if you don't know anyone in it or find it engaging in some way, you are not obligated to keep it.

DIGITAL VERSUS ANALOG IMAGES— NOT AN EITHER-OR PROPOSITION

There are advantages and disadvantages to both film and digital photography, whether you're a professional or amateur photographer. So I'll leave it to you to decide if you prefer one medium over the other and why. More important is the question of how you organize prints or digital images, and the answer is that you organize them exactly the same way: you use One Home for Everything and Like with Like as your guide.

PHOTO ALBUMS — FUN OR FRUSTRATING?

To answer this question, take a few minutes, check in with yourself, and answer the questions below:

- Are you someone who is already organized and motivated to make positive changes in your life?
- Are you curious or tenuous when you step outside of your comfort zone?
- Are you, for whatever reason, still searching for something to unlock that well of potential creativity inside?
- Are you relentless in the pursuit of your goals, sometimes to the exclusion of other priorities?
- Are you constantly on the go and moving from one project to the next?
- Do you dream of doing projects but seldom actually get them started and then typically don't finish them?
- Do you complete some things but lose interest when you encounter an obstacle or resistance?
- Are you easily distracted?

If you answered no to the first four questions and yes to the last four, I don't want to rain on your parade, but you may not be a photo album type of person. Not to mention, who is going to actually look at them?

If you are a scrapbooker or like this kind of project as an expression of your creativity, go for it. Just always keep in mind that you're doing this for yourself—not your grandkids or a museum. But if you've never created a photo album in the past, be honest with yourself about how much time you have to devote to this kind of project.

A great alternative to photo albums (and scrapbooks) are memory or keepsake boxes—they're distinct from Sentimentaland but in the same hemisphere. These boxes allow you to corral photos (and other related sentimental objects) into one container, creating a mini time capsule of a trip or an event. They come in many sizes and colors and are a no-brainer when it comes to keeping things together—open the lid, fill the contents thoughtfully, and store them away.

DIGITAL FRAMES

A digital frame is a great way to stream a slideshow of your favorite images; it's like creating a photo album, only here it's much easier to update images whenever you want and you never need to turn a page. You can easily load hundreds of pictures into one frame and enjoy them as a rotating slideshow of a single event or multiple events. The only limits here are storage space and your imagination. Some even have built-in speakers, so you can stream music or a personalized narration as your photos rotate through their cycle.

Digital frames make great gifts for less tech-savvy friends and family who still want to see your photos but are not so great at streaming or accessing shared servers or services online. And their size, portability, and the ease and speed with which you can update them make them a viable alternative to creating photo albums the old-fashioned, time-intensive way.

NOTABLE NOTE

Albums can be small enough to fit just one trip's worth of pictures or large enough to hold multiple years of photos. What makes the most sense for you? Many people choose the easiest route and just insert photos as they get them, adding new pages or creating new albums as required. If this is you, make sure to label pages with dates to provide some structure, both for organizing and to offer some context for the viewer.

For those interested in creating photo albums, here are a few tips:

- Basic photo albums or blank-page scrapbooks can be bought at most drugstores and greeting card or stationery shops.
- Consider albums with a window or frame on the front

cover. Then insert a decorative card or evocative image to introduce the album's content.

- Label the binder's spine for easy reference.
- All pages and any adhesive should be acid-free and lignin-free and should have passed the Photographic Activity Test (PAT) to avoid destruction to the photos. Any product that has passed the PAT test will state so on its packaging.
- Avoid magnetic and self-stick photo albums—they damage your photos.
- Any plastic sleeves should be made from uncoated pure polyethylene or a similar material. Plastic containing PVC generates acid as well. Read the label carefully for composition.
- Select photo albums that are expandable. You may want to add pages in the future.
- Do not overstuff photo albums—this can cause the pages to buckle and damage the photographs.
- Select an organizing principle (chronological order, by subject, etc.).
  - Chronology: Put a beginning date in each album and a final date when the album is full.
  - Subject: Examples include baby albums, travel albums (either each trip in its own album or a large album of all travels), and holiday albums (a year of holidays or every Christmas for the past few years).
- Always plan the layout of each page before permanently affixing images.
- For all photos, create typed or printed labels that describe the setting and the subjects. You can also clip phrases or names from magazines for captions. Any label should be attached to the page and avoid contact with any photographs.
- Whenever possible, store albums vertically. Laying them on their side can warp the photos.

- For the most protection, store duplicate prints separately whenever possible to minimize potential loss.
- If you're drawn toward scrapbooks, consider using a big blank book. Then add keepsakes to the pages, such as ticket stubs or other paper-based memorabilia, even swatches of fabric or locks of hair. Use caution with glitter or sparkles to ensure that they will not decompose or come loose over time and damage your photos. As with photo albums, always use an acid-free adhesive.

THE DISEASE OF I-MADE-IT-ISM

I have several friends and clients who are photographers, and many of them have the same particular ailment: I-made-it-ism. Far on the other side of "I might need it someday," I-made-it-ism endows anything and everything created by the afflicted with an unwarranted significance just because it came from their hand. It's possible that this illness was first contracted at a summer camp upon the artistic creation of a ceramic ashtray or maybe a God's eye made from yarn and Popsicle sticks.

In the adult photographer, it manifests itself in the need to keep every photograph and negative ever shot. The photo could be out of focus, it could be a partial exposure, it could be a duplicate of another shot. The simple fact that some effort of theirs produced the picture seems to them reason enough to hold on to it.

Artists working in other media also sometimes suffer from this condition, but it seems particularly acute with photographers. What I find doubly remarkable is that while they won't let anything go, they are hyperselective about what they will actually exhibit or display. So the bulk of these photographs, once printed, never see the light of day. They are stored in any number of flat file boxes and kept indefinitely. When I've asked several of them about this, this is how the conversation often plays out:

Andrew Mellen: So tell me about all the photos.

Photographer: I took them.

AM: [chuckling] Okay. Got it. What are you intending to do with them?

Photographer: Nothing.

AM: Nothing now or nothing ever or . . . Can you be a bit more specific?

Photographer: I don't know. I mean, I took them. I'm not getting rid of them, if that's what you're thinking.

AM: Well, I don't think I was implying just tossing them out willy-nilly. I guess I was thinking that maybe you'd go through them and keep the images that you like or that are useful or that you might or would print again or . . .

Photographer: Yeah. I'm not going to do that. I took them. They're my photographs.

AM: I understand that. No one's trying to do anything to you or take anything from you. I'm just trying to understand, and I'm trying to relate this to other art forms. When I write something, for instance, I'll go through several drafts until I arrive at a completed manuscript. And then I don't really have the need for all the previous drafts. I pull out phrases here and there that I might be able to use somewhere else, but then the rest of it is either redundant or just not needed, so I end up deleting it or tossing it in the trash.

Painters, too, will sketch things out and then begin a canvas, and unless the sketch was significant in some way, once they start working on the canvas, the sketch is set aside and eventually discarded. Chefs pick out the choice parts of their ingredients and then use the remains for either a stock or compost.

Photographer: I don't know what to tell you. I took all these photographs. I don't want to get rid of any of them. I made them. They're little parts of me.

AM: Hmm, really? I think I'm going to disagree with you on that. And if you think about it, they're not really even extensions of you. They're certainly expressions of you, but they are not in any way actually little pieces of you. [pausing] Okay, then. Let's move on.

Whether you're an amateur or professional artist of any kind, you might relate to how these photographers feel. If so, I encourage you to talk to other artists about how they manage all of the by-products of their art over the years.

If you've achieved some degree of fame or visibility, someone may be interested in creating an archive of everything you've ever created. That's probably the exception here, not the rule. And if that is the case, like any other element of an estate plan, nailing down details sooner rather than later is the best choice here, too.

For everyone else, it comes down to your end game. What do you intend to happen to all these things when you're gone? Making this one decision ensures that whoever comes behind you will know exactly what has significance and what is still here only because you refused to make any other decisions at the time. There's no shame or reason for judgment in not deciding—but there are stuff consequences.

And that leaves us with answering the question of how you want to store them while you're here. When everything is precious, nothing is precious. And without a sustainable system for organizing these bits and pieces, you will very likely end up drowning in a sea of photographs or rough drafts or sketches that will interfere with your creative process and even crowd you out of your studio. Again, these are some of the very real consequences of avoiding critical decisions in the moment.

NOTABLE NOTE

There are numerous online photography resources—too many to list here. Whether you're looking to purchase supplies, develop your film, store and share your photos online, or get a custom book made of your photographs, a quick search will show you multiple options, so do your research carefully.

When it comes to online storage, remember that parking things in the cloud does not negate the need for redundant storage on your hard drive and an external drive as well. Never rely on some company's technology to protect and save your images for you. There are enough horror stories of servers crashing and other technical glitches to validate an electronic version of the adage "Don't put all your eggs in one basket." Just like with investments, when it comes to backing up, diversify.

APPROACHING SORTING AND HOW TO SORT

When you're ready to sort through photos, find a quiet place to examine them where you will not be disturbed. Remember that this is a task—not an unpleasant task but a task. Every task has a beginning and an end, and the result of a task well done is the *only* goal. A delightful by-product may be a pleasant experience.

There's far too much emphasis these days placed on having fun at all times—thanks, social media. I'm all for amusement and enjoyment. When they occur organically as part of this work, that's great. But their absence doesn't mean that you've failed or are missing an essential element of your process. Don't equate the absence of amusement as then becoming drudgery. Tasks can be challenging or interesting or demanding without being unpleasant. So do yourself a favor: Don't torment yourself unnecessarily by heaping expectations on top of a process that may already be loaded with some procrastination and skepticism.

To start, set your timer for a comfortable length of time between 30 minutes and an hour. It helps to have a time limit—that way, you'll stay focused on moving briskly and deliberately and are less likely to stray into reminiscing, which is dangerous territory when sorting photos.

Do this every time you sit down to sort them. Do not try to be a hero or think yourself exceptional by assuming that time limits are for mere mortals, and since you're so motivated, you'll be able to work for hours uninterrupted without stopping for food or rest. Let the timer help you. Trust me on this. No more than an hour at a time.

Even if all you do during breaks is get up and stretch and walk around the house, it clears the head. You should expect a certain amount of reverie when handling photos. The key is to work steadily so you don't fall down any rabbit holes on memory lane.

ACTUALLY SORTING

If you haven't already done so, gather up all your physical photos now. Find them wherever they live—in boxes, in drawers, in piles. Bring them all together. You do not need to take apart or undo photo albums already created; just collect them together with all the other photos.

Now, decide which categories you want to use for sorting them. When I did this project myself, the following are the categories I used. Your companion workbook contains these categories in worksheet format, or you can download the same worksheet at unstuffbook.com/photos.

Old Family Photos: These are typically black-and-white and are pictures of people who are older and even possibly deceased. These are photos of whom I would call "ancestors."

Current Family Photos: These are typically in color and feature blood relatives. I don't sort further than that, meaning I don't distinguish between my nuclear family versus my extended family and then further sort into various nuclear versions of the extended family, but you could. I don't have so many relatives that distinguishing between cousins is that important, at least photographically.

Friends: These are pictures of friends that transcend a particular event or were taken at no event at all, just because I or some other photographer wanted to capture something specific yet random.

Travel: These are sorted by trip, so all the India pictures are together, the camping-in-Canada pictures are together, the summer-spent-backpacking-through-Europe pictures are together. They are then arranged in either alphabetical or chronological order. I chose alphabetical.

Events: These, like Travel, are grouped by specific event (for example, piano recitals, bar mitzvah, senior prom, high-school graduation, shows and gigs during college, college graduation, significant birthdays, wedding, work gatherings, etc.). Mine are in chronological order of events as well, so piano recitals (when I was nine or 10) are grouped before high-school graduation, and so on.

Theme: These are images whose relationship with other images is based on an external or abstract theme. I did a series once of single riders reading books on the NYC subway. I took another series of photos of roadside produce stands. So a theme or common subject ties them together, not my relationship with them.

Utility: These are not pictures of the gas meter. They are photos of valuables in my home that I've taken for insurance purposes or photos I've taken of water lines running through newly constructed walls when those walls were still open. By *utility*, I mean that the photos' only purpose is utilitarian or functional.

In your workbook, notebook, or on the worksheet you downloaded, write down your categories. With all your photos in one place and clarity on your categories, you're ready to set the timer and begin. With each photo, ask yourself the following questions to determine if it is a keeper or a leaver:

1. Is the print properly exposed, meaning neither under- nor overexposed?
   Yes. Go on to the next question.
   No. The photo can go in the trash.

2. Is the subject in focus?
   Yes. Go on to the next question.
   No. The photo can go in the trash.

3. Is the subject completely in the frame?
   Yes. Go on to the next question.
   No. The photo can go in the trash.

4. Is the subject obscured by anything (thumbs, straps, signs, etc.)?
   Is any part of the image obscured by anything?
   Yes. Go on to the next question.
   No. The photo can go in the trash.

5. Is the photo flattering?
   Yes. Go on to Question 7.
   No. Go on to the next question.

6. If it's not flattering, is it amusingly unflattering?
   Yes. Go on to the next question.
   No. The photo can go in the trash. If it's uncomfortably unflattering, it's not worth keeping. Spinach in the teeth might be okay, runny makeup following a fight, less so.

7. Do you know everyone (or anyone) in the photo?
   Yes. Go on to the next question.
   No. The photo can go in the trash.

8. Do you care about everyone (or anyone) in the photo?
   Yes. Go on to the next question.
   No. The photo can go in the trash. Really think about keeping pictures of exes. I'm not a fan of cutting people out of a photograph to reflect the way you've cut them out of your life. Toss the whole thing instead. Several clients took great pleasure in shredding pictures of their exes—it was very liberating for them.

9. Would you be embarrassed for anyone else to see this image?
   Yes. The photo can go in the trash.
   No. Go on to the next question.

10. Is it a photo you would rather not remember?
    Yes. The photo can go in the trash.
    No. Go on to the next question.

11. Are you keeping the photo because you're afraid of something or someone?
    Yes. The photo can go in the trash. And while you're at it, identify what you're afraid of. Say it out loud—name it, know it.
    No. Go on to the next question.

12. Will you ever want reprints of this image? Would anyone else?
    Yes. Go on to the next question.
    No. The photo can go in the trash.

13. If it's a close duplicate of other shots, is it superior to those?
    Yes. Go on to the next question.
    No. The photo can go in the trash.

14. Do you have an immediate positive emotional response to the photo?

Yes. Keep the photo and place it in the appropriate category.

No. The photo can go in the trash.

You only need one disqualifying answer to determine a photograph's fate, so after the first response that identifies the image as a clunker, stop and let the picture go. Any photo that fails any of these questions should be discarded.

Also consider letting go of duplicates or near-duplicates. If you have good double shots, give them to family members or to anybody else who might appreciate them.

NOTABLE NOTE

If you're a perfectionist or at all fussy, you may find yourself imagining how a particular photo could be improved by cropping it or making other adjustments to it and so be tempted to set it aside for a future project. Be realistic. In project management terms, this is scope creep. You probably have enough to do just organizing the photos in front of you, let alone creating more work for yourself, right? How feasible is it that you'll have the time *and* willingness to prioritize investing that time into editing images? Of all the things you want to do, how important is this by comparison? Would you be willing to invest your money into having someone else do it for you instead?

To help you make this decision now and future decisions later when something similar occurs, put things into perspective by considering this: What's something you love to do that you already don't have time for or make time for right now? Let's call that activity X. So, if you had to choose between doing X and editing photos, which would it be? How about editing photos versus visiting family or gardening or exercising?

Very quickly, you should be able to see that things you're already interested in and possibly neglecting or not doing enough of would be better places to invest your time (and money) rather than whatever your new bright idea is. Entertaining these kinds of ideas for more than a moment creates mental clutter, distracts you from the task in front of you, and possibly even derails your enthusiasm for your current project. So it's important that you evaluate these thoughts quickly and clearly, then prioritize them or let them go just as quickly.

In this case, a better choice would be to celebrate your keen aesthetic sense and then lean into the fact that you have neither the time nor budget to take this on now or in the foreseeable future. Yay! You had a curious idea, you determined it wasn't a good fit, and you're ready to get back to what you were doing in the first place. Great. Ring your bell and move on.

Once you've determined whether a photo stays or goes, you could label each image you're keeping with some key information if that helps you avoid going through them twice. Either way, sort the photos into the categories you identified. If the final destination for your photographs are photo boxes, create one for each category and sort the pictures directly into each box. That may be all the sorting and organizing you need or want to do.

If you're planning to store them in acid-free sleeves or pouches with their negatives nearby, once you've completed your categorical sorting, you can begin to assemble these sleeves or pouches. The same is true for albums or scrapbooks. After applying the categories, you'll have your raw material for your individual books.

There is no one perfect way to sort and organize photos, so there's no need to stress about this process. What you're doing is creating a system and some order where there was previously chaos. So all progress is good progress. Aim for completion rather than perfection since no one really cares if you end up with a few pictures out of order.

This doesn't give you permission to be sloppy, though—pay attention so you only have to do this once. The goal is for you to end up with a photo collection that is organized in a way that makes sense to you where you can find the photos you want easily and quickly. Don't overreach and create a monster. If you design a meticulous, highly structured organizational system for your photos and it becomes so complicated that you'll never use it again, you've defeated the purpose.

Once all the photos have been culled, sorted, and labeled, and they are in either photo-safe boxes, sleeves for storage, or sleeves headed for scrapbooks or albums, it's time to put them away. Using One Home for Everything and Like with Like to guide you, find a place to store them all that is climate-controlled, easy to access, and large enough for them all to live alongside each other. This way, whether they're in photo boxes, albums, or sleeves, they'll be together, not scattered throughout the house or even the room. Keep them together, and you'll always know where to find them, day or night.

ORGANIZING DIGITAL PHOTOS

Digital photography has revolutionized the world of photography, but it hasn't revolutionized photo organization or storage just yet. We've traded in piles of prints for random images scattered across our hard drives, on current and retired phones, in and out of digital folders and smart cards, etc.

For the average person, the odds of finding the exact picture you want instantly is almost impossible without a razor-sharp memory, excellent computer skills, and a bit of luck, too. For all the advances with facial recognition and AI, your devices still "name" each picture or file with numbers, so your only hope of finding the right picture is either rapidly scrolling or at least isolating every file with a .jpg, .png, .heic, or .tif suffix attached to it and starting there.

If that bit of alphabet soup has you overwhelmed, confused, or both, do not freak out.

By applying the exact same principles and process for sorting and organizing your digital photos as you did for print photos, you will end up with a manageable and functional system going forward. That said, completing this process does require some basic computer skills such as creating folders, importing photos, and labeling and naming files. If you don't feel confident in these areas, recruit a tech-savvy friend to help, hire a local expert, or give yourself extra time to search online for instructions.

Gathering All Your Historic Digital Images Together

Start by creating a folder on your best-working computer and label it 20XX Photo Organizing. This is the equivalent of the table or area where you initially brought all your print photos to start sorting them.

Then find all your loose images on any phones, tablets, retired computers, flash drives, and memory cards, import them to the computer, and move them into that folder. Once you've confirmed that they have all been successfully added to the new parent folder, make two backups of this folder and label them 20XX Photo Organizing Backup 1 and 2, then set them aside in two different locations, like an external hard drive and the cloud.

Next, take the bold step of deleting all the photos from their original locations. I know this sounds scary, but if you skip this step, you could end up wasting a lot of time organizing duplicates and never completing this project.

Best Practices for New Behavior

What you just did was momentous, right? And the best way to make sure you don't have to do it ever again is to create new behaviors for when you take new digital photos. Going forward, make it a practice to regularly download new pictures onto your computer. Do not procrastinate or rely on any particular app or program to sort and organize them for you. If you use a digital camera, it's almost guaranteed that at some point you'll be rushing out the door with no time to check your camera, and when you go to take that first picture, you'll discover that your memory card is full and you don't have a spare.

I have a client who never downloads his images; he simply buys new memory cards. As a result, he's yet to enjoy a single image he's ever photographed—they're all still on their cards in a drawer. Worse yet is that the longer he waits to download those images, the more memory cards he'll have to deal with and the longer the sorting and organizing process will take.

If you typically use your phone to take pictures and don't regularly download them to sort and organize them, you also likely have way too many images and have probably already discovered that trying to organize them on that small screen is a hassle, even with the help of any apps.

So, if you take my advice and harvest photos from your devices weekly—or monthly at the latest—this is how you should do it: When transferring photos to your computer, direct them into specific subfolders immediately. Do not dump them all randomly into a parent folder labeled My Pictures or Pictures or Photos, thinking you'll come back later to clean them up and organize them.

Instead, create subfolders that accurately describe the photos you're about to deposit into them—like 20XX 08 21 Billy's Birthday or 20XX Summer Cape Cod. A short description is more likely to jog your memory than just a date, so be sure to include both.

Every computer has a location it defaults to when you plug in a camera or phone. You can either globally alter that under a Preferences or Options tab or manually redirect the download each time you plug the device into your computer. If you're transferring them wirelessly, most computers will default to either your Downloads folder or the last location you imported a file to. It should tell you or ask you what that folder is, and in that moment, you can select a different folder to import the photos into. So, instead of just dumping the images randomly into My Pictures, create a series of subfolders inside it as follows:

My Pictures (parent folder)
→ 20XX (subfolder)
    → 01 01 20XX New Year's Day (subfolder of a subfolder)
        → Nancy & Dave Smith (photograph)

NOTABLE NOTE

If you post any photos online, make sure to save the original, hopefully-higher-resolution version as well. Most platforms will automatically compress your images to reduce storage space. So if the online photo is your only copy and you decide to print or share it somewhere else later, you'll only be able to download its smaller, lower-resolution image at that time.

If you already have historic photos randomly living inside your My Pictures parent folder, schedule a block of time (or several) to create subfolders as described, and then slowly and deliberately sort your photos into the appropriate subfolders.

You may be using cloud-based storage services like Apple iCloud, Google Photos, Dropbox, or Microsoft OneDrive to automatically upload and sync photos taken with your smartphone. These are great for saving you the hassle of transferring digital photos to your computer, but using them makes it even easier to avoid organizing your images.

In addition, some of these platforms rely on AI, facial recognition, tags, and other alterations to the metadata of your photos. If you ever unsubscribe or remove your photos from their platform, any organization the system provided will be stripped from the photos as you are migrating or downloading them.

And as with all deferred decisions, by only uploading images but never reviewing or deleting any, it may not take long before you've run out of storage space and have to pay to upgrade. So do yourself a favor and apply the same best practices of sorting, deleting, and organizing your photos into specific folders on a weekly or monthly basis.

Renaming, Tagging, and Photo Apps

RENAMING PHOTOS

As advanced as technology is today, when you download (or sync) pictures from any of your devices, they still have names that are numeric—sometimes starting with DSC and other times just a number that represents its position among all the images currently on that device (e.g., DSC000014). This is why, going forward, it is so important for you to name at least the folder you're downloading or moving them into so you have some way of finding what you're looking for without having to look through all your photos every time.

Eventually, if you want to find specific pictures, you're going to have to do at least one of these three things, and possibly two of them: rename them, tag them, or run them through a sorting app.

The easiest time to rename photos is as you move them into their new folders. I'm not going to lie to you: renaming photos can be a tedious process, especially if you have a lot of them to rename. But if you don't know how or care to learn how to apply tags or use software that can sort them for you, this is the easiest of the three techniques available to you.

Fortunately, you don't need to rename each file one by one. Most operating systems will let you rename your photos (or any files) in groups. Just select all the images you want to rename, right-click on them, choose Rename, type in whatever new name you want to give them, then press Enter. The photos will all be given that name along with a sequential number tacked onto the end.

If you're looking for third-party software to speed up renaming your files, look for a program that gives you access to the metadata associated with each file. That way the information, including any names, becomes embedded into the photo's data file.

The time you spend now putting in good systems will almost certainly save you confusion and frustration in the future, not just in being able to quickly track down images that you want but also when it comes to backing up your data. Please trust me when I say the time you invest now will pay dividends in the future. The next time you go looking for a photo and can find it in 15 seconds or less, you will be grateful for the time you spent organizing these images.

Now, you could just stop at putting them in a properly labeled subfolder—the only problem with that is if or when they get separated from that subfolder. If you're the only person with access to your computer, the risk may be minimal. If you share your computer with others and they are not particularly careful or attentive, that's when the risk becomes bigger. Whenever possible, it's better to rename each photo file with something clear, consistent, and recognizable.

Remember that a folder or filename doesn't need to contain too many details to be helpful. It used to be standard practice to separate each word in a filename with a hyphen or an underscore because some software couldn't read the spaces. While spaces are no longer an issue, it's still best to avoid using any other punctuation or symbols such as commas, exclamation marks, or apostrophes.

Here's a good formula for naming digital photos: Start with the year, followed by the month and then the day. This will ensure that your files are always in chronological order when you list them alphabetically in a Finder or File Explorer window. For example, your naming sequence could look like this:

20XX 06 21 Summer Solstice Party 001.jpg
20XX 06 21 Summer Solstice Party 002.jpg
20XX 06 21 Summer Solstice Party 003.jpg

If you're renaming more than 99 images at a time, start your numbering sequence with 001 so you allow for three digits rather than two. Also, if you're renaming images that have multiple sizes or have been edited in any way, be sure to include that detail in the name. For example, if you've reduced the file size to share on social media, you could name the file like this:

20XX 06 21 Summer Solstice Party 001 social media.jpg

Once you have established your naming conventions or lexicon and set up your relevant subfolders inside the parent folder My Pictures, you have built yourself a simple, sustainable system for organizing historic photos and importing new photos easily and quickly.

TAGGING PHOTOS

Tags are essentially keywords or categories used to identify a piece of digital data—in this case, a photograph. *Tagging* means writing to the metadata—that's the information embedded in each digital image file—so that any computer can more easily search and sort going forward.

While you may be able to visualize sticking a tag or a series of tags on an image, like a Post-it or the label your mom sewed into your underwear when you went away to camp, you don't actually see tags displayed anywhere. You have to open the backside of the image—its metadata—to add, view, or edit the tags. Curiously, when using some of these apps, you literally drag a representation of a tag to drop on your pictures—even though that tag won't be displayed when you view the image itself, only when you are viewing the metadata.

If this all sounds too involved for you, then it may be. In this case, simply renaming your files and putting them in the right folder is all you need to do to organize your photos.

If you do decide to use tags, don't go overboard. Even if you have 200,000 photos, you still only need about 20 keywords or tags. With a little care and thought, create a list of categories that will become your tags. There are no hard and fast rules for creating your tags, so keep it simple and use keywords that will help you find the photos again later.

For example, they can include:

- Who is in the photo?
  - » People, pets
- What is in the photo?
  - » Landmarks, buildings, landscapes, flora and fauna, food and drink, and other subjects or objects
- Where was the photo taken?
  - » Names of locations
- Why was the photo taken?
  - » The event that made this day and these photos important
- When was the photo taken?
  - » Time of day, time of year

Before you start applying tags to photos, write up the list of key-words you would use to search for your photos. Be consistent and watch out for overlap. You don't want to use Auto and Car to describe the same kind of vehicle. You should also decide on singular or plural so you don't end up mixing them. For example, don't use Dog, Cat, and Horse and then later create Dogs, Cats, and Horses. Likewise with verbs, you'll want to stick to a single form: Running, Biking, and Swimming rather than Run, Bike, and Swim.

Use these tags to get you started:

- Family (If you have a small family, you may consider creating a tag for each person's name.)
- Friends
- Travel
- Holidays (or Holiday #1 Name, Holiday #2 Name, etc.)
- Biking
- Boating
- Skiing
- Birthdays
- Headshots
- Gardens

- Shows (or Concerts)
- Home (or use the street number and name)
- Investment Property (or again, use the street number and name)

Use too many and the list becomes unwieldy, too few and there's little distinction between images.

The power and ease of tags is apparent as soon as you start searching for a particular photo or photos. Instead of sorting through various folders trying to remember what you may have called the folder or photo, especially if some digital number is the photo's only name, you just think of one of your tags, like Skiing or Birthday or Family. Search on that tag, and all the photos associated with it will come up.

If you do use individual names as tags, you'll be able to search for and find every picture of a particular person instantly. You can further refine any search by including or excluding additional tags. For example, a search for Gary and Ethel will bring up all photos in your collection of Gary and Ethel. By excluding Wedding from the same search string, you'll end up with all the photos of Gary and Ethel except for those also tagged Wedding.

APPS THAT CAN HELP SORT YOUR PHOTOS

These days, most of our devices have software that accurately recognizes faces, places, and common visuals, like a kiss. So you can leverage machine learning and artificial intelligence to identify the what, who, and when in your photos.

There is still a bit of upfront work you need to do, though; you will have to "teach" the photo app how to accurately recognize people, places, and things in your photos. For example, if you want the app to identify Andrew Mellen in your photos, you'll have to give it a few examples to reference. From there, it will be able to identify Andrew Mellen's face in all other photos in your collection.

Whatever program you choose, make sure it offers the ability for the tags to remain with the image so that if you change software or give the image away, its tags stay with it. The language to look for is anything that describes embedding the tag into the metadata of the photo.

If you're wondering if I have a recommendation for the best app to use, I don't. There are many options on the market, and they change rapidly. Your best bet is a quick search online for "What is the best photo organizing software?," and you'll get plenty of results to review. Some software requires an up-front fee or an ongoing subscription, and some offer perfectly fine free options. Do some research, talk to your tech-savvy friends, see what looks user-friendly, and pick something within your budget.

MISERLY MEAN APPS THAT STRIP METADATA OUT OF FILES

As I mentioned, many photo apps now have facial recognition and also let you add keywords or tags to your photos. But some of these same apps will strip that information out of the file's metadata if you export your images away from that app. It's a mean and shortsighted policy driven by greed, so don't fall for it. Be sure to find an app that keeps the file's metadata intact regardless of whether you're viewing the metadata with that app or another app.

And of course, facial recognition isn't for everyone. You may be opposed to it on principle, or you may just find it difficult to use. Either way, no harm, no foul.

One Last Plug for Folders

Regardless of whether or not you use photo-organizing software, you still want to sort your photos into subfolders by year, category, and subject. There will always be times when you want to get to a specific photo directly, and having it labeled in a folder is one of the surest ways to do that.

I suggest that with tags and/or subfolders, you keep a simple list of them someplace, perhaps in a notes app or right on your hard drive in your My Pictures folder. You can always print the list for easy reference, but keeping the original in digital format makes updating it very quick and easy. Whatever categories, tags, or folders you use are less important (they can be completely idiosyncratic to you) than recording your choices so you always remember them and use them consistently.

MAINTAINING THE SYSTEM

Once you take the time to sort through all your old photos, either film-based or digital, put them in appropriately named folders or boxes; then tag, label, and/or rename the images, and you'll be finished with that historic challenge, however large. This now becomes your base for future organizing.

Use the following steps to keep the system working. Remember that each task has a beginning and an end, so complete each step in order, and if you are diligent and consistent, you will never *not* find a photo again. Ever.

For new film-based photos, follow these steps:

1. Develop film in a timely fashion.
2. Review prints and keep only the best, discarding the rest.
3. Label each image with some sort of information: who, what, when, where.
4. Transfer the keepers from the developer's sleeve into an acid-free sleeve or the appropriate photo-safe box, accurately labeled.

For digital photos, follow these steps:

1. Download the images from your device or sync them with your cloud-based storage.
2. Sort the images into appropriate subfolders, creating new folders when necessary.

3. Rename the picture files from gobbledygook to a few actual words that make sense to you.
4. Label or tag all images.

For a comprehensive and easy-to-use guide for all your photo sorting and organizing dos and don'ts, check out your companion workbook. You'll find a simpler free version available at unstuffbook.com/photos.

Back Up Your Digital Photos Regularly

Anyone who's lived through the nightmare of having their computer crash knows the necessity of backing up their files and pictures on an external drive. As the saying goes, "Back up early; back up often." Most external drives come bundled with backup software that simplifies the entire process. You select which folders you'd like to back up, select a schedule for the backing up, and leave it alone. As long as the drive and computer are powered up and connected at the appointed time, the drive will scan the computer and back up all the folders indicated. Some even scan for additions, adding just those files to the folders already stored.

In addition to an external drive, send an additional backup to the cloud. You may think that redundant backups are overkill, but they're not. More than a few clients and even I have suffered through failed hard drives and the anxiety of trying to harvest whatever data could still be salvaged after the technical failure. The only difference between my clients and me when that happened was that I had multiple backups, and they did not. Remember: it's always a question of when technology will fail, not *if* it will fail.

10

EMAIL · DIGITAL FILES · SOCIAL MEDIA

Programming today is a race between software engineers
striving to build bigger and better idiot-proof programs and
the Universe trying to produce bigger and better idiots.
So far, the Universe is winning.
–RICK COOK

Diamonds are forever. Email comes close.
–JUNE KRONHOLZ

WHAT WE'RE GOING TO COVER IN THIS CHAPTER

- What Email Is and Isn't
- One Home for Everything and Like with Like
- Establishing an Email Policy
- Managing Incoming Email
- Managing Spam—and Not the Potted Meat Kind
- Communication Vampires
- Online Shopping—a Potential Personal Hell
- Organizing Your Bookmarks
- Older Forms of Digital Media
- Organizing Your Computer
- Backing Up!
- Social Media—What's In It for Me?
- Texting, Direct Messaging, Video Conferencing, and the Like
- Identity Theft
- Boss or Drone: Who's Running This Show?

THIS CHAPTER is not a how-to instruction manual on using or repairing technology. What we're going to cover in this chapter is how to organize the *contents* of your devices, meaning your files. You'll get some basic information on organizing apps and software, too.

Your digital files are the modern counterpart of paper documents that traditionally would've been found in an office or filing cabinet. Organizing your digital files assumes that you already possess some basic computing skills. That means that you know what your hard drive is, you know where to locate it on your computer, and that locating, navigating, and modifying the hierarchy of your computer's subfolders are things you feel are within your grasp.

We're not going to hack or modify software or apps, remove viruses or worms, and we're not going to optimize your computer so it can run faster. We're going to optimize you so that you can run more efficiently and actually find things when you're looking for them.

Like any other tool, whether a drill or a chain saw or a dishwasher, your computer can be leveraged to buy you back some time and speed up processes. If productivity is your jam, you'll find even more detailed instruction in my book, *Calling BS on Busy*, available at cbobbook.com and everywhere books are sold.

What we want to avoid is any situation where this tool, your computer, ceases to be useful and becomes a burden and an obstacle to efficiency and speed. Specifically when it comes to email, your use of it should align with your core values and provide some fundamental benefit to you rather than overwhelm you or drain your energy. In essence, we want you running your email rather than your email running you.

We're also going to address social media and text messaging. Many people use them both in the most basic or personal ways to keep in touch with friends and family, and as such, they can each either suck time out of your day or increase productivity depending on your intention and your ability to stay focused. Hanging out in cyberspace chatting and scrolling all day can be fun, but knowing how to quickly and succinctly reach people with focused and precise communication is also possible with the same tools. If that ability would serve you well but you currently don't have it, you will have it after this chapter.

If you are afraid of or intimidated by machines, at least half of that fear is based on your current mindset. Since most of us are not programming these devices, we're just using them, getting familiar with their most basic functions just takes a bit of practice. Like everything else you've ever learned to do, from tying your shoes to driving a car, you just need to spend enough time repeating certain actions until they no longer feel foreign. The more you do it, the faster you become and the more familiar it becomes. And unlike chopping onions, the more you do it, the *less* likely you are to end up in tears.

So reading this chapter will help you establish good work habits and ensure that even if chaos and confusion are the current condition of your electronic devices, that will soon be old news, and you'll be able to consistently find any file on any machine quickly and easily.

Things You Will Need for This Work

- A computer and/or smartphone or tablet
- Internet access
- Timer and stopwatch
- At least a bit more patience than you usually muster for technology

WHAT EMAIL IS AND ISN'T

Email (noun): A method of exchanging digital messages, designed primarily for human use; a system for sending and receiving messages electronically over a computer network

Email is not a siren call; it is not an emergency broadcast system; it is not the fire department banging on your front door. It's a string of symbols that have been electronically transmitted between devices for the benefit of humans (and in a few labs somewhere, probably by chimps).

NOTABLE NOTE

The average frontline worker spends up to 8.8 hours a week on email, which amounts to nearly two hours each day.[8] The typical office worker receives more than 120 emails each day. Thirty-eight percent of these workers report that "email fatigue" is likely to push them to quit their jobs.[9] Email junkies, take note.

Unless you're a surgeon and the way that you are called to the operating room is via email (unlikely) or you are on a clearly articulated deadline and you're awaiting key information in an email message (possibly), you are not obligated to check or answer email constantly. I know that the speed with which email travels around the globe can be seductive and intoxicating. But just because email arrives almost immediately into your inbox does *not* automatically require an instantaneous response.

---

8 Microsoft, 2023 *Work Trend Index: Annual Report; Will AI Fix Work?*, May 9, 2023, https://www.microsoft.com/en-us/worklab/work-trend-index/will-ai-fix-work/.

9 Edward Segal, "Survey Finds Email Fatigue Could Lead 38% of Workers to Quit Their Jobs," *Forbes*, April 21, 2021, https://www.forbes.com/sites/edwardsegal/2021/04/21/survey-finds-email-fatigue-could-lead-38-of-workers-to-quit-their-jobs/?sh=643997a625d9/.

The one exception is an email exchange in a customer-focused business or job. In those cases, customers have come to expect quick responses, but if you're in this type of role, you can be speedy with your responses for customer inquiries *only*. You don't have to be Johnny-on-the-spot for the rest.

Just as you don't have to leap for the phone every time it rings, you *can* break the cycle of obsessively checking your email and responding like one of Pavlov's dogs to notifications of new messages. Snail mail still arrives once a day, six days a week, and that hasn't changed since the 1890s. While your creditors would prefer to contact you electronically (under the guise of saving the planet by saving paper when it's really about saving printing and postage costs for them), even they seldom require an immediate response.

So it's okay to slow down—you are not under attack, and arriving messages cannot hurt you. And regardless of what other people might think, moving more slowly and deliberately when reading and replying to email does not mean that you don't care or that you're irresponsible or rude.

ONE HOME FOR EVERYTHING AND LIKE WITH LIKE

When it comes to digital files and emails, these two rules may be even more important than they are in your physical spaces. Because digital files take up such little space comparatively and because it's so easy to accumulate them, it's essential that One Home for Everything and Like with Like guide you in organizing them along with keeping track of all your email, too.

You need to know where every file on your computer lives—because unlike your desk, you'll never move a book or folder to discover a stray receipt lying there that you had been looking for just minutes ago. Even with robust search functions, the chances of randomly stumbling across a misplaced digital file are unlikely. That's why it is imperative that you always pay close attention when saving or moving files and folders around on your hard drive. This is a time when you do *not* want to be multitasking.

I've tracked down files that clients have inadvertently grabbed and dragged to the oddest of places, all because they were talking on the phone or not paying attention when moving something. Using One Home for Everything to set up your digital filing system and maintain it will save you hours of frustration.

ESTABLISHING AN EMAIL POLICY

Most companies have email policies for their workers—we should follow their lead, whether we're using email professionally or personally. In establishing your email policy, it's important to remember that you are in control of your email. You may not always be able to control what ends up in your inbox, but you can control when and how often you check your email, when and how often you reply, and what you say when you choose to reply.

It's likely that email is not going anywhere, regardless of its volume and limitations. Given that, here are my suggestions on how to better manage it. Feel free to use or modify this list as it serves you. I strongly urge you not to alter the first rule, however—when used correctly, it's a time management and sanity saver.

Check Email Only When You Can Read It and Reply to It

Just as discussed in Chapter 2—don't open physical mail if you don't have time to process it—do not scan your emails and click on random messages if you don't have time to also answer (or process) it at the same time. Here's what I mean.

If you read an email without enough time to respond to it, at best you're wasting the time reading it since you'll have to reread it when you do have the time to reply. At worst, if the content is at all unexpected or upsetting, it may become all you can think about regardless of what else you need to be doing at the time. I have certainly ruined more than one night's sleep by reading an email I was too tired to deal with but not too tired to be upset by. So when you do decide to check your email, start and finish dealing with each new message when you first see it.

Of course, if you read anything that is too emotionally charged for you, set it aside and ideally make an appointment with yourself to compose a thoughtful and measured reply when you're a bit less agitated. Prudence of pen and tongue is a great guide when replying to emotionally charged emails; you don't want to commit to something in writing that, with some distance, you could come to regret.

Excluding the emotionally fraught exception, follow these three steps for dealing with each email:

1. Read it.
2. Reply to it.
3. File it (or delete it).

Check Email on Demand Only (Disable Automatic Checking)

When you're not actively reading and replying to emails, close your email program completely and/or turn off automatic mail checking and all notifications. Unless you're on deadline or expecting something specific from someone specific, you don't need to see or know about each email's arrival.

Don't Read and Answer Email throughout the Day

I easily receive between 50 and 200 emails each day—how about you? Some are subscriptions I've opted-in to that are related to my work or a subject I'm interested in, like meditation or weight loss. Others are actual correspondence that will need to be answered, but very few of them need to be answered immediately. I've let everyone important to me, meaning friends, family, and private clients, know that for anything urgent, the best way to reach me is to either text or call me.

No one can be productive and constantly interrupted at the same time. So you need to establish a particular time or times each day when and for how long you'll check email. I used to schedule 30 minutes three times a day until I discovered that I usually only need 15 minutes for each session.

I do put buffers on the back end of each session in case an email reply needs a lot of crafting or consideration, but often those buffers become free time for something else. To see an example of how these sessions show up on my calendar, visit unstuffbook.com/resources.

For each session that you're checking email, set a timer, and when the time is up, you're finished. You don't have to prove to anyone else that you're always available, and you don't need to be sitting online waiting for some email that may never come.

Let go of any obsessive worrying about appearing rude—instead, focus on that major project sitting in front of you. If you have a customer service job or business where your customers are particularly demanding and needy, give them alternative ways to contact you so they always feel like they can reach you when they need you.

I remember calling author Suzanne Pharr years ago and being struck by the directness of her outgoing message. It announced that if you had phoned between certain morning hours, she was writing and would not be answering the phone. It made an impression. Now I often do the same; I modify my autoresponders for both voicemail and email to state that until X date or until Y project is finished, I will not be checking emails and will reply as soon as possible. This little hack has saved my sanity and a lot of time over the years. Thank you, Suzanne!

Once you've figured out how long *you* need to answer the volume of emails that actually require a response, schedule those appointments in your calendar and stick to them. I find that three times a day—once midmorning, again around lunch, and just before the end of the work day—works best for me. Whatever you decide, make it a part of your routine, and only alter it when needed.

Don't Answer Email at Your Most Productive Time of Day

I'm a morning person. I'm up early and at my most productive between 7 and 11 a.m., so I prefer not to get lost in email first thing in the morning. I check in with my assistant between 9 and 10 a.m., and by then she's already been in my inbox screening for anything urgent and important.

Complete the following statement for yourself:

I'm most productive between [time of day] **and** [time of day] .

And now that you've defined it, that time is sacrosanct. Not only should you not be answering emails, you really should not accept any commitments for that time that aren't of the highest value to you. Schedule less demanding tasks, including managing email, outside of your optimal work time to ensure you're making the most of your day.

For me, the distraction of email is sometimes a welcome shift from more rigorous brain activity when I'm losing steam or getting fatigued from extended focus on a particular project. In general, though, I save my most productive time for my most important work.

Inbox Means Inbox

Ideally, your inbox should only include unread messages. I know this is a big ask. It can certainly be a goal if not a constant reality. What you want to avoid is using your inbox as a makeshift task list, a shopping list, or a reminder area where lingering to-do items hang out until they're forgotten or deleted.

I have one client who had more than 60,000 emails in her inbox, and searching through them for emails she meant to read but never got to would waste hours a week. We spent several long work sessions eliminating duplicates, redundant subscriptions, and spam to get her down to a reasonable number of emails in her inbox, meaning 50 or less. This leads us directly to the next point on the list.

Let Technology Manage Your Email

Saving time, reducing digital clutter, and successfully managing your email must include setting up and using filters. All email apps or programs offer the ability to configure email rules or filters to direct emails to specific folders based on any number of criteria: the sender's specific email address, the sender's domain, keywords in the subject and/or body of the email, etc. For instance, you could set a filter to direct any spam immediately to the trash, although you may want to check your Spam and Trash folders at least weekly for emails that were wrongly misdirected there.

I have many subfolders I've create for specific categories of emails. My email program automatically filters all incoming emails and directs them to the appropriate folder whenever a message is a match for one or more rules I've set up. Here are a few examples.

Books: All correspondence from my agent, editors, designers, proof-readers, etc. is immediately directed to this folder.

Events: This folder contains correspondence from any person or organization who's looking to hire me to speak at an event or has already booked me for an event.

Finances: All bank statement alerts, billing correspondence—including payment alerts and postings—and all digital bills and invoices are directed here.

Andrew Mellen, Inc. Team: While the bulk of internal communications between my team members happens on Slack instead of email, there are a few messages that will occasionally be forwarded or need to be in an email rather than posted to a public/private forum.

Shopping: These are notices, invitations to special events, and coupons from online and brick-and-mortar stores that I've purchased from or follow online. While I don't shop often and never on impulse, there are a few vendors whose aesthetic or marketing strategy is inspiring to me, and sometimes both are. If you are too tempted by these kinds of emails, don't even let them show up in your inbox. Immediately unsubscribe from their lists.

Family: This is correspondence from anyone I'm blood-related to.

Clients: Within the Clients folder, I actually have several subfolders:

- **Active Clients:** Each of my active clients (organized by name) has their own folder.
- **Casual Clients:** This is where any of the clients who I work with occasionally live. They aren't inactive, but I don't do weekly or even monthly work with them.
- **Inactive Clients:** This where any of the named client folders get moved to when I complete a project and either the client or I am taking a break. If the client becomes active again, their folder is moved back into either the Casual Clients or the Active Clients folder.

In addition to creating these kinds of folders, you can also customize the appearance of incoming mail. For example, you can bold the subject line and color-code all emails from all your clients, an individual client, or your boss.

Filters can also be used to clean up after you by setting them to automatically move all read email out of your inbox after 24 hours. That way, even if you've forgotten to file them, the computer won't.

Another way to distinguish among emails is to flag them. Like tagging photos in Chapter 9, you can create associated saved searches for each flag. That way, you don't need to recreate frequent searches each time you want to find all emails bearing a specific flag.

Finally, using the preview pane at the bottom or the side of your incoming email list allows you to quickly scan through new emails that your filters may have missed to then manually redirect them to their proper folder.

The More Emails You Answer, the More You Receive

It doesn't seem logical that as soon as you clear your inbox, it fills up almost immediately again. Like rabbits, emails seem to breed at a tremendous speed and volume.

I have found that the more I reply, the more they send, so I only reply when necessary. For emails that don't require a response, I will typically send a thumbs up or other emoji. That seems to be a good way to signal "I got it" while also ending what could otherwise become a never-ending thread of nonessential communication.

When an actual thank-you is needed, send it. But we've all been caught in these kinds of exchanges, and no one seems to want to be the first one to stop:

"Thank you!"

"Thank you."

"You're welcome!"

"No problem."

"Cool."

"Don't mention it."

"You bet!"

Someone has to stop volleying, and it might as well be you. Figure out where your tolerance for busyness meets your sense of etiquette, then establish some guidelines and stick to them. If everyone is as busy as you are, they are not going to be judging you as rude; they'll be silently thanking you for your courage.

And whether a digital hoax shows up in an email or on social media, while we all appreciate your desire to stamp out misinformation, that could easily become a full-time job. Just point your misguided friends and acquaintances to any online fact-checking sites, and let them find out for themselves how false those stories are. For links to online fact-checking resources, visit unstuffbook.com/resources.

Reply When Necessary

While there are many emails that don't require a response, some certainly do. So even if the answer is "no," "no, thank you," or "I can't," send that reply ASAP to anyone waiting to hear from you before they plan their next action. Delaying your reply is not helpful to the sender.

The impulse to thoroughly investigate something before replying is noble, but since the other party can't read your mind, all they know is that they haven't yet heard back from you. Do them a favor and let them know. Even if all you do is let them know you're working on a larger or more carefully considered response, any news is better than no news.

If you aren't the right person for the request or you don't have the information but know someone who does, forward it on to the appropriate person and cc the sender. That way, you've facilitated a solution and gotten yourself out of the loop—a double win for you and your sender.

Read the Entire Message Thread before Responding

Have you ever answered an email only to discover that someone else has already answered it and the conversation has moved on since then? If you've been out of your inbox for a while, it's possible that several emails have stacked up on the same thread, so be sure to review all related messages before answering any of them. This will save you time and face.

If your email app is currently set up so that you are viewing condensed threads rather than individual messages, you may want to change that setting to avoid confusion.

Use Complete Information in the Subject Line

Help your recipients anticipate what you're sending and you'll also make filing or filtering easy for both of you. Avoid using personal shorthand, any private secret language, or overly abbreviated subjects like Update, Checking In, or Status, particularly without including the day's date—they are ambiguous and confusing. Be thorough but succinct, to the point and direct. You're sending an email, not laying an ambush. There's no reason to be cryptic or vague.

And when you're not fully present for the task at hand, you might leave out important words because you're moving too fast or just assuming that everyone already knows what you're referring to. But again, since your recipient is probably not reading your mind, they actually can't fill in the missing words or meaning behind your staccato subject line. So instead of sending an email in response to a request for a file with the subject line "Your request," send one with a simple yet descriptive subject line like this: "Volunteer Opportunities File Attached Per Your Request, 3-30-XX."

Automate Responses to Frequently Asked Questions

If you often get emails asking the same questions, you can create standard replies to those frequent questions and either make them stand-alone email signatures or include them in your primary email signature. That way, you just have to pull down a menu to select your precomposed response and hit send. There's no need for a personal message when there's no need for a personal message. Here's an example of a signature that does double duty:

> Thanks for requesting more information on upcoming events and the possibility of me speaking at one of yours.
>
> I am always eager to help businesses and organizations simplify their operations and increase productivity. The quickest and best way to proceed is to hop on a quick call, so we can discuss your programming needs and how I can best serve you and your audience.
>
> Here's a link to book a call: https://calendly.com/andrewmellen/speaking.
>
> If you have any problems with that link or can't find a time that works for you, please send an email to hello@andrewmellen.com, and someone on my team will get right back to you.
>
> Thanks again for your interest. I'm looking forward to connecting with you very soon!
>
> Here's to more love and less stuff,
> Andrew Mellen
> CEO, Andrew Mellen Inc.
> AndrewMellen.com

For emails like this, you may then want to file them someplace where you can follow up in a timely way. For others that are more informational or, really, any email where a paper trail, digital or otherwise, isn't needed, the next step is to delete it and move on.

Publish Your Preferred Methods for Contact

Let people know via your website, in your signature, or through some other means the best ways to reach you. Some people use auto-replies pointing folks to alternate channels like WhatsApp or their mobile phone for texts. You get to decide when and how you want to communicate with others.

Personally, I still think a phone or video call is the quickest and most efficient way to answer multiple questions at the same time. Media companies often send a list of questions for me to answer, and I'll either send them back a video recording or hop on a call to get them the information they're requesting.

Particularly for articles and other content requests, great ideas inevitably come up in the back-and-forth exchange that wouldn't happen with me just writing out my responses. And for one-off requests that prompt follow-ups, I don't have the patience or time for those single questions pinging back and forth, when in five minutes we could wrap up every question and any follow-up questions, too.

Reduce Your Use of Email as Much as Possible

As I mentioned, my team moved all internal communications from email to Slack several years ago, and it was a game changer for us. Conversations are much easier to track and reply to, and the threads inside individual channels keep everyone updated on the status of ongoing projects.

I suggest this all the time when I'm speaking on productivity and organization to companies around the world, and I'm still amazed when this is something they hadn't considered before I mentioned it. Breaking your dependence on email to communicate both at work and home will immediately free up an hour or more every day.

For broadcasting messages to your network, consider where they are already spending their time; maybe it would be faster and more direct to post the information there? If you don't need a response from the recipient, where can you publish publicly so you get more traction and visibility? This will accomplish several things at once:

- It gets the answer online with less chance of you needing to personally share it more than once.

- It provides a URL that could be relatively permanent and reliable. This helps with SEO and other searchability factors.
- It encourages people to return to the information instead of relying on an email request for additional information.

When All Else Fails, Declare Email Bankruptcy

As attached as you may be to your email address(es), sometimes you just have to throw in the towel. Email bankruptcy lets you abandon an address and start over. But as with other forms of bankruptcy, this is a last-ditch effort. Carefully consider whether something as final as bankruptcy is going to be the solution you need or if you've got a bigger problem to solve: effectively managing your limited time and how and where you want to invest your attention.

If your problem is less about spam and more about the number of emails received versus your time and ability to answer them all, you'll want to put some things in place to cure this problem so you don't quickly find yourself back in the same situation with a new address. Study the other earlier suggestions and try them on as you shift your relationship with email. The result should be more time for what matters and less time in your inbox.

If you do decide to declare email bankruptcy, there are plenty of articles online that detail best practices for ditching an email address and starting fresh. For starters, you'll want to send one last email informing anyone you want to stay in touch with that, come tomorrow, you'll be abandoning this email address and no longer checking it or replying to messages. Then you'll need to figure out who you'll share this new address with, how you'll limit subscriptions and other nonessential mail, and when and how often you'll check email to avoid a backlog from piling up.

MANAGING INCOMING EMAIL

Now that you've considered how you'd like to use email going forward, it's time to make some decisions. Visit unstuffbook.com/email or see your companion workbook for a worksheet that will walk you through a step-by-step process of

- identifying which email addresses you have and use,
- deciding which email addresses you may want to retire and which you'll want to create,
- determining the kinds or categories of email you currently receive,
- figuring out which categories, if any, you want to continue to get,
- unsubscribing quickly from any lists you're finished with,
- creating subfolders for your emails, and
- setting up filters, including directing your emails into your new subfolders.

After you make these critical decisions, you can quickly configure your email to better serve you.

I use two email addresses—one for personal and professional correspondence and one for all online subscriptions, banking, and shopping. This way, I'm not bombarded all day with nonessential emails in my primary inbox. I can check the second email address once a day or once a week—there's never anything there that requires my immediate attention. These are the kinds of email that I direct to my secondary address:

- Banking and finances
- Airlines and travel in general
- Shopping, including online catalogs and vendors
- Marketing strategy and other business development resources
- Podcasts and blogs
- News sources
- Product registrations, codes, and warranties
- Social media accounts
- Personal interests—real estate, home improvement, gardening

As you sort through any email lists you've subscribed to, get clear (and honest) about which ones you actually read and enjoy. Remember, we're talking about emails here, not precious and rare jewels. So even if you err on the side of unsubscribing to almost everything, it literally only takes a click to opt back in.

This may help you in your process: If you have a bunch of emails that you haven't already deleted or unsubscribed to, create a new folder now and then manually drag them into the new folder. Name it Email Subscriptions to Delete. Then set aside 15 minutes a day to go through them and click on the Unsubscribe link at the top or bottom of each message until you finish them off. If you have already deleted the most recent ones, as each new one comes in, follow the Unsubscribe link at the top or bottom of each email and kill them in real time. Either way, it shouldn't take more than a week or so for you to eliminate the bulk of them.

If you're feeling at all hesitant right now, thinking, *Yeah, I hate them, but "someday" there might be one that contains something really important, and I'd hate to miss it just because I was impatient,* consider the following. First, "someday" doesn't actually exist, remember? You can't live in the future and in the moment at the same time.

Second (and less philosophically), the content or information that they are delivering will still be available somewhere—on their website, somewhere else online, or in actual printed form within a book, catalog, or magazine. Carefully consider what you're actually choosing by deferring to take action on these emails. Their arrival and presence in your inbox demand at least some of your attention. Is this really where you want to invest it?

If the content is not information you need for work or life to complete a project or meet a deadline, go ahead and unsubscribe. Free yourself from the idea that you're missing something important. You're not. Think about it: you're already missing lots of things all the time—a soccer match in South America, a trade show in Dallas, a going-out-of-business sale down the street. It's a given that you can't be everywhere at the same time, so accept it, and let that panicky feeling fall away. At the same time, recognize that whatever you actually need to know or find out, you can and will actively pursue. The rest can be recognized for what it is—a distraction and some visual noise.

When you finish this exercise, you should be receiving emails only from actual people or companies and organizations you have a strong affinity for. If it takes you a few passes to complete this process, that's fine. Don't judge it, just celebrate your growing freedom from inbox clutter.

MANAGING SPAM— AND NOT THE POTTED MEAT KIND

If you haven't yet been bombarded by spammy emails, you are either incredibly lucky or maybe a spammer yourself—because I don't know anyone who hasn't complained at least once about the volume of unsolicited junk email they receive.

So while these suggestions won't be able to stop spam, they can certainly help you slow down spam—which may be a big enough victory to make this worthwhile.

Let's start with a list of email address prefixes that are magnets for spam bots. Whenever possible, don't set up or use email addresses containing these:

contact@

help@

home@

sales@

support@

webmaster@

info@

Generic email addresses like these are assumed to exist at every domain. For spammers, they're a no-brainer, so any accounts with these prefixes are bound to get hit often.

Now let's look at the most common types of spam floating around.

Nine Common Types of Spam

ADS AND PROMOTIONAL EMAILS

Unsolicited bulk emails are pretty annoying and one of the most common types of spam. Every day, hundreds of millions of advertisements and promotional emails are sent to anyone and everyone with an email address. These emails come from legitimate businesses as well as shady ones.

I'm not talking about emails from companies you've done business with; while you may not necessarily want promotional emails from them, they technically aren't spam. Most websites ask you if you'd like to be included in their communications, and they often do this with an offer to give you something in exchange for the privilege of adding you to their email list. Other companies default to adding you to their list through an opt-in feature like a checkbox, or they just assume that since you bought something, you want to continue to hear from them with other offers.

In any case, if you no longer wish to receive these emails, the previous section walks you through unsubscribing, which I strongly encourage you to do.

The problem arises when companies you interact with sell your data—including your email address—to anyone willing to pay for it. That's how you end up on spammers' lists. This is why having a secondary email address you can use for purchases and subscriptions makes so much sense. Using this email address when you sign up or shop online will reduce the amount of spam being sent to your primary email inbox because spammers won't have it on file.

PHISHING SCAMS

These emails are designed to look like official emails from financial institutions or big, established companies. They direct readers to scam sites that look like the real thing but are actually designed to capture the unsuspecting victim's username and password or other sensitive information. Those credentials or personal details are then used by the scammers to gain access to the victim's real accounts.

There are two easy ways to spot these sites before you enter your personal details. First, look closely at a few pages and see if you can find any typos or grammatical errors. While few legit sites are error-free, the errors on phishing sites often read like they were written by non-native speakers of the site's parent language.

Also, do a quick search for the company online and compare the URL you see in the legit site's address bar to the URL you see in the phishing site's address bar. It's usually easy to spot the differences.

EMAIL SPOOFING

A cousin of phishing scams, these emails try to fool you by impersonating someone you know or a company you have a relationship with. The emails look like they were sent from a familiar email address, but that is just a skin they are wearing. The scammer dresses up a fraudulent email address so, naturally, you trust the sender and are more likely to do what they ask you to do, which is often included in the email's message.

When in doubt, right click on the email address and see if the sender's address is actually displayed as the email address it claims to be from. If you still have doubts, follow up by asking the person or company directly by phone or text if they actually sent the message. Do this *before* sending any personal information or money.

MONEY SCAMS

These come in several flavors as well. There are the get-rich-quick emails where you've just been discovered to be the only heir to a fortune. There are the pleading emails where someone is fleeing an oppressive regime, and they trust you to manage their money until they can get free. A variation of that email comes from someone claiming to have been mugged while traveling and just needs you to send them some money so they can get home. In all these cases, you are asked to send money directly, purchase a gift card, or provide banking details. Please do none of these things.

Another version is triggered by any item you're selling online. Out-of-town buyers will promise to wire you the money and trust you to send them the item, and for helping them out, they're happy to pay you handsomely. Yet another version involves asking for money for children or families abroad or for communities who have suffered losses as a result of a natural disaster. Always keep in mind: if it sounds too good to be true, it is too good to be true.

TROJAN HORSES

Email worms not only infect your computer but they also clone themselves and fire off a new email containing the same disgusting worm to everyone in your contacts. The most infamous email worm came with the subject line "I love you," since most people would be tempted to open an email from someone they know with that message, right?

So, while we don't want to become overly paranoid or reactionary, the best practice with any email attachment from someone who either doesn't typically send attachments or isn't particularly tech-savvy is to get offline immediately and then call or text the sender to confirm it's a legit attachment before opening or downloading anything.

CHAIN LETTERS

As dangerous as some other types of spam are, these are actually the ones I hate the most because they prey on people's easily exploited feelings and vulnerabilities. All of these follow the same formula. Someone got superrich or fell in love or got superrich *and* fell in love, and you can, too, as long as you copy the message and send it to 25 of your favorite people who are just as gullible and pliable as you are.

These are very popular on social media as well. The premise is the same: Show me how much you value our relationship by copying this and spamming a bunch of other people (like the sender/poster just did to you), and if you really love me, you'll send it back to me, too. That's not all, though; if you break the chain, you'll die a speedy and horrible death. Of course you will.

While you probably don't want to flag these as spam since they came from someone you know, throw them in the trash and try not to resent the sender too much.

POLITICAL OR TERRORIST

In the U.S., we know that the IRS doesn't leave voicemail messages or send emails. That doesn't stop criminals from appearing to be a politician or a well-known government agency and sending you an email claiming that you're either in trouble or in danger. These fake government emails are usually about you being in hot water or about some group needing to be stopped before they destroy the country. Either way, these messages claim the only resolution is for you to send off a bunch of money to pay penalties, interest, or legal fees or to make a political contribution.

If you ever receive anything like this, don't panic, but also do not reply.

Instead, you can forward the email to reportphishing@apwg.org. This address is used by the Anti-Phishing Working Group, which includes internet service providers, security vendors, financial institutions, and law enforcement agencies. You can also report it to the Federal Trade Commission at reportfraud.ftc.gov/.

If you think there's any chance the email is authentic, contact the alleged sender at a phone number you know to be genuine and then verify the information on the call.

PORN, SEX, AND HEALTH AND WELLNESS HOAXES

Whether the email offers you pornography, a cure for Erectile Dysfunction, a surgery for enlarging penises or breasts, or any other health-related miracle cure, every one of these topics is designed to get your attention and then direct you to a malicious website.

Porn, as a huge global industry, is not surprisingly also a leading source of malicious content. From sleazy ads to identity theft, porn scammers will try every way possible to get your contact and credit card information. All the other get-in-shape-without-changing-your-diet-and-never-exercising emails are preying on your desire for something for nothing. So thoroughly research any product or service before buying or subscribing and be hyper-cautious with anything that shows up in your inbox that you didn't proactively seek out.

MALWARE AND ANTIVIRUS WARNINGS

Apple, Dell, and other technology companies don't contact their customers to warn them about malware. So whether it's a phone call or an email earnestly warning you about a possible malware infection on one or more of your devices, a scammer is behind it. Of course, no one wants a virus, and if you tend to run a bit anxious, it's easy to lean into the fear that your computer is infected.

In some cases, the email claims to have the solution to your problem; you just need to provide some information or download an attachment. The disgusting irony is that instead of downloading security software once you click install, you're actually doing their work for them and infecting your device with a virus they sent you. Then, the only way to get rid of the virus is to pay them for additional software that will magically clean up the virus you just installed.

You'd be much better off using comprehensive antivirus software from a trusted company. The good news is that there are many great free and paid versions out there that run on all operating systems.

Reducing Spam

In addition to avoiding those types of digital garbage, here are some other ways you can further reduce spam. While it's impossible to completely eliminate spam, the following suggestions can alter its grip on your inbox:

- **Don't use AOL, Hotmail, Yahoo!, Gmail, Outlook, iCloud, or any major web-based email providers for your primary email address**; get a domain name instead. Creating a domain is very easy, and many hosting companies will walk you through the simple process. So instead of being BettySmith@icloud.com, you could be Betty@BettySmith.com.

  Spammers know that there are almost endless accounts at the big email providers, and they target those accounts with their most aggressive spamming efforts. If you must use one of the major providers, choose an obscure email address that has some combination of letters and numbers.

- **Opt out of email lists**, and don't do business with merchants who share or sell your email address or other personal data with others. Read the privacy policy of any site before purchasing anything or corresponding with online merchants.

- **Never open spam.** Never. Simply opening a piece of spam informs the spammer that your email address is valid.
- **Never reply to spam**—even to unsubscribe. Spam often offers false unsubscribe options as another trick to confirm the validity of your email address. As a result, clicking on the unsubscribe option actually increases the amount of spam they send. In the case of hijacked email addresses used to send out spam, your reply would be sent only to the innocent victim of the hijacking.
- **Never purchase anything from an unsolicited email message.** Spammers send out spam because it's profitable, either through perpetrating fraud on unsuspecting individuals or through the sale of junk to unsuspecting individuals. If the profits dry up, spammers will find new ways to scam the public, but they'd at least give up on spam.
- **If you don't have spam protection, get some.** If you have it and you're not using it, set a timer for 15 minutes now and set it up.

Most internet service providers and web-based email applications offer some sort of external spam filter. Log in to your email on their server, which you can do by going to their website and following the links for webmail. Once there, look for a Preferences tab or something similar and select it; then look for anything that is labeled Spam Filter or Spam Blocker or something with the word *spam* in it.

Once you find that, you can play around with the settings to configure the filter until you get it the way you want it. Setting the sensitivity level too low will continue to let the bulk of spam slip through. Set the sensitivity level too high and even your friends and family might get caught from time to time depending on what's in their emails to you. The filters monitor for keywords, images, and other triggers, so even if you know the sender, if their email contains enough triggers it will get snagged.

- **If you are really struggling to control spam, you can use a third-party spam-filtering program.** Since spam and the apps designed to stop it change so quickly, I won't recommend any particular products. Like with most things, there are some free choices out there as well as others that you'd have to purchase. Whichever one you opt for, make sure it's easy for you to use, easy to customize, and powerful enough to do what it claims to do. Do some research online, talk to friends who have better computing skills than you do and ask for their suggestions, and then take your choice for a test-drive.

If none of these suggestions significantly slows down the volume of incoming spam, your last resort may be to abandon the email address that's being swamped—declaring email bankruptcy as discussed earlier. No matter how fond you are of your email address, you are not your email address, so keep that in mind. If breaking free from spam's grip means you have to send one email to everyone in your address book alerting them to your address change, it's a small price to pay for that freedom. And as a side benefit, it reinforces the temporal nature of all things, even email addresses.

COMMUNICATION VAMPIRES

Do you have a friend, relative, or client who seems to suck the life out of you with their communication? They sometimes fire off multiple texts or emails in a row that seem increasingly fraught. At other times, they start a conversation and then disappear for days or weeks only to surface with a sad story about why they've been out of touch. They'll offer another feeble, self-deprecating apology about what a crappy friend they are—often including declarations of their love for you and a promise to do better in the future.

How about "experts" and influencers who send you random texts, emails, or direct messages on social media? They never reply to your responses, *even when they ask for a response*; they just keep up the barrage of one-sided communication. Between bots and clueless humans, the implied entitlement to our time from some people and businesses is truly shocking.

Some people never reply to an email with facts or answers, only more questions. They claim to be interested in clear communication yet avoid addressing key points laid out in your replies. They ask you annoying questions that only exist to qualify you to buy one of their products, join their latest get-rich-quick scheme, or validate their latest conspiracy theory.

They focus only on themselves unless trying to convince you that the world is a hostile place where everyone is always being wronged and misunderstood. They are quick to point out how unfair something is while never taking any responsibility for their present circumstances. And one- or two-sentence emails or texts from you are answered with novellas.

These are all signs of a communication vampire.

Similar to other time vultures, these communication vampires experience reality as either one big soupy mess of hurt and betrayal or a shining beacon of hope and opportunity. Either way, you have become their latest target.

Before the internet, these people would fire off angry letters to the editor of the local paper or take hostages at a cocktail party, a PTA meeting, or the grocery store checkout line. Now they simply dominate your communication channels. And the more you try to shut them down and get away from them, the more fiercely they try to keep the dialogue alive.

Well, just like their fictional counterparts, a stake through the heart is often the only solution to this problem. Ignoring all communication only intensifies their pursuit. You have to not only cease all communication with them but sometimes take the extraordinary step of blocking them on whichever channel they've been chasing you.

Now, if someone is in genuine need, unless you are a trained therapist or other medical professional, you may want to point them toward professional help. It's hard to walk away from suffering. This is where the expression "detaching with love" is useful for us, if not for them.

To them, we're likely to become another link in their chain of unbroken misery and disappointment, more proof of how unfeeling the world is in response to their pain. With perspective, we can see that this unhappy conclusion was inevitable. They had already choreographed the entire relationship before we even entered into it. While not puppets, we were certainly cast for our affinity to our written roles. Without guilt or shame, we can recognize the role we played as enablers for as long as we did and move on with some grace for ourselves and compassion for them.

ONLINE SHOPPING—
A POTENTIAL PERSONAL HELL

I have a client, Barbara, who has a shopping problem. She seldom enters brick-and-mortar stores because she doesn't have time. But at 2 a.m. when she can't sleep, she's surfing online while also streaming Home Shopping Network in the background. It would seem that at this point one venue for uncontrolled impulse shopping is no longer sufficient.

She gets at least 75 emails a day from online vendors promoting sales and special events. Algorithms ensure that anywhere she goes online and certainly on any social media platforms, she's tracked and presented with a constant feed of anything she's shown interest in or anything that's remotely similar to anything she's purchased in the past six months. The overwhelming volume of these kinds of messages crowd out important communications from her daughter's school, neighbors, friends and family, and, perhaps most significantly, correspondence from her work.

Her dining room table and her entryway, living room, and kitchen floors are all stacked with boxes of products in various states of examination and return. The hours she spends processing returns is overwhelming—I've spent more than one eight-hour day packing up 30 to 40 boxes to hand off to UPS while 10 new boxes arrived on the same day. She tells herself that it's an efficient strategy to get something in various colors and sizes at the same time, believing that, in spite of overwhelming evidence to the contrary, returning things is simple and effortless.

Sadly, this doesn't even account for the many items that overstay the time limit for returns because she has trouble making decisions. Those items become gifts or are donated to local charities. Her neighborhood thrift stores are grateful for her excess purchases, but the cost of that generosity is over $150,000 in unsecured credit card debt. Even with her multiple six-figure income, she is often delinquent and over the limit on many of her credit cards.

She gets collection calls throughout the evening. Her mail often includes threatening letters from creditors. Her credit score is trashed. She's a nervous wreck. She knows it's a terrible way to live, but she is also unwilling to stop. At least not yet.

Perhaps the most disturbing part is that Barbara already owns a three-bedroom apartment's worth of everything. She has plenty of high-quality, well-cared-for clothing, costume and precious jewelry, electronics, artwork, and furniture. She wants for nothing material. So what is the void that she's attempting to fill or trauma she is reliving—only now she's the perpetrator inflicting new trauma on herself—with this desperate behavior?

Barbara may not know, but only she can answer that question. And breaking this pattern is deep work that may be best addressed with a counselor or other mental health professional. Either way, the first step in breaking patterns like these is recognizing and acknowledging that it *is* a pattern.

Maybe you're feeling superior to Barbara and her choices because you don't get collection calls (anymore) and only have a few returns lying around. Or maybe you can relate to Barbara and her choices; perhaps you, too, are engaged in something similar, whether that's overshopping specifically or another self-destructive behavior you know you should quit but seem powerless to.

Whatever you're feeling is fine; there's no need to judge. I certainly don't.

If you're starting to hyperventilate, breathe slowly and consciously until you steady your pulse. Count to five as you inhale and five again as you exhale. See if instead of identifying with Barbara's desperation, you can start to identify with the willingness to shift your behavior. Any effort you exert to break away from compulsive shopping will loosen the chains of this kind of bondage. And consistent steps forward will liberate you, perhaps not overnight but certainly over time.

It is worth noting that what would be intolerable to me and quite possibly you doesn't seem to be sufficiently painful for Barbara. That is, she is not in enough pain yet to stop. What this demonstrates is that we are surprisingly strong and resilient creatures, even when dancing on a razor's edge. But clearly, the ability to sustain prolonged discomfort while hoping to either prove ourselves right or prove someone else wrong is not always an asset. It often comes down to being right or being happy, and many folks, regardless of the pain, choose being right.

The willingness to let go is the key to breaking this cycle for Barbara or for any of us. Willingness. Not strength, not stamina, not cleverness—just being willing to stop doing something that doesn't serve you anymore and becoming willing to do something else. You don't even have to know how or what you will do to break the cycle of this behavior; you just have to be willing to do something different.

Recognize the crafty ways you may be speaking to yourself about this, either minimizing the negative consequences or justifying your unique position and privilege. Crafty speak is usually just fear wrapped up in a baloney sandwich—fear of not having enough or not being enough or some other fear. That fear and its good pal desperation will frantically shove anything they can get their hands on as a wedge between you and different behavior.

And of course, it is that different behavior that will create change in your life. Waiting to feel better (whatever "better" is) or stronger or ready usually means doing nothing other than waiting. Changing your mindset is a great place to start, but if that feels too difficult, the quickest way to change how you feel is to change your behavior. That yields the most consistent and reliable results. AA cofounder Bill Wilson said it so well: "You can't think your way into right action, but you can act your way into right thinking."

If you truly want to break the cycle of compulsive shopping and recover your financial well-being and mental health, not to mention the hours wasted aimlessly wandering around the infinite shopping mall we call the internet, the first step is to immediately get offline. Then remove yourself from every shopping email list.

Whatever deep discounts or VIP specials that you'll miss are not important. If and when you actually need something, you'll be able to find it with a quick online search. Until then, let someone else on their mailing lists benefit from the remarkable one-day sale they're advertising. It's nice to share, isn't it?

If you can't seem to stay away from online shopping sites and getting rid of your devices is not an option, consider using monitoring or "nanny" software. Originally designed to keep children from visiting sites with adult content, these apps can be configured to keep you away from whatever you want to block access to. That could be online gambling, porn, or any retailer with a website.

Whichever methods you use—and you may employ several to create a comprehensive plan of attack—remember that you are not alone. Shame, frustration, and fear can isolate you, and you may be feeling alone, but chances are there is at least one other person who cares about you and would be willing to help if they knew of your situation. Break the silence, open the door (or a window if the door seems overwhelming), and let someone in. Seek out appropriate help and support from friends, family, and/or professionals.

Just for today, *do not shop*. Whatever it takes. Play some miniature golf, binge watch your favorite show or movies, volunteer at a senior center or animal rescue or hospital, run errands for or with a friend—fill your day with something other than shopping and make the day about someone else. I promise you that, for at least today, you'll be sufficiently distracted, and the lovely by-product will be a feeling of usefulness and purpose—a feeling that is at best fleeting, if not entirely absent, when shopping.

ORGANIZING YOUR BOOKMARKS

Bookmarks are great for getting us to our favorite online sites fast, but without some organization and restraint, they can also slow us down and create chaos. Because they're so easy to create, they can quickly become more digital clutter.

If the way you currently create bookmarks is just to add one without then also saving that bookmark to a folder with similar ones, you're going to end up with a long list of all your bookmarks in no particular order. This means that your only chance of finding a particular bookmark when you want it is to scroll through that list until you find the one you're looking for. This not only wastes time, it doesn't take advantage of the convenience of actually bookmarking sites in the first place.

To organize your bookmarks, use the same approach outlined for paper filing in Chapter 4. Start by identifying the categories of subjects or interests that you want to group your bookmarks into. You can handwrite this list or create it as a note, a document, or a spreadsheet. Then open your bookmarks manager and create individual folders for each category.

Once you have all your folders created, begin moving your existing bookmarks into the correct folders, and going forward, make sure you always save any new bookmarks to the correct folder right away.

For a handy worksheet on creating and organizing your bookmarks and a screenshot of my bookmarks, check out your companion workbook or visit unstuffbook.com/resources. You'll find several pictures and a step-by-step guide that makes this process easy to follow and accomplish.

Your bookmarks toolbar is where you should keep the folders and sites you visit the most frequently. Even more convenient than organized bookmarks in expanding folders, these shortcuts live right in your toolbar so they are visible on top of every open browser window, making any site literally one click away.

Every browser lets you customize how windows and tabs are displayed, and that includes customizing your bookmarks and bookmarks toolbar. By investing a little time in this process, you can personalize and streamline how and when you visit your favorite sites online.

OLDER FORMS OF DIGITAL MEDIA

We talked about this in Chapter 4—on page 118—organizing your office, and it merits a mention here, too. The longer you wait to harvest files from any of those obsolete formats, the more likely it is that you'll run into issues when you do attempt it.

Also, be sure that you specify what format you want your media converted into before you send it out, and that it's always an editable file. Some services still convert old Super 8 and VHS family movies into play-only DVDs, which at this point is a total waste of time and money.

When you import these converted files to your computer, put them in the folder you created in Chapter 4, or if you haven't imported these kinds of files yet, create a new folder now and label it 20XX Files Import. This will be the temporary home for these files until you are ready to marry them into the updated digital filing system you're going to create in the next section.

ORGANIZING YOUR COMPUTER

Folder Names

For some of us, computers may just be really expensive email management systems or online shopping carts, but they are capable of so much more. Accordingly, they can also become digital clutter magnets if we're not careful.

Start by thinking of your computer's hard drive as a virtual filing cabinet. The fact that the files and folders are all data and not paper means that you can store so much more information on a computer than you can in even the largest filing cabinet. This is why having a working understanding of how to organize your files is essential.

Now, it's possible that you have not read or worked through Chapter 4 yet. It's also possible that you do not own a physical filing cabinet, or if you do, that you are underutilizing it. You may not own a single file folder, and you may be surrounded by stacks and piles of papers waiting for a system to make sense of them all. If that's the case, when you finish this chapter, your computer's organizational structure will become the blueprint for any future filing of actual paper you'll do.

To begin organizing your computer's files, please go to your computer now. Make sure it's on and that you are looking at Finder (on a Mac) or File Explorer (on a Windows PC). You should already have a folder called either Documents or My Documents on your hard drive. Please find it now. If you don't have one of these folders on your computer for some reason, create a new folder now and name it Documents.

This will now become your root folder for all your documents and personal files. By personal files, I mean all data that you have the ability to download, create, modify, and store on your computer.

Remember, we're not altering stand-alone software applications or programs—these, too, are stored in folders on your hard drive, typically inside a root folder called Applications. Unless you are a computer programmer, you should probably never be inside an application's folder altering or moving or deleting any files. Files with seemingly innocuous names could be pivotal pieces of code that will irreparably impair an application's ability to run on your computer if you mess with them. When it comes to folders containing applications or other pieces of software, remember this adage: when in doubt, stay out.

While your Documents folder is the foundation of your virtual filing cabinet, there is one major difference between a physical filing cabinet and this virtual one: there are no drawers to provide structure, only folders.

So we will create parent folders, such as Finances or Correspondence or Home Improvement, that define the first or broadest level of category that we're trying to contain. Then, within each parent folder, we will create more specific subfolders to further define its contents. For example, within Correspondence, we may have subfolders called Creditors, Family, Friends, and so on.

The rule for creating and naming file folders is to always make their names specific enough to be recognized by someone other than you but not so specific that they would contain only one file.

To see an example of best practices used to create a folder structure, please visit unstuffbook.com/filing. For an exclusive look at how I've laid out the contents of my computer, please see your companion workbook. You'll see my exact digital filing system, and I'll guide you step-by-step in creating your own.

For now, here's a preview of what a typical Documents folder could look like:

Documents (root folder)

- → Core Files (parent folder)
- → Current Writing (parent folder)
- → Medical and Health (parent folder)
- → Correspondence (parent folder)
- → Finances (parent folder)
- → Travel (parent folder)
- → Gardening (parent folder)
- → Office Supplies (parent folder)
- → Owner's Manuals (parent folder)
- → Photos (parent folder)
- → Recipes (parent folder)

Two things to note here: First, a few of the parent folders are not in alphabetical order. You can trick Macs into putting those folders at the top of the list by inserting a space (or several) before the names of these folders. Because the computer strictly alphabetizes the folders' names, those names beginning with empty spaces automatically rise to the top of the list.

Those spaces are discarded on PCs, so you can insert an underscore (_) to achieve the same effect. You can use this tip to "force" folders you use frequently to rise to the top of a list.

Second, many of these parent folders contain subfolders that further separate the contents into more specific groupings. Consider these subfolders within the parent folders:

Documents

→ Core Files

This includes password-protected documents like birth certificates, driver's licenses front and back, and social security cards. [Note: If you are unfamiliar with how to protect a file with a password, check out the instructions in your companion workbook.]

→ Current Writing

- → Medical and Health
- → Correspondence
    - → Personal Correspondence (subfolder)
    - → Professional Correspondence (subfolder)
- → Finances
    - → 20XX Credit Card Statements (subfolder)
    - → 20XX Checking/Saving Statements (subfolder)
    - → 20XX Retirement Account Statements (subfolder)
    - → Taxes (subfolder)
- → Travel
- → Gardening
- → Office Supplies
- → Owner's Manuals
- → Photos
- → Recipes

If we drill down one more level, this is how the folders look:

Finances (parent folder)
- → 20XX Credit Card Statements (subfolder)
- → 20XX Checking/Saving Statements (subfolder)
- → 20XX Retirement Account Statements (subfolder)
- → Taxes (subfolder)
    - → 20XX Tax Docs (subfolder of a subfolder)

Now, using the worksheet from your companion workbook or unstuffbook.com/filing, start to list the names of the parent folders you already have or will create within your Documents folder.

Great. Now for all of those parent folders, begin to outline the subfolders that would live inside them.

Once you have a workable list of folder names, use that list to actually create these folders on your computer. Ultimately, that's what you're going to want to do anyway. This exercise should get you thinking in these terms (folders and subfolders) and give you a visual map you can play with and alter without any consequences.

Continue to go down as many levels deep as you need to in creating subfolders so you can accurately and thoroughly corral each of your documents into an appropriate folder. Pay attention to whether you have created folder names so vague that they will probably contain many loosely related documents, or folders that are so specific they will contain only one document. In most cases, with a bit of careful consideration, you should be able to find the only-child document somewhere else to live. And if that is not the case, stick to your guns and maintain the folder with only one document.

Note at this point that we have yet to do anything more than create some structure on your computer; we haven't put any individual files away in their new homes. The actual sorting and organizing will happen shortly.

File Names

With few exceptions, such as a slash (/) and a colon (:), you can name files almost anything you want. Just make sure that you adopt a consistent language, style, or method for file and folder naming and that this naming lexicon is written down. Try to keep file names as brief as possible while avoiding abbreviations. Use common names that make sense to you and, when appropriate, include applicable model numbers, project names, or the names of key people.

Also, always add a date to the title of each document. Update the date each time you edit the document. If you have multiple revisions on the same day, also include the time as well. You can't rely on the modification date of the file to tip you off to the most current version of any file.

So rather than using My Card List as the name for your holiday card list, instead name it:

20XX Holiday Card List, (11-07-20XX)

This way, you know that it's the 20XX version of this list. It's also clearly named as the holiday list in case you have other lists of addresses or contacts. It's further defined by the date it was last modified, 11-07-20XX. Now if you search for either 20XX or Holiday, the files are sure to show up in the search. And when you review all possible documents, the date will further direct you to the most current draft.

The goal when naming files and folders is to make sure that each file name is easy to remember, easy to search for, and easy to tell apart from all the other files and folders. Once you've mapped out your naming system, share this with anyone who uses your computer and adds files to it. Consistency in naming files is the best way to ensure that you will be able to find files you haven't looked at in months or years.

Saving and Customizing Files

When you save files to any drive, external or internal, make sure to select the correct location when prompted to—this places your new (or edited) document in its appropriate folder.

Likewise when installing new programs, make sure you always direct the computer to put them in the Program Files or Applications folder. Pay special attention to *never* save files that contain text or information or data that you are altering and using in the same folder as any software application. That means do not save your Microsoft Word documents in any folder labeled Microsoft Word that contains the actual program or application named Microsoft Word. By always keeping document files separate from program files, you reduce the risk of accidentally deleting your documents when you install or upgrade programs.

NOTABLE NOTE

Avoid using common initials as identifiers in searches—many words may contain those two initials in their sequence. For instance, my initials are AM. If I use those as part of the name of a file (for example, AM Résumé, (01-16-24)), when

> I search for AM, every word in the name of a file that also
> includes AM in that order (name, game, amazing, etc.) will
> populate my search—certainly more files than I would want
> to sift through to find what I am looking for. Instead, searching
> for Résumé will bring up every file with the word *résumé* in the
> title—finding mine at that point will be much easier.

Don't save unnecessary files—be selective. You don't need to save every draft of a document once you've arrived at your final version. Lift any key sentences or ideas out of previous drafts and save them in their own file as a resource for future projects. Then delete the working drafts, retaining only your final version. Be sure to label it Final or Published or something that identifies it as the last edited version.

When it would be helpful to have the exact same file available from multiple locations, you don't want to create duplicate copies of the file. You run the risk of making competing edits in each version and losing valuable work. (I'm *not* talking about multiple backup copies; you still need those on an external drive and in the cloud.)

Instead, create as many shortcuts in as many locations as you need, all pointing back to the one original document. (For Macs, shortcuts are called aliases.) On all computers, right-clicking on your mouse while selecting a file will offer you the option to create a shortcut. These can then be dragged and dropped in as many other locations as needed.

If you are more of a visual person, you might find it helpful to associate thumbnails with your files. Thumbnails are little images you can apply (think two-dimensional electronic decoupage) right on top of a folder. Searching through folders in the thumbnail view (usually listed under the View tab in your toolbar) allows you to find things visually as well as by name. I've applied thumbnails to several folders—they're fun and help me distinguish particular folders from their neighbors with just a glance. For example, I've attached a bag of money icon to my Finances folder and a picture of a water meter to my folder named Utilities. They amuse me and make the folders stand out.

To apply an image to a folder, right-click the folder and click Properties. In the properties dialogue box, click the Customize tab. In the folder pictures area, click Choose Picture. (For Macs, you do this under Get Info.) You'll see an icon on the top next to the file name—just paste the icon or image over the generic image of a file folder and you're done.

If you still need more customization for your files, there are third-party programs (some free and some for a fee) that allow you to color-code the names of your folders and files. For example, finance or money files could be colored green. This is useful for quickly recognizing and accessing folders and files you use frequently.

Organizing Your Files and Folders

Now that we've gone over how to create folders, properly name them, and even have a little fun decorating them, it's time to actually organize them.

If you're not in front of your computer, please return to it now. If you're still there, make sure it's up and running and not sleeping. Get your timer out and set it for 15 minutes. Starting with 15-minute blocks of time when it comes to this kind of comprehensive organizing lets you make progress without getting too fatigued or sloppy.

When your timer goes off, shift your focus and change your physical position. The eye and body strain of prolonged uninterrupted computer use is debilitating. And if 15 minutes is too long, work in increments that feel good to you. At any time, if you need to, pause your timer, get up, get a quick drink or snack and resume working.

Once the timer starts, find and open up your Documents folder. For this process only, you'll want to create a new folder inside Documents and call it Temporary Dumping Ground, which we'll refer to going forward simply as TDG. Open this new folder and then resize it so it's the full height of your screen but narrow enough that you can have another window open beside it.

Now you have one open folder on your desktop named TDG. Next, open up your hard drive as a folder (Finder on Mac, File Explorer on PC) and resize this window wide enough to view several levels of the file hierarchy without having to keep adjusting the window's dimensions.

Begin searching for all files and folders that may be currently located anywhere besides inside the Documents folder. As you find these files and folders, drag them to TDG. Keep repeating this step until you are as certain as you can be that you've found everything and relocated it.

Now, close the hard drive window and open up your Documents folder. The Documents folder and TDG should now be side by side.

Review the folders and subfolders inside the Documents folder from your work creating those folders earlier. Refer to your worksheet or workbook for your naming lexicon and the comprehensive list of your folder names. Compare the names of any folders you've just found and dragged into TDG with the folders inside your Documents folder. If there's a perfect naming match, open the folder in TDG and review its contents. If there are files that you know you can delete just by looking at their names, do so now.

For the rest of the files that you want to keep and that are in the correct folder, drag them into the folder with the same name in your Documents folder. This includes both loose files as well as any subfolders that are in the correctly named folder, just not in the new version of that folder. Once these actions are completed, move the now empty folder from TDG into the trash.

Once you've moved each folder's contents from TDG to the correct folder in Documents, all you should have left in TDG are a bunch of loose files. If they are properly named (you can preview the files to confirm that), decide if you still need or want to keep each one, and then either drag them into the correct folder in Documents or toss them.

For any files that aren't properly or accurately named yet, preview the file, confirm it's worth keeping, and then either rename it and drag it into its new home folder in Documents or toss it in the trash. You may need to create a new folder for a file or series of files. Just make sure when you do that you also update your naming lexicon.

Each of these is a rinse-and-repeat activity. You'll keep doing this for each folder and file until the TDG folder is empty and everything has either been reassembled within the folders you've created in your Documents folder or been discarded.

Depending on the volume of files and folders on your computer, this exercise may take a few hours, a few days, or even a few weeks. Whatever it takes to complete this task, the goal is to properly name every file, place each file inside a folder with its brothers and sisters, and properly name that folder so it accurately reflects its contents.

When you have sorted and organized all your files, you may now empty the trash or recycle bin and delete all the extraneous files you've discarded. Congratulations—your computer is perfectly organized. For today.

A Few More Thoughts on Keeping Your Computer Organized

I am strongly opposed to your desktop serving as a catchall for files and folders. If you are working on a few projects, it's fine to create shortcuts on your desktop to those folders or files, but under no circumstances should you be creating new files or folders and defaulting to leaving them on your desktop. One Home for Everything means the folders need to be created as subfolders within the appropriate parent folder from the very beginning, not later or "someday."

The way to keep your computer tidy and current is obviously to move slowly and deliberately when creating files and folders. Always name things accurately at the time of their creation and store them in their proper home. Like with Like ensures that you'll keep similar files and folders together.

If you don't make a mess, you won't have a mess. Keep that in mind when you're inclined to rush or feel so pressed for time that you tell yourself, just this once, you'll cut a corner but you'll come back soon to clean it up. Bad habits breed more bad habits. Take the time to do it right the first time, and you won't need to make a promise that begs to be broken down the line.

BACKING UP!

Hopefully, I convinced you back in Chapter 9 to back up your digital photos regularly, and now I'd also like to convince you to do the same with all the contents of your computer(s). Along with copying important information to flash drives and storing them in a cabinet or a safe-deposit box at the bank, you'll also benefit from having an external hard drive that you'll attach directly to your computer with a cable, typically a USB cable. These drives can be used manually with you just dragging and dropping key files and folders onto the drive, or, as I mentioned, you can run special back-up software that allows you to establish routine backups of your files. You set the parameters for which files, when, and how often they get backed up, and the drive (and its software) does the rest. My preferred setting is for the drive to always be scanning and updating in real time so any files I modify are immediately backed up, too.

> **NOTABLE NOTE**
>
> Create and maintain a folder that houses an inventory of your home in digital form. This is a great resource in the event of a fire, flood, or other disaster. This way, you have digital pictures of all of your belongings, along with a description of each item.
>
> For major purchases, a scanned copy of the receipt or credit card statement is useful. You should also have a scanned

version of appraisals for all jewelry, artwork, and antiques—
any item whose worth exceeds basic limits on your insurance
policy. When suffering a loss, you don't want to be haggling
with insurance adjusters about the value of Great-Aunt
Grace's 18th-century secretary.

Keep this inventory in several places, at least one of them
off-site, either in a safe-deposit box; at a friend, neighbor, or
family member's home; or in your office. You wouldn't want to
do all this work and have only one copy of the folder sitting
on your now-melted hard drive.

There are also reliable online cloud-based backup services available. Some offer a limited amount of space for free and charge a fee for
greater amounts of storage, while others charge for any access to their
servers. Either way, these sites can also be configured to automatically
back up your computer at any interval of your choosing.

Flash or thumb drives are too unstable and unreliable to be your
primary backup source. One too many drops on the floor, accidentally stepping on it, leaving it in your pocket and then washing it while
doing laundry—any of these can render your drive unusable. They're
fine as portable transfer devices—I just wouldn't rely on one as the
only home for important data.

Again, remember to back up early and back up often. And as I said
before, it's always a question of *when* your hard drive will fail, not *if*.
Having lived through my own and clients' computer hard-drive failures and multiple-thousand-dollar data retrievals, I insist on multiple
backups in multiple forms—external drives, internal servers, and
cloud-based backups, too.

Do not put all your eggs—or in this case, files—in one basket.
Learn from others' misfortunes and avoid unnecessary heartache. It's
an awful feeling when a computer fails before you've had a chance to
save your personal files.

One caveat: As long as you have a license for any original software or apps, there's no reason to ever back up applications. In the event of a computer failure, you'll want to install any programs cleanly anyway. It takes only one missing piece of code to render a complete application useless.

SOCIAL MEDIA— WHAT'S IN IT FOR ME?

That is an excellent question. And if the answer turns out to be not much, that's okay.

I've written extensively about social media and its impact on our time and well-being in my book *Calling BS on Busy*, so there's no reason to repeat that information here. As it relates to unstuffing your life, carefully consider how much time you'll need to declutter and get organized and how much time you currently spend online. If you need to find more time in your day or week to dedicate to getting out from under the clutter, the time you spend on social media seems an easy place to find it.

As for the things shared on social media, if there are photos or other media that you've uploaded directly to the platform that are not filed anywhere else or there are things that have been shared with you that you have not downloaded and filed yet, add either or both of these activities to your to-do list. Technically, many of these platforms hold the position that everything posted on the platform belongs to them. I'm no lawyer, so I can't speak to the legality of that. But as an organizer, I'd say if you want to be able to access items off of the platform, harvesting the photos, videos, and other media should definitely be budgeted for—sooner rather than later.

Additionally, as you're building new habits, setting one up to immediately download any media you want to keep when you first see it will save you significant time. The same goes for uploading media. File it before you post it and you'll always know where it is. Scrolling back through various threads and feeds to track down something from a few weeks, months, or even years ago can be frustrating and is definitely a waste of time when that could have been done sooner with a new habit.

Finally, just remember that nothing posted online is private. By now, we should all know that schools and employers search online to learn more about prospective students and employees, right? And that's just the tip of the iceberg.

Dating sites are overflowing with catfished images and profiles, and chances are someone close to you has already been a victim of this kind of fraud. As more people struggle with memory and cognition issues, a compromised mind coupled with loneliness makes for a very vulnerable heart. So navigate this virtual landscape with caution and attention, and help your friends and family who might fall prey to scammers to avoid or minimize the negative consequences, too.

Support, friendship, and community are all possible online. So is getting ripped off. You can find contractors, plan a party, or learn helpful information on a health condition you have. You'll find and meet people who have common interests and goals or common dislikes and aversions.

For some of us, social media will never replace face-to-face contact. But for others, some of whom may be limited by mobility or geography, the possibility for connection and resource-sharing is as real as meeting at the general store on a Sunday morning for coffee and the latest gossip. Like most things, used in moderation social media has its purposes, so have fun—just stay present and alert and you'll probably be fine.

TEXTING, DIRECT MESSAGING, VIDEO CONFERENCING, AND THE LIKE

Text messaging and video conferencing are great ways to communicate and share media (e.g., images, videos, and other kinds of files). But text messages can also become a bit of a puzzle when trying to track down things that have been previously shared. With video conferencing, once the call is over and the window closed, any tangible things that were shared are no longer accessible.

So just like with social media, setting up new habits around sending and receiving media will save you a bunch of time and make your life so much easier. When something is shared that you want to keep, save it in the moment. Take a few moments and download it so you can file it with its siblings on your device. During a call or chat, you may be so in the moment that you don't want to take the time to properly name the file and put it away, so just make it part of your routine to finish putting things away as soon as the communication stops.

Likewise, if you want to transfer things from your phone to your tablet or computer or vice versa, hand it off now rather than later. Because these devices are so easy to use and the speed with which they process data is so fast, we can get fooled into thinking we have plenty of time later to put stuff away. That's a lie. What's more likely is that without a simple system or habit in place, these amazing tools will just become sources for new clutter and chaos when it comes to stuff.

IDENTITY THEFT

We touched on identity theft in Chapter 4 as it relates to paperwork, but unfortunately, your privacy is even more at risk online. And because digital thieves are often trendsetters when it comes to new ways to hoodwink the vulnerable, anything specific included here would be obsolete before the ink dries. So instead I'll offer some general guidance you can implement as you are organizing your digital files and managing your online presence:

1. **Protect your Social Security number.** Avoid entering it on a web form unless you are confident in the site's security features and legitimacy. If providing your SSN seems unnecessary, ask for clarification on how it will be used and stored before sharing it.

2. **Never give out your personal information unless you made the contact.** Legitimate organizations will not reach out to

verify your account number, username, password, PIN, etc. If an email, text, or direct message requests such information, contact the business by phone instead of replying to the message. Do not click any links in the message until you've confirmed the sender.

3. **Use strong and different passwords for all your accounts.** With the many online accounts we have these days, it's easy to get lazy with passwords. But weak passwords are one of the easiest ways for identity thieves to access your personal data. If you struggle to keep track of all your passwords, use the Perfect Password Formula included in your companion workbook—you'll never forget a password again.

    If you would rather delegate this responsibility to an app, you can invest in password management software. Just make sure you never forget your master password or you may find yourself locked out of your account.

4. **Be careful what you click on and download.** Just because a friend posted a link on social media or a family member sent you an email attachment doesn't mean those things are safe. It could've been sent by a hacker, or your loved one may have been tricked. If it looks at all suspicious, don't interact with it. Better yet, use antivirus and spyware protection software on all your devices, and run a scan on any unknown link or attachment. If it is malicious, the software will quarantine the offending item until you can delete it.

BOSS OR DRONE: WHO'S RUNNING THIS SHOW?

Modern electronic devices offer us many clever, fun, streamlined, and convenient ways of interacting with information and with one another. So embrace each advance in technology while holding firmly to the awareness that these machines exist to serve us and not the other way around. I don't mean this in a dystopian, science-fiction-y way where they take over our lives and literally imprison us. I mean it in much subtler ways where their demands on our time and energy, their constant tug for us to keep up with the never-ending stream of information and media no longer offer convenience and entertainment but threaten to drown us in a new but very familiar flow of stuff.

Just because you *can* feel connected 24/7/365 and spend hours scrolling online doesn't mean that you *need* to. You can remain calm, unhurried, and proactive in determining exactly when and how you use any of these tools and how you want to handle the particular challenges of keeping current with your digital files. The choice is yours. The only thing that's certain is that if you don't make a choice, that is in fact a choice and one that is sure to create more digital clutter.

11

NEW THINGS AND THE REST OF YOUR LIFE

Before we passionately desire what another enjoys, we should examine into the happiness of its present possessor.
–FRANÇOIS DE LA ROCHEFOUCAULD

It is through creating, not possessing, that life is revealed.
–VIDA DUTTON SCUDDER

Don't cry because it's over. Smile because it happened.
–LUDWIG JACOBOWSKI (NOT DR. SEUSS!)

WHAT WE'RE GOING TO COVER IN THIS CHAPTER

- New Things
- Impulse Shopping and Kicking the Habit
- Something In, Something Out
- One Home for Everything and Like with Like
- Happy Holidays! But Where Do I Put All the New Stuff?
- The Value of Stuff
- Time: The Commodity Not Traded on the NY Stock Exchange
- Needs Versus Wants
- Spiritual Materialism
- Belief as Definition
- "I Think I'll Miss You Most of All"

IN THE WORDS OF Robert C. Hunter, "What a long, strange trip it's been." We've made it from your front door out into cyberspace and back in one piece. Congratulations! In some ways, it's now that the real work begins. You have some awesome new habits. You have touched everything you own or are the steward of, and you now know where everything lives.

And just as you may enjoy a night out on the town and then return safely home for a good night's sleep, so should your possessions. Take them out, use them, share them, be prepared for them to occasionally break (and then to let them go), and in the meantime, always put them back where they came from—One Home for Everything and Like with Like have become your new mantras.

Your computer is a digital microcosm of your home or office, also neat and tidy, with things in their proper place. And you finally know where that proper place is. You should now be starting to spend more of your time doing things that are important and meaningful to you rather than just scrambling around looking for things that have been misplaced or distracting yourself with unconscious shopping or other subtler forms of consumption. You're on a path of consciously living each day. Perhaps you'll find yourself smiling at strangers, unless they're stealing your parking place—and then after a momentary scowl, you'll find ways to smile about something else.

If this works for you, don't keep it a secret. If your friends, family, or colleagues comment on these shifts in large or small ways, let them know what's changing for you. Allow your enthusiasm and newfound freedom to inspire others. Celebrate your successes without boasting or lording your progress over your friends, especially if they are still struggling with clutter themselves. Be a powerful example rather than a smug know-it-all. Avoid offering unsolicited feedback or advice, but if asked, share freely. That's the way a quiet revolution starts.

NEW THINGS

Oh, boy, who doesn't love new stuff? Even as we wrestle with tamper-resistant wrappers that slow us down, we giddily celebrate the glossy, unblemished, yummy freshness of "the good stuff" we're about to make our own.

I want to say that new things are great. Really. I'm not suggesting anyone other than a monk actually live like a monk. Have enough of anything and everything that serves you, and have nothing that doesn't. The core of my philosophy is based on reaching stuff equilibrium. And this book has been all about leading you through a process for gaining that equilibrium. A curated and well-edited life is what I'm advocating, a life where thoughtfulness and mindfulness guide your consumption, and where experiences are valued over things.

If having fewer things allows you to have nicer things (i.e., nicer to you), that doesn't sound like an unpleasant compromise. Luxury is not inherently bad. The opposite of extravagant consumption may be some form of puritanical asceticism, but we're not seeking the opposite. We're seeking an antidote, and the antidote to extravagant consumption is modest (in terms of volume), tasteful consumption.

If you can afford them, or if someone really loves you and gives them to you, enjoy Frette or Anichini linens—they're fabulous—but you don't need 12 sets of them any more than you'd need 12 sets of any other designer's linens, even if you can afford them. You can sleep on only one set at a time. (See Chapter 5 to learn more about linen closets and how many sets of sheets are appropriate.)

The idea of simplifying your life doesn't call for renouncing all purchases, just an insistence that each purchase be selective and carefully considered. Focus on quality, not quantity—and not from a status point of view but from a practicality point of view. We don't want to make choices about consumption based on fear, certainly not a fear of keeping up with the Joneses. We want to make our choices based on what we feel is sustainable, responsible, practical, enduring, and aesthetically pleasing, whether that's food or art or countertops. The rest doesn't matter.

IMPULSE SHOPPING AND KICKING THE HABIT

Seldom are the criteria I detailed—sustainability, responsibility, durability—considered when impulse shopping. Impulse shopping is one of the root causes of tremendous amounts of clutter and is the perfect collision of nonessential items running into ill-considered snap decisions.

Regardless of your financial situation, whether you can afford to buy whatever you want whenever you want or you need to monitor each purchase's impact on your bottom line, the end result is the same—more clutter and things you don't necessarily need. For anyone closely watching that bottom line, you would think that the squeeze caused by spending money on nonessentials would be enough motivation to curb unnecessary spending. And, yes, money can certainly be a powerful motivator in kicking the impulse-shopping habit, but unfortunately, sometimes fear around debt and declining resources spurs a spiral of shame that drags people further down into depression and additional self-destructive behaviors.

So let's interrupt that pattern before it becomes any more entrenched. I mentioned a few ways to do this in Chapter 10, but let's look at a comprehensive set of tips and tricks to help you avoid impulse shopping. You'll also find this guide in your companion workbook.

Shop from a List

And stick to it. Everyone agrees—from shopping for home improvement materials to buying groceries—you don't walk into a store without a list. And don't get sidetracked by something you think you meant to put on the list. If you actually need something that didn't make the list, complete the rest of your shopping first, *then* go back to collect the forgotten item.

Don't Zone Out While Shopping

Stay alert—shop mindfully and deliberately every single time you venture into a store, real or online. Don't multitask while shopping. No chatting, checking email, or texting with a cart in front of you. Each item should be vetted before it enters your cart: Is it on your list? Does it serve a real and immediate purpose, or are you stocking up for "someday"?

Avoid Shopping Carts

Use a handheld basket or just your hands whenever possible. If you've run into the store for milk, grab the milk and go—don't also grab a bag of chips, some ice cream, and some chicken that's on sale. Likewise, if you've run into the office-supply store for paper, don't then grab a new printer, stapler, and some folders just because you can.

Start at the Rear of the Store

Go deep and then head for the exit. The faster you're in and out, the less likely you'll get drawn in by something random.

Buy It Next Time

This is the only time I think "someday" is a good idea. When you come across some groovy gadget that you *must* have but isn't on your list, jot it down on the bottom of your list for next time. Then check at home to see if this is a valid purchase or an impulse buy. If you determine that it's an appropriate purchase, add it to your new list.

Take a Picture

Instead of actually buying something that isn't on your list, take a photo of the item with your phone and carry it around with you. Live with it for a week or two to see if, after the initial blush has faded, you still need to purchase it.

Get a Shopping Buddy or Two

Set up a mini support group with a reliable friend or two who are usually available. (Your best friend the flight attendant who's often on a jet is not a viable candidate.) Make a pact to hold each other accountable for good shopping habits. And then actually pick up the phone when you're tempted. Call first, and then purchase only *after* you've had a complete conversation. You can't say, "Oh, just a few things," when your arms are overloaded with stuff. Be honest, and then listen when your friend asks pointed questions, such as, "Do you absolutely have to buy this now?"

Send Someone Else

It may feel like cheating, but sending someone else is a surefire way to get the errand done and avoid temptation. Wait in the car outside the store or stay at home while a child, friend, or partner runs out to the store. If there's no one you can send to the store, you can order your groceries online so you just need to pick them up or have them delivered to your house. Temper whatever disappointment you feel at not doing the actual shopping in store with enjoying the surplus cash that's still in your wallet.

Pick Your Checkout Aisle Carefully

Do a little study of the checkout lines where you shop. Find the one in each store, usually toward the end of the row, that has fewer displays and make this your go-to line. Self-serve lines seem to have the fewest promotional items of all.

If you're a magazine buyer, carry something to read in your bag so you resist the urge to pull one off the rack and start reading it while waiting in line. Likewise, if you're a snacker, carry a healthy snack with you to avoid grabbing a last-minute candy bar.

Shop with Cash Only

A reliable way to spend less is using only cash to pay for things. Bringing a limited amount of money with you accomplishes two things: it keeps you within your budget, and it prevents you from running up the balances on your credit cards.

The key to this technique is leaving your credit and debit cards at home. Try leaving the house with just the amount of money you've budgeted for your shopping. When you run out of money, return home. This forces you to pay closer attention to each purchase as you spend your cash.

Stop Reading Catalogs, Sales Flyers, and Email Solicitations

Stop "rehearsal" shopping. Read a book or magazine instead. Go for a walk. Go to the park. Volunteer somewhere. If you know you need a new laundry basket, start the search then, not before. At unstuffbook.com/resources, you'll find a list of websites where you can remove yourself from catalogs, junk mail, and junk email lists.

Don't Shop as Entertainment

Window-shopping and killing time are two expressions that completely minimize the reality of what you're doing. You're not actually shopping for windows, are you? And no one has enough time to murder it. Aimlessly wandering through the shopping district or your local mall is not an appropriate pastime. Remember that you can't keep stepping into a barbershop without eventually getting your hair cut.

Eat before Shopping

Eat a full meal before heading out to the store, whether grocery shopping or running errands. People who shop while hungry are more easily distracted and tend to shop emotionally—see below.

Do Not Use Shopping as Therapy, "Retail" or Otherwise

Many people shop the same way they eat: emotionally. Take the time to get to know yourself. You may not need to spend long hours on a therapist's couch to discover why you buy what you buy.

Perhaps shopping distracts you from feelings you don't want to deal with. Many people buy something because it feels good to buy things. While you may have felt overly passive in a recent encounter, you're now engaged in an activity, making choices, exercising your will, and taking control.

Rather than automatically shopping as a way to get some relief, take a few moments and write about your feelings. You don't need to write a book, but sit still long enough to jot down "I'm angry with my girlfriend/ husband/partner because . . . " or "At work, I've been feeling . . . ".

By making a list of the things on your mind and noting what's bothering you, you interrupt the loop of things racing around inside your head. Write until you've exhausted all the things you've been thinking or possibly obsessing about. Of the things you've written down, what has an easy fix and what involves time and another person? Take on the easiest things first, and then build up some momentum to address the more complex issues you've identified.

If you often feel isolated and shopping facilitates a fantasy life in which you're entertaining or going out and showing off your new purchases, consider having people over to enjoy your home as it is. Look through your wardrobe, find a flattering outfit, dress in it, and head out on the town, even if you're just going to the library or for a walk.

If you find that the intensity of your feelings intimidates or concerns you, consider seeking out a support group or therapeutic setting where you can work through those feelings with peers or professional support. Just like anything else we know little about, there's no shame in seeking guidance and learning skills in areas where we find ourselves lacking knowledge.

Track Your Spending

Figure out exactly where your money is going. Create a log or spreadsheet, or use a financial app to record all your transactions. Flag all the purchases that weren't absolutely necessary, and total them up. Look at other areas of your spending that have been limited because of these purchases, and see how you could shift your impulse buys into either more immediate needs or saving for big-ticket items, such as a vacation or a new appliance.

Own Your Behavior

You may be adept at arguing your case for choices you make, but even if you're an attorney by trade, no one besides you really cares why you did something. There is no better reason for a choice than because you wanted to. So make choices you can stand behind without excuses or explanations. You can't fall back on "the devil made me do it" nor are you punishing someone or teaching anyone a lesson by shopping impulsively. Shopping is not a form of revenge.

In all instances, as soon as an excuse, explanation, or justification starts rumbling around, pause and reflect. See if you can then say, "I did it because I did it. I can see now that I may want to make a different choice. In the moment, I wasn't considering these consequences."

SOMETHING IN, SOMETHING OUT

Along with curbing impulse shopping, whenever something new comes into your life, it's important to ask why and what purpose it serves. Whether the item was mindfully purchased by you, found on a curb somewhere, swapped at a friend's house, or arrived lovingly gift-wrapped (with or without a gift receipt enclosed), always ask yourself the following questions, even as you're doing your happy dance:

- Do I absolutely need this?
- Do I absolutely need this *now*?
- What purpose does this serve?
- Where will this live, and do I have the room for it?
- What is it replacing?
- Am I willing to replace that with this?
- If it's something that was previously owned and in need of refurbishment, will I actually do the work necessary to restore it to full functionality (or get it to someone who will)? When?
- Can I see myself owning this for many years to come?

These are not trick questions, and they are not intended to shame you or to pry something lovely out of your hands. They are here to ground you and keep you responsibly present. These questions are designed to slow you down so when something new enters your life, it's carefully considered, not only in the moment but also from a long-term perspective.

You've come so far; you don't want to start accumulating new things just when you've finally created some clear space for yourself, do you? All that time and effort would be wasted if you now create more clutter in exchange for a quick rush. Describing these possible lapses in attention as deadly may be hyperbolic, but calling them counterproductive is an understatement.

A little side trip into acquisition euphoria may feel innocent enough and fun in the first flush of excitement, but it is a very slippery slope. Just like skipping flossing for one night will not cause your teeth to fall out, one quick dance with unfettered consumerism and unconscious spending is not going to create chaos. But it does reopen the door to "later" and "someday," and maintaining your current system becomes harder to do with any new item that slips past you without some thoughtful consideration.

Add to that any concerns you have about your environmental footprint and the proper disposal of things already in your possession, and you can see how a moment's diversion can have lasting consequences that far outweigh that breathless bubble of bliss.

Once you are present and settled within the knowledge that you have enough, that you have useful tools and functional machines, a wardrobe that flatters you, and pretty things to look at and enjoy, you should be able to begin shifting your thinking from accumulating to swapping out.

Enter the third leg of The Organizational Triangle: Something In, Something Out. This is how we stay organized, and it's the surest way to maintain stuff equilibrium. It simply means that whenever something new comes in to stay (not something that's just passing through), something that's already here leaves.

Unless you are setting up a new home, you already have things. And hopefully those things are useful and increase your comfort and ease of living. If not, replace a lumpy, uncomfortable mattress when you can. Eliminate nonstick coated cookware from your kitchen when the finish begins to flake off into your food. If a friend gives you her patio furniture, pass yours along to someone else.

So, because you probably have enough of everything already, you're either replacing things when they fail or swapping something that still works for a newer version of it that offers better features or some other improvement. When the need arises or the opportunity presents itself, replace, update, or upgrade. Just don't make it a sport. Remember: shopping is not therapy, regardless of what pop culture and influencers say. We didn't create this opening of time for you to fill it with constantly rotating through or fretting over stuff.

ONE HOME FOR EVERYTHING AND LIKE WITH LIKE

New stuff doesn't have a home when it arrives, so if it looks as though it's staying, find it someplace to live. Someplace comfy and cozy and not too crowded. In any instance where something new is not replacing something existing, find the new item a home alongside its siblings. Whenever new things are replacing existing things, the old item should be recycled or discarded and the new one put in its place. Equilibrium remains.

HAPPY HOLIDAYS! BUT WHERE DO I PUT ALL THE NEW STUFF?

Birthdays and holidays provide particular challenges to stuff equilibrium. Whenever friends or family gather for a special occasion that includes gift-giving, grab bags, Secret Santas, or other exchanges of items at a particular time of year, chances are that you'll end the event with more things in front of you than you started it with.

Once the wrapping paper is off and the flush of excitement quiets down, when you're alone and feeling steady, refer to the earlier list of questions and apply them to your new things. Things that do not improve the quality of your life are not required to stay in your life. They're allowed to just pass through. Even when they were given to you by people you care deeply about. You can still feel that deep connection to the gift-giver without transferring all that affection and significance to the item itself.

If the item doesn't serve you and keeping it will create clutter, it is okay to let it go.

THE VALUE OF STUFF

So now let's talk about how we assign value to stuff.

While there many types of values, for our purposes in looking at stuff, let's focus on four: monetary, sentimental, aesthetic, and functional. And we'll start with sentimental value since it's often the stickiest.

You are not required to automatically assign more value to an item solely because of who brought it into your life. You can choose to, but you are not required to. And in some ways, doing so reflexively may cause you to keep things that don't serve you simply because of who or where they came from.

Imagine you got two scarves at the holidays—one from your grandmother and one from your kid's second grade teacher.

One scarf is not automatically or intrinsically more valuable than the other because it came from your grandmother rather than the teacher—if they are of equal size and quality, as a neck-warming garment, they'll each do the same job.

One scarf might *mean* more to you having come from your grandmother, but that significance may not be constant—because feelings are subjective and likely to change over time. What if you have a fight with your grandmother next week and now she's on your not-a-fan list? Did the scarf's value decrease as a scarf?

So, in deciding which scarf to keep, you can give the scarf from your grandmother more weight, but then the other values need to come into play, too.

Is one prettier than the other? Softer? Better quality? Do you like one more than the other? If you didn't know where they came from, if all things were equal, which would you choose?

By tilting the scale with sentiment, you may complicate a process that otherwise would be quite simple. And by seeing the sentimental attachment for what it is, you are now free to choose whichever scarf you like more based on all its values rather than only one—the sentimental one.

When sentiment is in its rightful place, it is easier to acknowledge and derive pleasure and satisfaction from each individual act of kindness, each demonstration of affection that's expressed through a gift, regardless of who gave it to you or even whether the gift remains in your life.

Any conversation about the value of a thing must also include its actual practical value to you, its usefulness. On some level, an expensive gas range has little-to-no value if you live somewhere where the only hookup available for a range is electric.

Even monetary value is not constant. When looking at familiar assets like real estate, fine antiques, fine art, precious stones or metals, or some other item commonly known to be a reliable investment, once something has been purchased, there is no guarantee it will retain its value *beyond* its use. The previous examples seem exceptional because enough people agree that these things typically retain some value beyond their functionality.

But if everyone decided tomorrow that all a diamond was good for was etching glass and refracting light, the market in diamonds would shift, and they'd be no more valuable than a crystal prism or a glass cutter. When I'm trying to read a newspaper, my dime-store reading glasses are worth a lot more to me than a Rolex wristwatch.

The value of some new thing is not exclusively its retail or wholesale price nor is it the *difference between* its retail price and what was paid for it. Some people might call that number a bargain, but it's not a bargain if you don't need it.

The system we've created—or rather, the system that has been created for us—that overvalues certain stuff and undervalues other stuff does not need to make our decisions for us. Likewise, just because something arrived at a particular time of year in a particular kind of wrapping does not suddenly change the rules, either. So pay attention to conversations you might have with yourself about how much something is "worth" when trying to determine its place in your life. 'Tis the season? Maybe and maybe not.

As an exercise, rather than reinforcing the idea that stuff is inherently valuable, let's experiment with shifting our view to one in which stuff is basically worthless. Perhaps even a liability. Sounds crazy? Stay with me.

Recall all the time you've spent in the past carting stuff around, sorting through stuff to find other stuff, and being responsible for stuff. Then consider the following questions:

- Have you ever made decisions about where to live or how to relocate based on the amount of stuff you owned?
- Have you spent time and resented it while just maintaining your stuff?
- Have you ever ruled out certain homes because they couldn't house all your stuff?
- Have you avoided certain neighborhoods that otherwise seemed appealing only because you feared for the safety of your stuff?
- Have you ever fantasized about chucking it all and heading out with just a backpack and some cash?
- Have you then abandoned that fantasy, not because of other people's potential reaction but because of some attachment to your stuff?

If you answered yes to one of more of these questions, doesn't that indicate that your stuff is (or could be) a liability or at least an obstacle? And if so, doesn't that mean its value isn't as high as it feels?

With this shift in perspective, you can now return to assessing actual usefulness. Ask yourself, *Can I use it, and if I can't, what's the best thing to happen to it next?*

TIME: THE COMMODITY NOT TRADED ON THE NY STOCK EXCHANGE

In previous chapters, we've talked about living deeply and being present for experiences rather than simply accumulating objects to either remember the experience or represent the experience. Previous chapters also offered detailed instructions, tips, and guidance on how to accomplish certain tasks. It's time to expand the conversation. Now that we know where things live in your spaces, let's focus on where things live in your life.

We want to avoid any situation where maintaining stuff equilibrium is an unpleasant chore or where monitoring things occupies too much of your time—that is not the point of this work. We don't want to replace disorganization with obsessive organization. While you may no longer be drowning in clutter, simply managing your things is the least desirable outcome of the previous chapters' efforts. All the work to get your possessions down to a manageable number and into consistent locations, and establishing habits of using and returning those possessions back to their homes *is meant to free up your time to do and pursue the things that you love.*

So don't sell yourself short. Don't settle for just knowing that the knives are now always in the knife drawer. That achievement is not insignificant, so feel appropriately proud of your accomplishment. But compared to the tremendous amount of time you used to spend hunting for things, maintaining this system should require much less energy. The time you would have spent searching for a knife is now free for other pursuits.

All that time saved is what this work is about, and time is the one thing you can't buy or accumulate. The clock is always ticking, and since the only thing we can truly be certain of is this moment, let's not waste a bit of it hunting for a knife. Let's spend every minute we can doing the things we love, whether that's curing cancer or baking a cake or weeding the garden or drawing a picture with a child or watching the sunrise. How much nicer to do any of those things without the nagging thought that you have something else to be doing, such as finding a knife. You know exactly where the knife is.

Let's also shy away from imperatives such as "spend time wisely," as that implies if you're not hypervigilant, you may end up spending it foolishly. Rather, let's focus on spending it mindfully. Let's make some conscious and active choices, and then let's not take the evaluating and judging any further.

If watering the garden typically takes 20 minutes and you're still at it two hours later, we may say that you've not been efficiently watering the garden. But perhaps this day you were observing a swarm of butterflies traveling from flower to flower, and then you were drawn to the sight of a mother bird feeding some chicks in a nest. Suddenly, two hours had passed. I'm not comfortable labeling that as time spent foolishly. All we know is that you spent two hours outside while doing something that usually takes 20 minutes. That's the fact. The rest is a story.

When my father died, I watched a lot of movies—particularly old Westerns, which he loved—and napped a lot and ate a fair amount of egg foo yong, his favorite dish. And cried a lot. I was not very productive in the traditional sense of the word during that month I took off from work, but that time was meaningful and well-spent.

The key element in both of these examples is choice. I chose to spend as long as I needed mourning my father's death and celebrating his life. The fictional person in the garden chose to linger and observe nature. In both cases, we were the agents of those decisions, not reacting or worrying that there was something else more important that we should have been doing. Many other things could have been done, but none were more important than what we chose to do at that time.

And that's what I wish for you—enough time to make choices that satisfy you in the short term, leaving you with no regrets in the long term. I want you to get the business of running your home and your life down to a mechanical, easily maintained system so the bulk of your day, when you're not trading your time for money at work, is filled with things that feed your spirit.

NEEDS VERSUS WANTS

With a better understanding of the value of stuff versus the value of time, it may be useful to distinguish between two other often-misunderstood concepts: needs versus wants. These two ideas often get jumbled as people plead for something they desire with a plaintive, "I really *need* it."

Need (noun): Anything that is necessary but lacking

Want (noun): A specific feeling of desire

One is required and missing; the other is all about longing. So now, when you evaluate something new by running through those questions on page 401, you'll understand that what you're asking yourself about is need—not want, not desire.

I'm all for some good desire but not at the expense of my sanity. I've chased after plenty of things that I thought I needed only to find out that once I got them, not only did I not need them, I didn't want them, either. And in some cases, cleaning up the mess I created in the wake of those pursuits took even longer than the pursuit itself.

Language is important. How we talk about things is important. We, as well as other people, are actually listening very carefully to the words we use, and if in some hazy moment we mistakenly refer to a want as a need, it will be heard, if only by our subconscious minds. Then we'll be off and running after something that we no more need than I "needed" five-inch platform shoes in 1974. I really, really wanted them, but nobody could ever be persuaded into thinking that I needed them. Except me.

And that is the point. We will deceive ourselves even if we deceive no one else. I believe strongly that how we think about stuff and how we talk about stuff significantly informs how we relate to stuff.

To better align what you say with what you truly need and want, try this exercise. Get your companion workbook or notebook, and write the following sentence in it:

Right now, I need _____.

Take a few minutes and repeat completing the sentence until you've run out of things to write down. And remember that we're talking about something that is necessary and currently lacking. Think in terms of antibiotics if you have a bacterial infection or money to pay the rent or tuition.

Once that's finished, let's look at the things we desire that are not essential. In your workbook or on a separate page in your notebook, write down this sentence:

Right now, I want _____.

Again, continue writing until you've exhausted the list of things you desire.

Were you able to list 15 things that you need—actual necessities that are lacking from your life? Were you able to list more? If you are lacking basic needs, then I strongly encourage you to seek assistance in getting those needs met promptly. Clean water, adequate nutritious food, heat in the winter, and clean clothes are available, and there are agencies that will help you to obtain them. You can find a list at unstuffbook.com/resources. Be diligent in your pursuit, and do not give up until you get what you need to survive.

What about wants? Did you fill the page? Did you find yourself writing on several pages because there were so many things to list? That's great. Desire them. Just don't fool yourself into thinking that you need them.

In six months or six weeks, come back and review these lists and see how many of your needs have been met and how many of your wants have either been satisfied or replaced with new things you now desire instead. If you're like most people, your needs will be few and your wants will be a merry-go-round of ever-changing items—which is the point of this exercise.

By moving slowly, being deliberate, and looking at new stuff objectively, you're likely to see a pattern emerge: many things you initially thought were "must haves" are not essential at all, and what is essential seldom lives inside a physical thing.

SPIRITUAL MATERIALISM

You are not going to buy your way into heaven. Led Zeppelin wrote that song already. Nor are you going to buy your way into serenity. Surrounding yourself with crystals and statues and inspirational sayings can bring you only so far. Lighting candles and hoping that something will shift without you moving another muscle is perhaps overly optimistic and possibly misguided. You can lay the groundwork for change this way, you can create an environment that is peaceful and calm and pretty, but then you actually have to take some action— some peaceful, calm, and pretty action—if you want to see those qualities reflected in your life as well.

You might think you're "in the zone" when you're shopping, you might feel at one with the universe, but the act of shopping is not the same as sitting and meditating. If it were, you'd see shopping malls filled with Buddhist monks and monasteries filled with shopping bags.

So be mindful of what the actual goal is. If you want a calm and peaceful and pretty life, make choices that don't create chaos or drama. Simplify your life, and you're more likely to experience peace and serenity than if you compulsively shop for crystals or incense or robes. Like most things of significance, creating a peaceful life is an inside job. Keep the inside of the drawer tidy and clean, and all you need to keep the outside looking good is a quick wipe down of the drawer front.

Regardless of how serene the photo spreads in housekeeping or home improvement magazines look, we don't have a clue as to how people actually live in those spaces on a day-to-day basis. If you've ever opened the spare-room door, thrown every nonessential item lying around the house into that room, and then slammed the door before company arrived, you too may have presented a calm and so-called Zen environment to your guests. At least for a few hours.

So let's not judge a book by its cover. If what you want is a clean, crisp, uncluttered home, create one. If you want a clean, crisp, efficient, and uncluttered life, create one of those, too. Less stuff rather than different stuff is probably going to bring you closer to gentle and restful stillness. It has for me.

BELIEF AS DEFINITION

What do we believe about ourselves, and how does that define what we feel, what we think, and what we do? Are there things we don't attempt because of a particular belief? Are there things we continue to do, even if the results are less than desirable, because of a particular belief?

We can know certain things definitively. For example, I know I'm six feet tall, my eyes are brown, my hair is brown—although my head is now shaved—and I weigh 170 pounds. Those are facts. But belief is a whole different entity.

For example, I believed at one time that I was going to work in the theater for the rest of my life. I loved my work, was good at it, and while many other things came and went over the years, the theater remained constant. I had no reason to doubt that would ever change. I genuinely felt called to be an artist. But clearly, that's not how I make my living these days. What changed?

Flash back to 1995. I was laid off from a theater I was running in Seattle. If I wanted to add some drama to the story, I could tell you it was a few weeks before Christmas. Either way, I spent six more months there acting and directing and looking for administrative work before I decided to head back to the East Coast.

Almost immediately, I got a gig coproducing an awards ceremony at the Kennedy Center in Washington, D.C. One of the awardees was a prominent author and Nobel Peace Prize winner. I went to New York to collect some photos from his office, and what I found was a mess. The photos were in complete disarray—some were mislabeled, some had been lent out and never returned, others were missing entirely.

After a few hours in the office there, the Nobel Peace Prize winner's wife asked me into their apartment for a soda. We talked about life and what I had been doing most recently and my plans to move back to New York after the awards presentation. She asked me if I wanted a job organizing their photographs. I started to tear up; I was so moved by her offer and at the thought of coming to work for such a remarkable humanitarian. We made arrangements for me to start in late December once I had returned to the city. I took the photos I needed and headed back to D.C., giddy with possibility and excitement.

The day before I was to start work, their assistant called me and said something unexpected came up and we'd need to reschedule for a month later. Sure, no problem. A month later, though, the day before I was to show up, the phone rang. Same thing.

For three months, we scheduled a start date, and all three times their assistant phoned me to reschedule, the last time with no new start date. She said, "When we're ready to proceed, we'll get in touch with you."

When another month passed and I still hadn't heard back from them, I let it go. I couldn't bring myself to call them a fourth time—it just seemed too desperate. I figured if they knew how to reach me to cancel, they knew how to reach me to reschedule. So I never went to work for them.

But in the meantime, I had told everyone I talked to that I had this great gig creating a comprehensive photographic archive for this Nobel laureate. I mean, what an honor! And I was thinking big. After I got all the missing photos back, after I found the misfiled and mislaid photos from around the office and everything was gathered together, I was imagining publishing a coffee-table photo book. From the few images I had seen, I thought that book would be a slam dunk.

My enthusiasm must have been infectious because a friend referred me to her accountant who needed a filing system created. And when that work was completed, I started getting calls from some of the accountant's clients who then showed up at my home with duffel bags full of receipts. They hadn't filed taxes in years, were overwhelmed, had letters from state or federal tax authorities, and were so frightened and tardy that they didn't know where to begin. I organized the receipts, entered them into the computer, and created reports for the accountant.

This kind of word-of-mouth momentum continued to spread. Each new client led to three more.

In addition to organizing gigs, I was still freelancing as a director and a producer. I even had a play that I wrote presented off-Broadway during this time. But as busy as I was with theater work, it felt as though my life was shifting in some way. The work I was doing with clients was immediate and powerful, and I could instantly see the impact my efforts had on their lives. There was no metaphor between us, just clear communication, direction, and results.

In 1998, I had just finished directing a play off-Broadway that was a critical success but a less-than-satisfying creative experience. And at the same time, it was as if there was a huge neon sign in the sky right in front of my face saying, "You're really good at this organizing thing, and you should see where it leads."

It felt wrong somehow to turn away from that sign simply because I had this historical belief and expansive résumé that said I was a theater artist. I couldn't look away from that sign, because what I had come to know after many years was that, more than anything, I was supposed to be useful in the world. And I had also discovered that I couldn't always know the best way to be of use, that it was often revealed to me in small increments without warning or a recognizable pattern.

My work in the theater had been in alignment with that sense of service for many years, and I'm certain that I positively affected people's lives through my work as an artist—they've told me so in restaurants, on street corners, and in shopping malls. Yet here was this new opportunity.

Was I going to hold fast to a belief that seemed to be growing obsolete but had been with me, had comforted me, and had guided me for so many years previously? Or was I willing to lay down that belief in service of something else—something for which the outcome was unpredictable but that felt so appropriately seated in my body and my heart that it would have felt like a betrayal to ignore it?

Indeed I couldn't ignore it, so I made a decision to pursue this work full time.

I think by now you can sense how not woo-woo I am. So when I tell you that this decision to open my hands and let fall the one thing that had defined me for more than 20 years had nothing to do with my analytical abilities and everything to do with my feelings, I'm as awed by it today as I was when it first happened.

This was not a decision for which I could make a pro-and-con list and calculate my risk. But what's amazing is that when I think back to that time, I can tell you that I wasn't frightened. I was uncertain, I was confused, I was curious, but I was not afraid. It just felt like the next thing I should be doing.

And while this story is about a large-scale belief shifting, regardless of the scale of the belief, the point is still the same—that space for something new requires letting go of something old.

So if you began reading this book believing that stuff brings you happiness, would you consider shifting that belief now if you haven't already? After working your way through this book, after experiencing some relief as a result of letting things go, of finding things the first time you looked for them, of walking into a room and not wanting to turn around and run out because it was so suffocating, could it be possible that stuff does not in fact bring you happiness? At least, not in the way you thought? Is it possible that something else does instead? Wouldn't it be great to find out what that is? And imagine if what that is doesn't even cost any money? Wow!

I'm not suggesting that you discard everything you've ever believed in. I am suggesting that anytime you are about to turn away from something that holds a promise you desire, and the only thing standing between you and the pursuit of that desire is a belief, you spend enough time making sure that what you believe in is solid and grounded in your belly.

Make sure it's not superstition or something you read in a book or overheard in a café or, like me, something you believed in and relied on successfully for 20 years and came to take for granted. Make sure that belief is as valid today as it was when you first adopted it. Then you'll never have regrets over choices made or paths not taken.

"I THINK I'LL MISS YOU MOST OF ALL"

We've come to the end of our time together, at least for now.

I feel you're strong and capable, thoughtful and alert, and ready for the challenges ahead of you. I am confident you'll find your way through whatever adventures lie before you. You have the skills, you have the knowledge, and if you also possess the willingness, you truly are a triple threat.

Remember the things we've discussed, honor the things you cherish that are not objects, and hold lightly the objects that you value. Do not expect or demand perfection from yourself. What you can expect is that if you are diligent about this work, if you are mindful and patient and kind and steady, you will always find whatever you are looking for, whether that's inside the knife drawer or inside your heart.

In peace and in simplicity, I wish you success and happiness in all you attempt, and thank you for spending this time with me. It's been an honor.

Here's to kicking the clutter habit once and for all!

Namaste.

ACKNOWLEDGMENTS

AS WE CLOSE OUT the second edition of this book, it's important to acknowledge that no book is a solo effort. The people I thanked in the first edition of *Unstuff Your Life!* still deserve all the praise and appreciation I shared back then.

With this latest edition, there are a few more people who deserve acknowledgment.

These excellent artists and technicians actually made the book: Carra Simpson, Jazmin Welch, Alex Hennig, Jessica Sherer, and Lynn Slobogian. Tyson Cornell has been a great friend, cheerleader, and advisor, both inside and outside the world of publishing.

You wouldn't be reading this right now if it weren't for my agent, James Levine. I couldn't do what I do without my team and collaborators, past and present, at Andrew Mellen Pro Organizing: Awilda Acosta, Kelly Case, Alice Chin, V.J. Corpuz, James P. Friel, John Gugliada, Kristin Hart, Maya D. Haynes, Drew Jacobsen, Lisa Lewis, Luke Nevill, Jess Reidell, Linda Schwader, Kevin Smith, Paula Thrall, and Johnny Walker.

Our amazing students and clients continue to inform this work and the information in this book. Let's acknowledge them here without naming names. You know who you are. Your kindness, generosity, and enthusiasm continue to teach me and the team about clutter, productivity, resilience, and the human heart. I'm grateful beyond words.

My dear friends Don Alden, Michelle Battista, Laurie Brown, Sarah Byam, Ileana Gomez, Jaime Grant, Stephanie Kelly, Carolyne Landon, Linda Lippner, Michael MacLennan, Jenifer Madson, Phil Rossiello, Tina Sabuco, Lisa Lapides Sawicki, David Stewart, Sé Sullivan, Jennifer White, and Victoria Whitfield—you feel like family. I'm a better writer and certainly a better person for your friendship, love, and support. Likewise, for my actual family—while we may be spread out geographically, I feel you closer than the miles would indicate.

As always, it's imperative to celebrate the strangers and friends, named and unnamed, who show me how to be a better person every day. It isn't easy being human some days, so I strive to pass on what I have learned without mucking it up or getting thumbprints all over it.

Until we meet again . . .

ADDITIONAL RESOURCES

If you haven't already checked out unstuffbook.com, I encourage you to do so. You'll find many additional resources there for getting and staying organized, including "Should It Stay or Should It Go?", a comprehensive list of which documents to keep and for how long. FYI, that list was the appendix in *Unstuff Your Life!*'s first edition.

You can also visit andrewmellen.com for information about my podcast, speaking and coaching events and programs, 1-1 coaching opportunities, and much more. You can also follow me and my work on social media, including Facebook, Instagram, X, YouTube, Pinterest, and LinkedIn.

ABOUT THE AUTHOR

ANDREW MELLEN is a speaker and coach, and the author of the *Wall Street Journal* bestseller and #1 Audible book *Unstuff Your Life!*, as well as *The Most Organized Man in America's Guide to Moving* and *Calling BS on Busy*.

He is the creator of the De-Stress Your Mess Challenge and the Unstuff Your Life System—virtual programs that have helped over half a million people and businesses worldwide change their relationships with stuff, time, and clutter for good.

Mellen has been a student of mindfulness and meditation since 1989. In a previous career, he was an award-winning actor, director, and arts administrator who toured the United States performing improvisational theater in prisons and penitentiaries. He splits his time between New York City and Treasure Island, Florida.

KEEP IN TOUCH

Did you benefit from *Unstuff Your Life!?*

SHARE YOUR PRAISE

Did this book help you get organized? Did you gain any new insights that have directly benefited your daily life and your relationship with stuff?

If so, a review shared through your favorite online retailer would be greatly appreciated!

A few minutes of your time will help others find this book and enjoy some of the benefits you've already received.

PLACE A BULK ORDER

Would you like to share this book with your company, team, or group? We offer bulk discounts for orders of 10 or more copies in most locations. Write to hello@andrewmellen.com.

WORK WITH ANDREW

Even better, would you like Andrew to speak or train at your organization, conference, book club, or event? Write to speak@andrewmellen.com.

KEEP IN TOUCH

For more about Andrew's books, programs, and workshops, please visit andrewmellen.com.

Once you're there, be sure to register for upcoming events, including the De-Stress Your Mess Challenge. Andrew and his team offer many events and opportunities to simplify your life and maximize your time.

ALSO BY ANDREW MELLEN

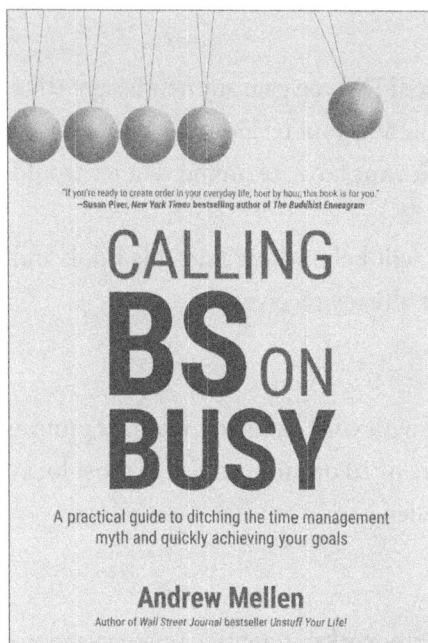

Calling BS on Busy: A Practical Guide to Ditching the Time Management Myth and Quickly Achieving Your Goals

Available in paperback, e-book, and audio

Calling BS on Busy unleashes the power of a radically positive mindset paired with simple, practical actions you can take to instantly reclaim your life.

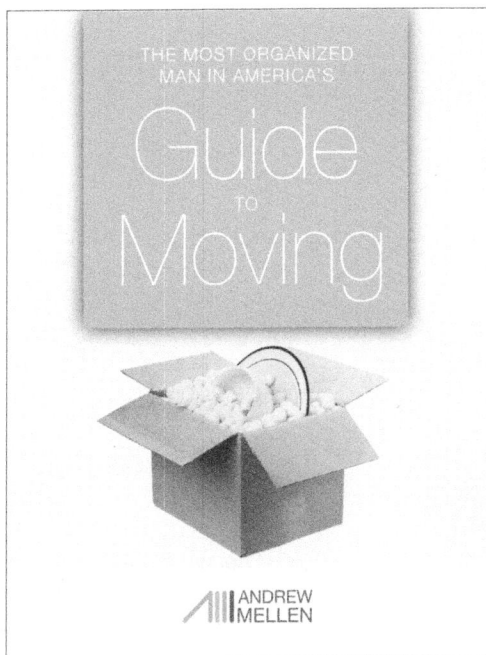

The Most Organized Man in America's Guide to Moving

Available in paperback and e-book

Moving house doesn't have to stress you out or overwhelm you ever again! Get step-by-step instructions, including a master checklist, from America's favorite organizer in this compact, foolproof guide.

Made in the USA
Las Vegas, NV
06 February 2025

17654289R00256